PROFIT
BEYOND
MEASURE

Extraordinary Results
Through Attention to
Work and People

H. THOMAS JOHNSON
ANDERS BRÖMS

Foreword by Peter M. Senge

THE FREE PRESS

NEW YORK   LONDON   TORONTO   SYDNEY   SINGAPORE

*f*P

THE FREE PRESS
A Division of Simon & Schuster, Inc.
1230 Avenue of the Americas
New York, NY 10020

The authors gratefully acknowledge permission from Ola Rollén to use the
comment and quote in the "Kanthal" box in chapter 5.

Designed by Lisa Chovnick

Manufactured in the United States of America

1   3   5   7   9   10   8   6   4   2

Library of Congress Cataloging-in-Publication Data

Johnson, H. Thomas
Profit beyond measure : extraordinary results through attention to work and people / H.
Thomas Johnson, Anders Bröms ; foreword by Peter M Senge.
p.   cm.   Includes index.
1. Industrial management.   2. Production management.   3. Managerial accounting.
4. Cost control.   5. Profit.   6. Automobile industry and trade—Management—Case studies.
I. Bröms, Anders.   II. Title.
HD31 .J554 2000
658.4—dc21   00-055124
ISBN 0-684-83667-X

This book is dedicated
to the memory of
Dr. W. Edwards Deming
1900–1993

May the
Seventh Generation
after us know a
world shaped by
his thinking

We are not stuff that abides, but patterns that perpetuate themselves.

NORBERT WIENER
The Human Use of Human Beings, p. 96

By learning the ways of the universe and by reflecting upon them as they surface in the daily life of family and work and community, we take the first steps into a new form of human understanding and existence.

BRIAN SWIMME
The Hidden Heart of the Cosmos, p. 7

If you want to be a great leader,
you must learn to follow the Tao.
Stop trying to control.
Let go of fixed plans and concepts,
and the world will govern itself.

LAO TZU IN STEPHEN MITCHELL
Tao Te Ching: A New English Version, chapter 57

CONTENTS

....

CHAPTER 4
Design to Order

– 115 –

How Scania, a highly profitable maker of heavy trucks, succeeds by embracing a natural "spirit in the walls"; managing product design from the perspective of nature's system of evolution, not managing by results.

CHAPTER 5
Assess to Order

– 141 –

How order-line maps and ratios may be fundamental tools for managing by means, in the same way that measurement and management accounting are fundamental tools for managing by results; how companies use order-line profitability analysis to assess their efforts at reducing structural complication in design, operations, and administration.

CHAPTER 6
Results Are in the Details

– 171 –

How any organization can learn to master the principles that guide living systems in nature; steps managers can follow to stop chasing quantitative targets and, instead, to manage by means.

CHAPTER 7
What's Natural Comes Hard

– 193 –

MBM practices not only improve the long-run financial performance of businesses, they also improve humankind's situation in the ecosystem that sustains all life on Earth.

Afterword by Leif Östling, President and CEO of Scania AB
– 211 –

Appendixes
– 217 –

Acknowledgments
– 229 –

Notes
– 231 –

Index
– 247 –

FOREWORD

....

Peter M. Senge

What is the most profitable auto maker in the world? Few within or outside the auto industry would have any trouble answering this question. For most of the time since the late-1980s, the market capitalization for Toyota roughly equaled, or exceeded, the sum of the "Big Three" in Detroit. Even with the depressed yen and explosive U.S. stock market at the end of the 1990s, Toyota's market value still continued to exceed that of its much larger competitors.

What is the most profitable maker of large trucks in the world? This is a question that fewer of us would be able to answer. In fact, it is Scania, a Swedish manufacturer that has had a remarkable string of sixty-five years of continuous profits.

What do these two preeminent companies on opposite sides of the world have in common? On the surface they differ in their core expertise. Toyota is renowned for manufacturing innovations. Scania's primary innovations have focused on a unique modular approach to product design. These innovations, though quite different, have brought each firm distinctly lower cost structures than their competitors, combined with greater product flexibility.

The interesting point is that neither firm achieves its cost advantage by trying to manage costs in the traditional sense, by management setting cost objectives and "driving" people to meet those targets. In fact, both firms dramatically outperform their competitors without many of the traditional forms of management intervention at all. What both firms have in common, Tom Johnson and Anders Bröms believe, is that they practice "management by means," a radical break from the "management by results" thinking that has come to dominate almost all large industrial-age firms. Moreover, they have come to this knowledge by discovering universal principles of living systems, principles by which nature works—principles relevant to all enterprises yet violated by almost all large institutions guided by "modern management."

To appreciate this startling conclusion, and to give it some credibility, it is necessary to put it in historical context—for it is the product of a long journey. In 1987 Tom Johnson and Robert Kaplan turned the financial accounting profession on its ear with their historic *Relevance Lost.* They argued that the profession of managerial accounting had lost its way. It had become a servant of number crunching with no clear picture of how to serve management's fundamental responsibility to build a healthy business. They argued that concepts, like profit and return on investment, once meant to inform outside investors about the status of their investments, had been co-opted as management tools—worse, they had become arguably management's core tools. Corporate managers had become like baseball managers trying to coach their team by looking at the scoreboard. They had lost touch with the actual processes responsible for creating profitability, and in so doing had created a generation of mediocre businesses, paradoxically returning modest financial returns by the very act of trying to manage by setting financial targets.

Relevance Lost became a classic not only for its diagnosis but for an antidote it prescribed, activity-based costing (ABC). Within a few years, ABC created a sort of religious revival for managerial accounting. Corporate CFOs espoused it as the proper way to assign overhead allocations and accurately assess profitability of different business lines. Management schools adopted it into their curriculum. Ten years later, the editors of *Harvard Business Review* declared *Relevance Lost* to be one of the seminal management books of the past seventy-five years.

Yet Tom Johnson regarded ABC as a small first step in rethinking the entire practice of performance management, not just accounting measures. In fact, over time, he became more and more worried that ABC was becoming just another management fad. Something was wrong, he felt, with implementing a new system of measures as the sole solution to transforming management. Moreover, ABC was achieving popularity in the age of shareholder revolts, an exploding stock market, and increasing pressures to manage financial returns. Would it just become one more management technique to boost short-term financial results?

It was during this time that Johnson discovered the writings of Gregory Bateson and the emerging field of living systems theory. Bateson and the other natural scientists like Humberto Maturana, Fritjof Capra, and Brian Swimme are hardly household names for managers and management students. Moreover, the writings of many like Bateson are barely accessible to experts in their fields, let alone lay people. Yet Johnson saw in their ideas an intellectual framework to underpin the radical changes he felt were needed in management. The real challenge was how to get the ideas "across the bridge" from the world of evolutionary biology, cosmology, and systems theory to people managing and leading in contemporary organizations.

Fortunately, about this time Tom was invited by managers at Toyota's Georgetown, Kentucky, plant to study their manufacturing processes. He was also invited to study Scania's approach to product design, where Anders Bröms and his colleagues had been working for many years. While Scania's management innovations are not well known outside Sweden, few have been more widely studied than Toyota's legendary production system. Yet it still eludes imitators. As one American manager at Georgetown says, after touring the facility visitors invariably ask, "You have shown us A, B, C, D, E, and F. Our own plants have these already. Now please show us G, the secret ingredient that makes you different." But there is no distinct "G." The secret ingredient lies in the relationships among all the parts, in the production process as a whole. While this might strike many Westerners as esoteric or even evasive, Tom heard it as a direct expression of the systems view he was beginning to understand.

Between 1992 and 1999 Tom made over thirty visits to Georgetown, gradually coming to understand how a set of particular practices brought the elusive Toyota system to life. For example, Johnson discovered at Toyota a complex web of local control, in stark contrast to the traditional infrastructure of centralized control in typical manufacturers. When you cut your finger, your body does not send a series of requests to the brain for permission to act. Coagulants are generated locally and flow immediately to the cut. Just so, each person's actions in the complex process of stamping, welding, painting, and assembly at Toyota are coordinated completely by what is going on directly around them, aimed at meeting the needs of their immediate customer, the person to whom their work directly flows. If they encounter anything they consider problematic, they quickly signal for consultation and assistance. By contrast, typical large manufacturing processes are centrally coordinated by MRP (material requirements planning) systems that send instructions to myriad shops all at once. Not surprisingly, this requires a complex information system to keep track of all these simultaneous activities, and the inventories of components they produce. Individual workers are typically discouraged from doing anything that would cause a slowdown, even if they see problems developing.

The Toyota system of local control achieves not only lower cost— requiring neither this expensive "information factory" and the associated staff overhead nor the large inventories created by centralized control—but extraordinary variety. This is possible because each vehicle is built according to the order of a particular external customer. That unique customer order enters the production process almost at the outset, versus near the end in typical manufacturing. In principle, every step in the entire Toyota process allows for the flexibility needed to create an unending variety of unique products for unique customers.

Remarkably, Johnson found the same blend of elegance and variety in the modular product design approach that has evolved at Scania over the past thirty years, which literally allows for the design of a unique truck to meet a unique customer's requirements. He recognized this capacity to blend simplicity and variety as a hallmark of nature's "production systems" as well. If you or I looked under a microscope, we would be hard pressed to distinguish the cell of a common plant from the cell of a human being, because the cell's basic design is so universal. Yet, this omnipotential cell is able to create the extraordinary variety we see in nature. The basic design of the cell bears evidence to evolution's continual quest for harmony between simplicity and variety—"rich ends from simple means," in the words of Norwegian ecologist Arne Naess.

Perhaps the most surprising feature of both Toyota's and Scania's management is the approach to measurement and goal setting. It has become almost an unquestioned tenet of contemporary management that bosses set quantitative targets and then create control systems (incentives, internal metrics, individual and group performance reviews, and budgeting) to assure that management goals are met. This practice has spread from business management to other institutions—witness the current fixation in American education on students' quantitative test scores. Toyota's management uses neither overall cost nor productivity targets to influence day-to-day operations. Even if such targets were set, they would have little meaning—for the simple reason that there is no practical way in the short run to speed up the pace of work simply to achieve such cost or productivity targets. Similarly, Scania employs a unique set of metrics, such as total part counts and part commonality indices, in managing its product design process, rather than relying on aggregate measures of cost and productivity. Both firms believe that the key to superior performance and to continual innovation lies in "the minute particulars" of how local work is done, not in sacrificing those particulars to the pursuit of management-imposed metrics.

Herein lies a core insight likely to shock a few modern managers. It is common today to talk about the "hard stuff" versus the "soft stuff," by which is invariably meant the numbers versus the people, the unambiguous quantified measures of performance versus the highly ambiguous, messy world of motivation, trust, and human capabilities. But just how *hard* is the hard stuff? If "hard" means tangible, I defy you to touch profits or productivity. In point of fact, these are abstractions, which we measure according to rules set by convention only. Indeed, one of the main points of ABC was to challenge the conventions by which profits were defined. When the conventions changed, *profits changed*—that is, businesses that had previously been "unprofitable" became profitable, and vice versa. The key point is not that most measures are good or bad, but that most measures employed by management are less close to fundamental reality than our contemporary management culture seems to realize—and, consequently, they may have much less leverage than we believe. The commonplace "truism"— "if it cannot be measured, it cannot be managed"—may have very different implications than most think.

W. Edwards Deming, statistician and management innovator, used to say that, if management sets quantitative targets and makes people's jobs depend on meeting them, "they will likely meet the targets—even if they have to destroy the enterprise to do it." Many of us have firsthand experience of the destructiveness of management by objectives — "management by results." But, what is it that gets destroyed? It is the web of relationships that determines the character of the enterprise, its capabilities, and its capacity to learn and grow. I believe it is valid to view this web of relationships as "more real" than most management metrics because it comes closer to shaping whether the system as a whole functions well or poorly. There is no doubt that abstract management measures affect what people pay attention to. But, if the aim is sustained superior performance and innovation, is meeting management's targets the key, or the booby prize?

If our established ways of organizing work around centralized control and quantified targets is problematic, what are the practical alternatives? Most of *Profit Beyond Measure* is devoted to answering that question, laying out "management by means," Johnson and Bröms's view of a living-system approach to management. An alternative term might be "management by attentiveness." Anyone who has ever achieved a level of mastery with a musical instrument, or in a sport, knows that performing to your potential is thwarted when you "tense up." You must relax. But, the ability to do so is greatly diminished if you become too concerned about how you are doing. Somehow, our potential is only realized when we settle into a state of non-anxious attentiveness—a state often associated with play or fun. Psychologist Mihaly Csikszentmihalyi characterizes examples of extraordinary individual performance as involving a mental state he calls "flow." But paying attention is no trivial task. Indeed, much of the process of mastering any domain involves continual refinement in the capacity to pay attention, while simultaneously performing.

What firms like Toyota and Scania have learned how to do is develop sophisticated methods of paying close attention in the production and design processes, so that high levels of performance and high rates of learning occur naturally. I believe all organizations must develop their own practices and disciplines for cultivating attentiveness. Tools and methods like those at Toyota and Scania can help. But they will be of little use without deep, intuitive understanding. This understanding starts with appreciating the distinctions between management by results and management by means.

Lastly, none of this means that results do not matter. On the contrary, I believe management by means is essential to realize extraordinary results in a sustainable way. To appreciate this seeming paradox, we need to understand one last distinction. Management by results creates "needs," goals that we feel we must achieve for our survival or for personal gain. Management by means nurtures aspirations, aims that we pursue because they matter to us. The difference is subtle yet profound. Once we become convinced that we must achieve a certain outcome, our universe collapses and we see everything through the narrow lens of the predetermined outcome. Our awareness diminishes. Our ability to invent totally new ways of responding to new challenges is lost. Fear of failure increases. The state of flow is destroyed. By contrast, genuine aspirations elevate us and call forth our highest and most imaginative efforts. It is a tragedy when we lose the ability to distinguish needs from aspirations. This, I believe, is one of management by results' greatest shortcomings. Conversely, it is management by means' most important contribution. As the poet Robert Frost put it, "All great things are done for their own sake."

We stand at the outset of building a modern knowledge base of management by means—as we stand at the beginning in understanding living systems. So long as they deviate significantly from the management mainstream, innovators like Toyota and Scania will be at risk, regardless of their business performance. *Profit Beyond Measure* points us in a direction and offers invaluable insight in getting started. But most remains to be done.

There is growing talk today about the new economy and even a "second industrial revolution." But what would be the basis for such a revolution? Globalization? e-business? These are significant changes in the playing field for business enterprises and are leading to dramatic changes. But are these changes in the essence of how society functions or only in the arrangements of commerce? The Industrial Revolution changed how society functioned, breaking up traditional seats of power and creating new ones. It gave rise to new types of institutions of work and education, which have come to shape how we think and act. Arguably, the Agricultural Revolution, which nurtured the view that the human species was distinct from and superior to the rest of nature, shaped social evolution even more so.

I would argue that the current changes being wrought by information technology are more akin to a second phase of the first industrial revolution, insofar as the underlying values driving the changes—to make money—and the key assumptions—new technology and private wealth creation benefit all—are unchanged. Yet, they may be harbingers of deeper changes to come. These deeper changes will get at the "DNA" rather than the arrangements of modern society.

I believe we can start to discern three elements of such deeper changes becoming evident. The first stems from seeing knowledge and knowledge creation as the cornerstone of what makes any organization successful. In business, there is a growing appreciation that the ability to generate and diffuse knowledge is the root of competitive advantage; and this viewpoint is gradually spreading beyond business organizations. The second comes from seeing all organizations as embedded in and interdependent with larger natural and social systems. A small but influential number of organizations are starting to see that they cannot be healthy if they do not contribute to the health of these larger systems. Johnson and Bröms's "management by means" may be the third element. How work is organized must be guided by principles of living systems. Together, these three elements could be the basis for a second industrial revolution that would close the circle and enable humans to live once again as part of, rather than apart from, nature.

Introduction

....

Toward a New System of Thought

> . . . thinking makes it so.
>
> —William Shakespeare[1]

> . . . 'tis only thinking Lays lads underground.
>
> —A. E. Housman[2]

Virtually all businesses today generate enormous amounts of waste, recognized and unrecognized. The waste appears primarily in two forms: excessive operating costs in the short run and excessive losses caused by market instability in the long run. A key message of this book is that any company can avoid this waste—can avoid vast amounts of cost in the short term and excessive losses in the long term. Any company can gain a richer, longer life if it will simply change how it thinks about work and, as a consequence of changed thinking, alter how it organizes work. The book shows that business leaders can achieve higher and more secure levels of profitability if they organize work according to the systemic principles infusing nature and cease to drive work with quantitative goals.

Typically, even today's "leanest" and most profitable organizations have not abandoned the conventional thinking that prompts companies to drive work with financial targets. Lean and profitable organizations do better than others at reducing costs. However, following the principles of natural systems as outlined in this book, even a lean and profitable company can organize work to greatly lessen its long-term earnings instability and to sharply reduce its short-run operating costs.

A company that follows such principles invariably connects every member's work with the needs of the specific customers it serves. In contrast, the defining feature of most organizations today is a chronic disconnect between the work and the customer. Such a disconnect increases long-term variation in earnings by causing work to be perpetually out of synch with customer needs. It also creates a need for additional people and time to process information, expedite flows, and schedule activity that would be unnecessary if all work were connected with customer needs at every point. It is not an exaggeration to say that in most organizations today, each person whose work eventually serves customers' needs is "shadowed" by another person whose job is to keep track of other people's work or to patch up mistakes that slip through because workers and customers are not connected. By eliminating virtually all need for such "shadow" activity, companies that stop driving work with targets and that adopt truly systemic work habits can probably cut their short-run operating costs by half.

The contrast this book draws between driving work with financial goals—"managing by results"—and organizing work systemically— "managing by means"—was framed by W. Edwards Deming many years ago in the following words: "If you have a stable system, then there is no use to specify a goal. You will get whatever the system will deliver. A goal beyond the capability of the system will not be reached. If you have not a stable system, then there is . . . no point in setting a goal. There is no way to know what the system will produce: it has no capability."[3]

Viewed from Deming's perspective, it is clear that the proper role of managers is to lead people to understand business as a system of work, a system that links each worker's capacity to serve with a specific customer's needs. The goal of a business is to nurture continually the creative talents of company members. By focusing on its members' activities, the manager will thereby improve the system's capability to serve the needs of customers. To help each employee and supplier realize his or her potential in the company, management's main job is to learn exactly what people do in their jobs and how what they do serves customers. Such learning is difficult, if not impossible, in companies that manage by results. Managers of companies that ignore systemic

thinking and drive work with financial targets, which is most companies in the world today, feel compelled to short-circuit the need for
learning. Instead of making time and providing opportunities for those
in the organization to learn, they focus on managing the outcome.
"Focus on outcome," Deming said, "is not an effective way to improve
a process or an activity. . . . [M]anagement by numerical goal is an attempt to manage without knowledge of what to do, and in fact is usually management by fear." The price of managing by fear rather than
cultivating systemic learning is higher operating costs and suboptimal
long-term profitability.

The past forty years of business history provide ample evidence that
companies do indeed pay a high price for putting the pursuit of quantitative financial goals ahead of genuine learning. Focused on financial
targets rather than on systemic learning, most large publicly owned
companies have incurred excessive costs and have made themselves vul-
nerable to periodic slumps in the economy. Instability is less of an issue
today than it has been for many years, but only because the economy
since the early 1990s has been riding the longest and most powerful
spending boom in history. Nevertheless, people so confident as to believe that the global economy makes the business cycle extinct will for-
get the history of the 1960s, 1970s, and 1980s at their peril. Indeed, as
recently as the 1980s and early 1990s, major automobile companies
recorded annual losses so large that some business journalists expressed
fears that Ford and General Motors would become bankrupt. Chrysler
in the late 1970s did become virtually bankrupt, only to be rescued by
the United States taxpayer. And cyclical booms and busts among commercial airline companies prompted the frequent observation in the
early 1990s that the U.S. airline industry as a whole had managed to do
no better than break even since World War II. Similar stories of revenue
and earnings instability could be told for companies in steel, petro-
leum, banking, insurance, truck making, electrical equipment, and
countless other major industries.

Causing the earnings instability and high costs that plagued American business so much in the fifty years after World War II is the tacit,
taken-for-granted thinking that influences how most companies organize work. While today's heady economic environment surely dulls
awareness of the consequences of that thinking, the next economic

downturn will rekindle such awareness as companies once again experience declining profits and, in many cases, severe losses. Predictably, desperate companies that serve financial targets will then run madly to catch the next wave of "solutions" to the "profitability and productivity problem." Companies that practice the natural systemic thinking proposed in this book, however, will experience relatively more stability when the inevitable downturn comes. Their resilience will reflect a new way of organizing work that reduces costs and earnings instability, making irrelevant most of the "solutions" that companies still committed to the old thinking will in a downturn rush to adopt.

Chapter 1 introduces the reader to this new way of organizing work by telling a story that contrasts the management thought of two different groups of automotive manufacturers in the decades following World War II. The story contrasts the goal-oriented thinking of America's "Big Three" auto makers with the more systemic thinking of Toyota. The Big Three view workers and customers as independent objects that respond best to incentives and targets—external stimuli. The role of managers in the Big Three is to manipulate those stimuli so that customers purchase enough products at appropriate prices and workers produce enough products at appropriate costs for the company to reach its bottom-line goals. Grounded in mechanistic principles reminiscent of classical Newtonian physics, this thinking has led companies to optimize cost with "economies of scale." They run large-scale plants as fast and as full as possible, to achieve the highest possible throughput for the existing level of costs. In contrast, the Toyota organization views customers and workers as parts connected in a web of interrelationships. Toyota does not drive outcomes by manipulating external stimuli, but by having everyone "produce to order" according to a few basic principles. In Toyota's system, all work at every moment is done to a specific customer order and all the information needed to guide work is in the work itself, not in separate information systems. With the same few principles always guiding its work, Toyota has operated for many decades at much lower cost and with far more stable earnings than any other auto company in the world.

Chapter 1 identifies the principles that guide Toyota's behavior with the same principles that modern science finds at work in natural living systems. In contrast to those natural systemic principles, conventional business behavior reflects conformity to mechanistic principles that have dominated Western thought for over three hundred years. According to the mechanistic view of things, order naturally and inevitably crumbles into disorder in the absence of external intervention. That fundamental belief informs the nearly universal conviction that managers must use quantitative controls to impose order in an organization. In contrast to those mechanistic principles, the new worldview emerging from modern science portrays the universe as a self-ordering system of billions and billions of adaptive, self-organizing subsystems, ranging from galaxies to subatomic particles and including living cells, human beings, and human organizations. Order reverts to disorder and living things die, of course. But order inevitably reappears again and again, according to a deep universal pattern. If business leaders accept these principles and view a business as a natural living system they will not attempt to impose external order on an organization, but instead will work to cultivate the organization's natural capacity to generate order.

Chapter 2 demonstrates how modern management accounting has actually hindered companies. It has prevented them from seeing the adverse consequences of practices designed to impose order. Because companies are inherently self-ordering systems, such accounting practices are injurious to them. Among those practices, none is more pernicious than that of using financial targets to drive work—the defining feature of managing by results. The chapter describes in some detail how management accounting practices have shaped the organization of work in most companies since the 1950s. It shows how those practices weaken and destroy companies because they inappropriately drive work with quantitative measures such as financial scorecard targets. Being one-dimensional magnitudes that can depict only linear cause-and-effect relationships, quantitative measures can direct action only in mechanistic systems. They cannot logically be used to manipulate results in an adaptive multidimensional and nonlinear system, such as a business organization. Chapter 2 stresses that companies must replace such use of quantitative measures with mindful reflection on natural systemic principles—the central feature of managing by means. Until companies understand how the use of financial targets long advocated by management accountants precludes systemic reflection they are not likely to carry out the steps needed to achieve the short-term and long-term benefits of "working to order."

The next three chapters of the book report on extensive field research showing how production, design, and assessment activities can conform to principles resembling those that guide the operation of natural living systems. Chapter 3 describes "production to order" as it is practiced in Toyota's largest American facility, Toyota Motor Manufacturing, in Georgetown, Kentucky. Chapter 4 describes "design to order," a concept developed by Scania, the Swedish builder of heavy diesel trucks and buses. Chapter 5 examines how a technique referred to as order-line profitability analysis enables companies to "assess to order." Taken together, these three chapters show business practices that reflect "managing by means" according to natural-system principles.

Chapter 6 offers a pathway on which companies can discover the natural-system principles that will enable them to manage by means. The chapter shows managers how to overcome the compulsion to chase after financial targets and, instead, to master the principles that guide living systems in nature. In a very provisional sense, the chapter provides a "how to" manual for achieving the "work to order" practices described in the previous three chapters' cases.

Chapter 7 concludes the book by indicating that the adoption of management-by-means thought and practice does more than just improve the performance and longevity of individual companies. Implicitly, management by means is synonymous with the ecosystemic thought and practice that will be required to sustain human life on Earth. Most proposals for "sustainable" business practices appeal to moral concern for the environment or they advocate technological and political solutions to problems such as pollution, resource depletion, and human economic injustice. While commendable in themselves, such proposals do nothing to challenge the fundamental assumption of management-by-results thinking that limitless growth in production, consumption, and wealth are necessary goals of business. Practices that enable companies to achieve endless growth are inherently incompatible with long-term sustainability. Manage-by-means thinking sets aside the assumption that quantitative growth is necessary for business success. The adoption of such thinking will make it more likely, therefore, that today's environmental goals will be reached as a natural by-product of everyday management practice. Notably, a company that manages by means will profit only by nurturing fundamental human and natural relationships, in contrast to the conventionally managed company that drives people to meet profit targets by sacrificing human and natural relationships.

The "profit beyond measure" awaiting companies that manage by means encompasses, then, the profit of individual businesses as well as the health and long-term survival of the ecosystem that supports all human life, including the human economic system. To the extent that it helps harmonize activities in the human economic system with "the way nature works," management by means helps resolve the persistent threat that human economic activity poses to the survival of human life in the natural ecosystem. The human economic system and nature's ecosystem both support human existence, but with a difference. Whereas nature's ecosystem supports all life on Earth, including human life, the human economic system promotes human interests without necessarily protecting the well-being of the ecosystem as a whole. It is now widely recognized that relentless economic growth has an adverse impact on the natural ecosystem—global warming, mass extinctions, decline of fisheries, loss of soil, and on and on—that threatens human existence in the long run. Causing those conditions is the thought that humans, through technology, can endlessly lift natural constraints on human growth and accumulation. That thought has shaped how companies organize work to achieve quantitative targets aimed at growth and accumulation. Management by means now proposes a way to organize work that is slower, quieter, and more likely to insure human survival in Earth's ecosystem, while being sufficiently profitable to insure the long-term survival of companies. Instead of viewing business as an institution that commercializes human technology at any cost to human and natural relationships, management by means views business as a living system through which humans use and transform technology to achieve a fuller life in harmony with other life forms and with the system that sustains all life on Earth.

. . . . .

For 15 billion years the universe has manifested a remarkable process that combines the reinforcing growth-oriented imperative of self-organization with the balancing imperative that all things interrelate. As a result of this process, a constant budget of matter and energy that emerged in a "big bang" of homogeneous heat and cosmic dust has evolved into a continually diversifying array of forms that ranges from subatomic particles, stars, and galaxies to bacterial cells, human beings, and business organizations. That process created the ecosystem on Earth that supplies all living things, including the human species, with everything they need to survive. That evolving natural process also created the power of thought that enables humans to aspire toward conditions that transcend mere survival. The human economic system and business organizations evolved out of efforts to apply thought to the problem of transcending the limits of what nature alone provides humans for survival. Working through those institutions, humans have evolved technologies for enhancing their food supply, for protecting themselves from natural predators, for extending the span of human life, for achieving comfort in all places and climates, and much more. Those institutions provide benefits that no human wishes to forego. But humans now recognize, increasingly, that their way of achieving those benefits threatens long-term human survival. The job now is to achieve the benefits of social and economic exchange without having the prevailing system of exchange lessen the chance for humans to survive in Earth's ecosystem.

Transforming business practices through the adoption of manage-by-means thinking will go a long way toward balancing and synchronizing human economic activity with nature's ecosystemic activity. Business practices identified in this book with "working to order" will do much to slow down the pace of human production and consumption, thereby helping to reverse the decline now occurring in every living system on Earth. Moreover, by reducing short-term operating costs and long-term earnings instability, these practices will do much to increase the longevity of business organizations. Indeed, were businesses to conform to nature's system, most would endure much longer than the people who work in them.[4] Given such longevity, business organizations might become a context for enhancing human creativity. Unfortunately, today most companies provide only an ephemeral setting in which the talents of many are sacrificed to sate the limitless greed of a few.

To capitalize fully on the benefits of nature's system requires no new technology. It requires new thinking. It requires the courage to abandon old questions and old assumptions. These old ways of thinking prevent people from enjoying their place in nature to the fullest. In particular, the thought that order emanates only from design and control must give way to the thought that nature's system, from which human life emerged, is wonderfully ordered. We must recognize that nature's system is in fact capable of sustaining our needs indefinitely. We have only to follow its principles rather than impose our own principles on nature. That is the key message in the chapters that follow.

1

....

Lessons from the Rouge

It is clear that the primordial intention of the universe is to produce variety in all things. . . .

—Thomas Berry[1]

He who would do good . . . must do it in Minute Particulars. General Good is the plea of the scoundrel, hypocrite, and flatterer.

—William Blake[2]

Managers of business organizations will find as a result of reading this book that they can no longer accept without question the conventional wisdom that says an organization will reach its bottom-line goals best if it drives its employees and suppliers to achieve financial targets in their work. Given this belief, a manager's primary task is to motivate people to reach and exceed quantitative targets defined by financial measures. If you are a manager who takes pride in your ability to cause people to reach quantitative targets, read on. This chapter and the next show that your success actually creates unseen and unnecessary inefficiency and instability. The new management thinking that will help you avoid such inefficiencies and instabilities is then discussed in succeeding chapters, where you learn how to lead your organization to profit beyond measure.

Managers who adopt the new thinking offered here will accept as second nature the idea that what decides an organization's long-term profitability is the way it organizes its work, not how well its members achieve financial targets. This chapter compares the long-term records of Toyota and the American "Big Three" automakers to demonstrate the truth of this proposition. It posits Toyota's principles as an example of new management thinking called "management by means." Managing by means is the antithesis of "managing by results," practices identified in this chapter with Toyota's American competitors. Those who manage by results focus on the bottom-line target and consider that achieving financial goals justifies inherently destructive practices. Those who manage by means consider that a desirable end will emerge naturally as a consequence of nurturing the activities of all employees and suppliers in a humane manner. Managing by means requires a profound change in thinking that is a bold alternative to conventional management thinking and practice.

The alternative to managing by results which this chapter advocates requires disciplined practices, sustained attention to how work is done, and nurturing every step of the work at every moment. Managing by means requires all managers in an organization to focus, as does nature, on minute particulars. Such attention to detail involves encouraging employees to cultivate their creative talents so they may best serve a customer's specific needs. This management behavior manifests the belief, not that the ends justify any means, as conventional twentieth-century management practice holds, but rather that *the means are ends in the making*. The job of managers who manage by means is to cultivate and nurture conditions that bond company talents and customer needs in a profitable union, not to drive work with destructive financial targets. Instead of a quest for relentless growth of quantitative targets that burns out companies before their time, managing by means, as this book shows, can enable a company to profit beyond measure for generation after generation.

To demonstrate what this change in thinking can mean for companies today, this opening chapter tells how differences in the way people think about work actually caused a significant difference in the long-term economic performance of real companies in recent decades. The story contrasts the consequences of acting on the belief that order must be externally imposed with the consequences of acting on the belief that order self-emerges from within. Specifically, the story tells how certain automobile manufacturers between the end of World War II and the 1980s responded differently to the problem of producing vehicles in varieties at low mass-production costs. One manufacturer is Toyota Motor Corporation of Japan and the others make up the group of American auto makers known collectively as the Big Three—General Motors, Ford, and Chrysler. The three American companies' practices differed from one another in many respects. But they are grouped here to emphasize similarities in their thinking and in their consequent styles of manufacturing that contrasted markedly with the thinking and manufacturing style found at Toyota from the 1950s to the 1980s—similarities and contrasts that persist more or less unchanged to the present day.

THE STORY: TOYOTA AND THE AMERICAN BIG THREE

In the early 1950s Toyota and the American Big Three struggled independently with a problem that confronted virtually all manufacturers following World War II. How could they satisfy customer demand for an increasingly varied range of new products, yet do so at mass-production prices? Replicating mass quantities of one variety of a product—as if each item had been stamped by the same "cookie cutter"—was the way many early-twentieth-century manufacturers, including automobile makers, had provided an abundance of material goods at prices average people could afford. Indeed, the auto maker Henry Ford helped pioneer the concept of low-cost repetitive mass production before World War I. He then pushed that concept farther than anyone else before or since in the giant facility he opened in 1919 on the banks of the River Rouge in Dearborn, Michigan.

After World War II, it was obvious that great opportunities lay ahead for companies able to offer customers the widest range of styles and models at the lowest prices. The different ways that Toyota and the American Big Three addressed this opportunity between the 1950s and the 1980s epitomizes the essence of manufacturing history in the second half of the twentieth century. To understand this crucial history, and its lessons about the impact of management thinking, we must know how executives of Toyota and the Big Three after World War II perceived the remarkably low cost at which Henry Ford's River Rouge plant produced automobiles in the 1920s. But to understand those perceptions, one must know the conventional story about how work was organized at the Rouge in that decade.

Henry Ford's River Rouge Plant in the 1920s

Probably the quintessential example of successful mass production was the giant Ford Motor Company plant built during World War I at River Rouge near Dearborn, Michigan. That plant and Ford's Highland Park plant in Detroit together produced some 15 million Model T cars by 1927. Dedicated to making one model, the Rouge facility operated virtually around the clock year in and year out until it literally sated the public's first-time demand for a basic automobile. The high profits Ford earned in that setting are usually attributed to the plant's remarkable efficiency, where "efficient" is equated with low cost per unit. The principle Ford ostensibly followed to achieve low cost was to build a facility to produce one variant of a product and then run it without interruption at full capacity until demand was sated. If the variant is referred to as A, then the most efficient and most profitable schedule for producing A is AAAAAAAA etc., where each A is assembled in a continuous flow, one at a time.[3]

A way to organize work to meet that schedule is shown in Figure 1–1, a highly simplified schematic of the flow of work in Ford's River Rouge plant in the early 1920s. An important point to observe in that figure is that the work more or less paced itself. Indeed, the schedule pushed material at a relentless pace that was sustained by having machines

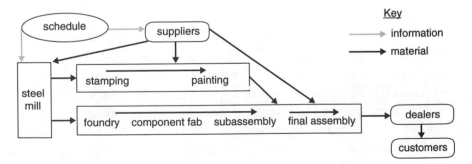

Figure 1–1: Mass Production Without Variety in the 1920s

and workers—the people themselves being little more than "cogs in the gears" of the system—perform repetitive tasks as fast as possible. Given the simplicity of the flow and the repetitive nature of tasks at each work station it was not necessary to spend extra resources on activities to control and expedite the flow of material. In effect, the flow was dictated by the plant's initial design—a design that promoted efficiency by allowing work to flow continuously from beginning to end and by having it consume at every point only the resources needed to advance one unit of output one step further toward completion. The River Rouge plant in 1925 produced about one vehicle per minute in a total lead time of about three days and nine hours from steel making to finished vehicle.[4]

A sign of the mechanistic roots supporting this mass-production system is the relation between information and the flow of work. The primary information influencing the flow of work originates *outside* the process, in the schedule and in the layout of the plant. Neither the material nor the workers who transform it supply any information to guide the process. Both material and workers respond only to outside influences, literally being "pushed" by external information. Underlying that information is a design, or abstract model, that defines the laws governing the motion of material and workers in the plant. The mass-production model features homogeneity of inputs and outputs (such as uniform material and interchangeable parts transformed by endlessly repetitive steps into identical black Model Ts), large scale, high speed of throughput, and uninterrupted flow of work. The design of the work process and the quality of incoming material insures an acceptable level of quality. The uninterrupted flow of homogeneous units at a rate as fast as possible insures the lowest possible cost per unit of output. The primary rule suggested by this mechanistic model of production—a rule enshrined in the phrase "economies of scale"—is that costs per unit fall as the speed and volume of output rise.

How Perceptions of Low Cost at the Rouge Shaped the Quest for Variety after World War II

Until the mid-1920s, Americans delighted in Ford's Model T, a private, enclosed, gasoline-powered alternative to bicycles and horse-drawn buggies. Few buyers expected or sought a variety of designs. The Model T's low price, sustained by the low costs Ford achieved at the Rouge, offset strong desires for variety, at least into the mid-decade. As time passed, however, and the car-buying public grew more sophisticated, they wanted cars with more features and styles. General Motors responded after 1920 by coordinating activities among its several divisions so as to provide a car for "every purse and purpose." But on the whole, such efforts were thwarted first by the Great Depression and then by World War II.[5] The solution to the problem of producing variety at low cost awaited the rise of the strong postwar consumer market.

After World War II, Toyota and the American Big Three addressed differently the problem of how to produce varieties of automobiles at low cost. Their distinctive responses to that problem reflected adherence—although perhaps unacknowledged—to basic differences in thinking. To appreciate the starkly different kinds of thinking that characterize Toyota and the American Big Three, consider the following meeting in 1982 between Eiji Toyoda, then head of Toyota Motor Corporation, and Philip Caldwell, then head of the Ford Motor Company. At that time, Toyota was emerging as the lowest-cost producer of the highest quality automobiles in the world. Ford and its Big Three partners were then plagued by falling market share, rising customer dissatisfaction with the quality of their vehicles, and unprecedented financial losses. Presumably, Caldwell visited Toyota in Japan in 1982 seeking new ideas. During Caldwell's visit, his host, Mr. Toyoda, is said to have toasted Mr. Caldwell by saying, "There is no secret to how we learned to do what we do, Mr. Caldwell. *We learned it at the Rouge.*"[6]

It must have been obvious to Mr. Caldwell in 1982 that he and his colleagues at Ford, as well as his counterparts in the other Big Three companies, had definitely *not* viewed the operations at Henry Ford's Rouge River plant in the same way as had Toyota. As Caldwell surely observed, Toyota by the early 1980s was using stunningly simple means to successfully produce a diverse array of vehicles at mass-production costs, while maintaining the highest quality and earning gratifying profits. Meanwhile, Chrysler, General Motors, and Ford from the 1950s to the 1980s produced an increasing variety of vehicles by using complicated means, generated products of variable quality, and often suffered disappointing financial results. Why did the Big Three apparently not discover the same key to success at the Rouge that Toyota claimed it did? When Toyota's managers considered that facility, what did they perceive? When executives at the Big Three companies contemplated that facility, what perceptions did they share? To understand the differences in how Toyota and the Big Three interpreted operations at the River Rouge plant is to understand the difference between Toyota's distinctive thinking and the thinking that has dominated management practice in most of the world's other businesses during the past five decades. How different *methods of thinking* affect long-term performance is the lesson to be learned from what follows.[7]

MASS-PRODUCING VARIETY IN BATCHES

What the American Big Three Saw at the Rouge

The AAAAAAAA mass-production schedule and the way to organize work shown in Figure 1–1 faced a challenge when companies realized that their economic survival demanded making products in more than one variety. By 1950, the growth of markets, and the even faster growth in demand for varieties of products, was convincing more and more companies that they could profit most by selling products in increasing varieties. One way to meet these demands was to build a new plant dedicated to each new variant. But the idea of replicating a plant as large and complex as the River Rouge facility for each variant seemed impractical, especially as the number of varieties increased. Therefore, companies searched for ways to make two or more variants of a product in the same plant, but do so efficiently and profitably.

In the past fifty years, most manufacturers who have strived to produce output in varieties have remained committed to the mass-production thinking that says high profits depend, ultimately, on producing at low costs by running operations without interruption at full capacity for as long as possible. But in the context of making products in varieties, they discovered that "running without interruption" and "running at full capacity" are not necessarily achieved as simply as they are when the production schedule is AAAAAAAA and work is organized in a continuous flow that consumes resources at the rate needed to produce one order at a time.

Look first at the effect variety has on the production schedule. Whereas the mass producer of one variety, A, can simply "turn on the faucet" and watch product flow at a steady pace such as AAAAAAAAA, that same producer must consider what to do about the time it takes to change from A to other varieties of product, if a decision is made to produce varieties. Were it possible to change instantaneously from A to B to C, then a flow such as AAABCCAACBB etc. could be achieved without "turning off the faucet." However, if changing from one variety to another takes time, then one cannot produce a second and third variant, say B and C, in the same plant as A without "turning off the faucet" from time to time to change from A to B to C. The key to understanding how the Big Three automakers and most American manufacturers addressed the issue of variety after World War II is to realize that they all took for granted the times it took to change over the various types of equipment used in their plants in the late 1940s and early 1950s. They apparently saw no benefit to reducing the time it took to do individual changeovers. Instead, as they increased the variety of output, they took steps to reduce the *total amount* of time spent changing over. They did so by separating the various processes through which material flowed continuously in the early River Rouge plant. With processes separated, material for different varieties could be batched and processed "efficiently" in long runs that economized on changeovers.

The System the Big Three Created in Response to What They Saw at the Rouge

As noted above, if changeover time is not reduced it causes delay, and the more so as varieties increase. Hence, variety is not produced by taking the daily production schedule from AAAAAAAAA, where every A potentially is produced to customer order, to something like AABAAABBCCCAAA, where each A, B, and C is also produced to customer order. Instead, following the same sequence, the daily production schedule becomes AA(delay)B(delay)AAA(delay)BB(delay) CCC(delay)AAA. Each transition from A to B to C requires stopping to change something, and often very many things.

Such delays are problematic to a mass producer whose rule is to "run without interruption at full capacity" as much as possible. Each delay not only requires extra work and cost, their number can extend the production schedule into another shift or another day—prompting yet more cost and delay. The general solution to this problem favored by most American manufacturers who regarded variety as necessary to survival after 1950 was to schedule production so that each variety could be batched separately and run without interruption as long as possible. Continuing the above example, batching each different variant would generate a schedule AAAAAAAA(delay)BBB(delay)CCC. This schedule reduces the number of interruptions and increases the percentage of time that the facility is up and running product, all of which reduces cost and, presumably, increases profitability.

However, producing varieties in long-running batches creates new costs because the mix of varieties produced does not automatically mesh with the mix of varieties that customers wish to purchase. Producing in batches means producing out of step with the flow of customer orders. Thus, to avoid having production deviate too much from consumption, time and resources must be spent on forecasting demand or, alternatively, on stimulating demand so that it fits what you are producing. Market forecasting and advertising become expensive necessities for achieving the low costs promised by batch-producing varieties of output. Even so, there is still a chance of being wrong much of the time. Sometimes a batch will contain more of a variety than customers ultimately want, which is a costly waste. At times, a batch will tie up capacity and prevent making something else that customers *do* want, which can lead to a costly loss of sales.

Most mass-production manufacturers addressed these added costs of batching varieties by speeding up the flow of output for each batch. More output in a given amount of time meant lower costs per unit, including the costs caused by batch production. Thus, manufacturers who reduced the total amount of time lost changing from one variety to another by producing varieties in batches adhered to the mass-production principle of "running without interruption as fast as possible," at least during the time each batch was running. By speeding up production and increasing output, thereby reducing costs per unit, they attempted to control the costs of forecasting demand, discounting prices on unwanted output, and losing sales. In this way they honored the mechanistic concept of "economies of scale."

Making varieties in batches led to new ways of organizing work that generated additional costs, besides those costs caused because batched production is invariably out of step with customer demand. In principle, material flows without interruption as one batch of components is being produced. However, all the batches of components that go into making one variant of a product do not flow continuously from start to finish, like the flow that occurs when work is organized as it is in Figure 1–1. Because of the widely different changeover times among operations such as stamping, painting, casting, component building, and final assembly, work on each variety of component will occur in separate batches *in each operation.* Thus, while the components needed to make each variant of a product eventually travel from raw material to final assembly, they do so by lurching through the operations in discontinuous fits and starts. In practice, components from each operation are produced in a separate department or plant and then sent to staging areas, such as warehouses, from which they are shipped in the appropriate order to separate final assembly departments or plants. While batch-produced materials may flow ultimately into varieties of finished products through a final assembly operation that resembles the pattern in Figure 1–1, the continuous flow in machining and component making seen at River Rouge in the 1920s did not exist in a typical American automobile final assembly plant by the 1970s.

To deal with the realities of batch production, mass producers who wished to manufacture automobiles (and other products) in varieties after World War II reorganized their operations in a completely different way than Henry Ford had done at River Rouge. As variety proliferated after 1950, most large manufacturing organizations in America and Europe separated their otherwise linked operations into separate departments, and allowed each operation to perform according to its own changeover rhythm. This "decoupled" batch production approach to mass-producing variety featured uninterrupted work only in each separate operation, followed by transit to a central staging area, or warehouse, where material waited until a schedule directed it to flow in varieties to a final assembly plant (Figure 1–2).

Making all the pieces in this complicated "flow" come together in

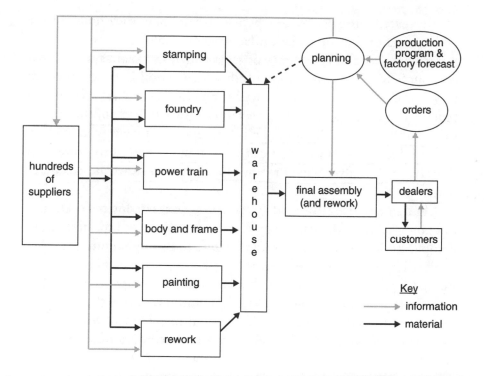

Figure 1–2. Mass-Producing Variety in Batches by the 1970s

the right places at the right times required people and equipment not employed in the actual making of the products themselves. These resources, referred to as "overhead," were employed in activities such as scheduling, controlling, expediting, storing, inspecting, transporting, and reworking. Particularly noteworthy was the investment of resources needed to profitably handle the material flows shown by solid lines and arrows in Figure 1–2. Those resources were invested in sophisticated scheduling and control systems, increasingly computer-based, shown by the dotted lines and arrows in that figure. One could say that all these resources represented an "information factory" that was separate from but alongside the material-flow factory. Ironically, this "information factory" was needed to impose order on a batch-driven system that had been created to minimize the costs of producing output in varieties. Eventually, the "information factory" in most companies would employ more workers than the *real* factory would employ to actually transform material into finished products.

However, company leaders believed that they could control the added costs of the "information factory" by applying the same mass-production logic of economies of scale and speed that says that cost per unit falls the more units you produce in a period. According to this logic, profitability is always assured if enough output is produced to reduce unit costs below the prices customers will pay. So, the answer to the added costs of building an information factory was to increase the speed and amount of output (i.e., "throughput") even more, and then engage in advertising or other incentives to stimulate customer demand.

cause of consumption & debts?

Most companies attributed the activities associated with batch production to complexity caused by *producing varieties* of product, not to complications caused by the way they *organized work* to produce that variety. Those activities were virtually absent from a continuously flowing mass-production system such as that shown in Figure 1–1. They were utterly essential, however, to the smooth working of batch-production systems that produced varieties of products as shown in Figure 1–2. The following list describes only a few examples of such added activities:

1. Separating parts of the system, to accommodate their different operating rates, made inventories and warehouses indispensable. All work, until final assembly, was forwarded to warehouse staging areas from which balanced flows to final assembly could be coordinated in the varieties desired. Mass production without variety does not require warehouses (Figure 1–1). By the end of the 1950s, however, most American manufacturing plants could not operate without them (Figure 1–2).

2. Separating the system into independent stages—decoupling—created a need for production controllers and schedulers to coordinate the movement of things between these stages and from inventory to final assembly. To cope with the added level of complication brought on by this work, by the 1960s and 1970s, most large American manufacturing organizations were using production scheduling algorithms, such as material requirements planning (MRP), made possible by the recent appearance of high-speed mainframe computers. Over the years, exponential growth of the capacity and speed of computerized information technology (IT) systems reinforced the illusion that computers always

made it possible to manage the complexity attendant upon mass-producing more and more variety.

3. Over long periods of time such as a model year, output from all parts of
the system in Figure 1–2 is expected to balance out with customer demand. However, that "balance" is often forced by means such as building
inventory, scrapping excess output, investing in advertising campaigns, reducing prices to clear out excess stock, and, in cases of severe imbalance,
eliminating parts of the system by laying people off and selling assets.

4. Workers in each independent part of the system, producing to schedule
for inventory, cannot receive immediate feedback from workers in the
next operation. Hence, many errors and defects either go undetected, or
are detected and intentionally ignored. Errors and defects must be remedied through rework at a later time, often at great cost. Not unexpectedly,
the number of uncorrected defects appearing in the final consumers' products rose dramatically in the 1960s and 1970s in most American manufacturing companies that adopted the mode of production shown in
Figure 1–2.

5. Compartmentalizing—decoupling—the flow of work to accommodate
different changeover rhythms creates a correlation between increasing varieties of output and decreasing the amount of time spent each day actually producing, as opposed to changing over. To meet annual output
schedules, therefore, work must be done at increasingly faster rates *during
those times when output actually is being produced.* This means that the
rated capacity of machinery (size and speed) must increase as variety (and
the consequent need for changing over) increases.

6. Rising costs encourage the belief that if performance incentives are offered
to workers, workers will hasten production, thus helping drive down unit
costs. Unfortunately, the outcome of performance incentives has proved
as a rule to be analogous to what might happen should each musician in
an orchestra be rewarded for playing faster and louder than the others. Cacophony would result, not the harmony arising from the interaction of
specialized instruments adhering to the same fundamental rhythm. Performance incentives invariably are a source of cacophony that translates
into yet higher costs.[8]

As variety and volume of output grow, the practice of separating the
flow of work into segments—decoupling—creates increasing delays,

and therefore increasing costs, in the overall system.[9] Changing over for more varieties generates delay, as does the time needed to inspect and rework parts, to schedule flows of work, to sort and store parts, and to move parts and material over longer distances. As an example of this impact, the overall lead time to make a vehicle went from three days and nine hours at Ford's River Rouge plant in the mid-1920s (Figure 1–1) to several weeks in most auto-making organizations by the 1970s (Figure 1–2).

Similar increases in lead times caused most American manufacturers after the 1950s to experience painful increases in total costs. These increases usually appeared in the accounting ledgers under headings such as "overhead" or "indirect costs." Most accountants before the late 1980s did not have, for various reasons, proper tools with which to analyze and explain costs that fell under those headings. Traditional cost accounting practices simply allocated such costs to departments, products, and other cost objects, and gave little or no regard to what caused the costs. Thus, accountants could show when, and by how much, costs rose, but they could not explain *why* costs rose, especially not overhead costs. Nor did it seem to occur either to accountants or to those managers using their numbers that *the way work was being organized* might itself be the primary cause of rising costs.

As noted above, executives in most manufacturing companies, following mechanistic principles of scale economy and mass production, believed they could address these costs, and keep unit cost (i.e., cost ÷ unit) in line, by *increasing* the scale and speed of output in each one of the various operations of the decoupled work system. In that regard, cost accounting and production planning became essential tools to help determine the necessary scale and speed to keep costs in line with targets. This scale-and-speed model enabled executives to further rationalize the decision to separate the system into parts. Moreover, this model encouraged subordinating the issue of how work is done in the parts. Instead, the model placed emphasis on the perceived need to get products out the door, without regard to any imbalance in the rates at which the various parts of the system operated. In other words, while great attention was paid to meeting output targets, slight attention was paid to how work was done to produce output.

A comparison of Figure 1–1 with Figure 1–2 suggests that the shift from mass production without variety to mass production with variety created a complicated and messy pattern of work in which it was difficult, if not impossible, to perceive any sense of order. Systems resembling the flow of work in Figure 1–2 were designed according to the same mechanistic principles as the continuous flow systems in Figure 1–1—that is, run without interruption and at full capacity—but they did not present the same appearance of order. Order seemed to be introduced, eventually, by computer-oriented production control, scheduling, and cost accounting systems. Production schedules (e.g., MRP) and standard cost budget variances, for example, provided managers with a sense of what should be done at any time, and how far actual results deviated from targets.

At first the abstract information compiled and transmitted by these computer systems merely supplemented the perspectives of managers who were already familiar with concrete details of the operations they managed, no matter how complicated and confused those operations became. Such individuals, prevalent in top management ranks before 1970, had a clear sense of the difference between "the map" created by abstract computer calculations and "the territory" that people inhabited in the workplace. Increasingly after 1970, however, managers lacking in shopfloor experience or in engineering training, often trained in graduate business schools, came to dominate American and European manufacturing establishments.[10] In their hands the "map was the territory." In other words, they considered reality to be the abstract quantitative models, the management accounting reports, and the computer scheduling algorithms that were used to make sense of decoupled batch-production systems.

With the rise of this new generation of managers after 1970, mechanistic and quantitative thinking began to shape management practices with a vengeance not only in large manufacturing firms, but in business, governmental, and educational organizations all over the world. The hallmark of this emphasis is the use of abstract economic models and quantitative measures to drive work and to evaluate individuals at all levels in organizations. Instead of paying attention to how work is organized and how the organization of work might affect financial results, managers increasingly saw workers and organizations as collections of objects, responsive solely to pressure to achieve external quantitative targets. This belief in quantitative measurement as the primary tool of management led to "management by results" (MBR), a subject that chapter 2 covers in much greater depth. MBR is perhaps the primary legacy of applying mechanistic thinking to business practice.

Indeed, the use of abstract quantitative measurement to direct work—the hallmark of MBR—spread rapidly after the 1970s. Beginning with manufacturers' efforts to control the costs of mass-producing variety with batches, MBR spread eventually to almost all types of business, regardless of size, type of markets served, or extent of variety produced. However, the decoupling of work into compartmentalized stages, the increased speed of work, and the increased size of batches inevitably drove a wide chasm between workers and final consumers. Not only did this not reduce costs, it led to rising costs and an accompanying decline in quality. After the late 1970s, these developments drove away customers in many cases when alternative suppliers appeared— often from Japan and Western Europe—who could provide variety, with quality, and low cost.

By the early 1980s, most manufacturers assumed it was nearly impossible to efficiently and profitably make increasing varieties of products for large markets. They believed they could profit by producing wide varieties *or* by selling in large markets, but not by doing both. Indeed, a cornerstone of strategic management thought since the 1970s is the belief that a company, to be profitable, must choose between differentiation and mass production. Presumably, a company that differentiates sacrifices scale economies by multiplying the varieties of its products. Therefore, it can be profitable only by selling in small niche markets where prices are high enough to cover the high costs of variety. Alternatively, the argument goes, a company that limits its product variety can sell large quantities profitably at low prices, because it efficiently mass-produces each variety.[11]

Proponents of this strategic thinking assume that variety spawns complexity and, therefore, extra costs that make it difficult to be profitable in large markets. They are right, at least up to a point. Variety does generate complexity, and lots of it, in most organizations. What strategic analysts have failed to consider is that such complexity may not be due to proliferation of product variety. Instead, it may be due to the way that work is organized. If work were organized to avoid complexity, then choosing between differentiation and mass production would be unnecessary. But to organize work so that it produces variety at low cost required a shift in thinking, from the mass-production thinking that was implicit in the American Big Three auto makers' methods to a different way of thinking that became embodied in Toyota's methods.

PRODUCING VARIETY IN A CONTINUOUS FLOW

What Toyota Saw at the Rouge

When Eiji Toyoda told Philip Caldwell that Toyota had discovered the secret to its success at the Rouge, his comment implied that what Toyota had perceived about operations at the Rouge was very different than what Caldwell and his Ford colleagues or their counterparts in the other Big Three auto companies had seen. For one thing, it seems that Toyota people did not view low cost at the Rouge in terms of its scale, its throughput, or its managers' efforts to impose external targets for speed and cost on workers in the plant. Instead, they seemed to perceive a holistic pattern permeating every minute particular of the system. On one level, the pattern that caught Toyota's attention was the overall continuous flow of work in the Rouge as a whole. But at a much deeper level, they observed that work flowed continuously through *each part of the system*—literally through each individual work station—at the same rate, the rate that finished units flowed off the line.

It is not difficult to see that this pattern has the potential to produce the superior costs, quality, and flexibility for which Toyota became so famous by the 1980s. If every step in a continuous flow works at the same rate, then at any moment each step consumes only the resources required to advance one customer's order one step closer to completion. In that case, for the volume of output being produced, *costs are as low as they can be*, given the total number of process steps, the work designed for each step, the design of the product, the prices of inputs, and the certainty that everything done in each step is done correctly.

Indeed, to Toyota's people, Henry Ford's River Rouge system achieved low costs because balancing every step in a continuous flow *conserves resources*. With all steps linked in a balanced flow, no worker did more than was needed to prepare only the work called for by the next step, and then pass it on. At the limit, each work station was scaled to meet the requirements of no more than one unit's worth of product at a time. Moreover, Toyota people perceived that if each worker could design and control the steps he or she performed, then workers could perform *different* steps on each unit that passed by them in every time interval. Thus, *variety could be achieved at no greater cost* than if all units were identical.

Toyota people saw low cost at the Rouge as a property of the system that emerged spontaneously from relationships among the parts—the individual workers and the steps they performed to meet customers' needs—and the pattern that was implicit in those relationships. Low cost was not forced by manipulating the speed at which individual workers performed their tasks. It was achieved by nurturing in each work station the conditions that maintained a balanced flow overall— the pattern that defined the whole system. Thus, perceiving the key feature of Henry Ford's system to be its ability to pace every step of the work at the same rate that finished units flowed off the line convinced Toyota executives after World War II that *variety had to be achieved in the context of continuous flow* if it was to be achieved at the lowest possible cost and highest quality. The question they faced was how to accomplish this goal.

To answer this question, Toyota concentrated more attention after the 1950s than did the American Big Three on exploring the implications of continuously linking and balancing steps in the system.[12] For them, the scale and speed necessary in a batch-oriented system that decouples work into separate compartments may have seemed to impose excessively high capital costs to achieve variety. No doubt the scarcity of capital and a concern to conserve resources prompted Toyota's executives to concentrate on resource-saving linking and balancing as their means of achieving variety. The scarcity Japanese manufacturers faced after World War II precluded Toyota achieving variety by decoupling and batch-producing because they lacked the means to store inventories in warehouses, to employ large staffs of schedulers, expediters, and production controllers, to inspect for and rework accumulated defects, and to tolerate weeks-long lead times from order to delivery of finished vehicles. Necessity required that they work on a smaller scale than the Big

Three, with smaller inventories, but still achieve low mass-production costs. Working carefully became their watchword. At Toyota, Taiichi Ohno and his colleagues identified reducing individual *changeover* times as the key to achieving variety of output while keeping all steps linked in a continuous flow.[13]

The System Toyota Created in Response to What It Saw at the Rouge

Toyota executives in the 1950s gave no credence to the notion adopted by the American Big Three that variety could be achieved at low cost by decoupling the continuous flow into separate parts and producing varieties in batches. Such separation and batch production would subvert the continuous flow system's inherent ability to conserve resources. Variety could be achieved at low cost, Toyota believed, only in a system where material and work flowed continuously, one order at a time. Brilliantly answering the problem of how to achieve variety in such a system, Toyota's executives realized that they had to make changeover times conform as closely as possible to the rate at which finished units flowed out of final assembly. They theorized that if the time needed to change over every step in the system were actually less than the time interval between units flowing off the line, then it would be possible for every unit coming off the line to be different from every other unit, and still costs per unit would be nearly the same as if every unit were identical. Those conditions, in other words, would make it possible build a unique product for each customer, at Model-T costs.

The gap between theory and practice is often gigantic, of course. To make theory coincide with reality, Toyota evidenced prolonged dedication. From the 1950s until the 1970s, they carried out an unremitting campaign to reduce changeover times in all steps of their manufacturing system. Although Toyota never achieved the goal of performing all changeovers faster than the rate at which output flows off the line, it did substantially reduce changeover times—by orders of magnitude in many cases. It also designed expeditious ways to use inventory buffers where changeover times did not mesh perfectly with the material flow rate. Consequently, virtually all work requiring changeover was incorporated as much as possible into the continuous flow.

By the mid 1970s Toyota had created a continuous flow that focused

on connecting workers with customers in self-organizing relationships
that are capable of continually generating unique outcomes—diversity,
in other words. A later chapter that discusses Toyota's largest American
manufacturing facility, located in Georgetown, Kentucky, describes
this production system in great depth. Without going into details,
therefore, a few general comments at this point can show how the main
features of Toyota's system contrast with features of the Big Three auto
makers' system depicted in Figure 1–2.

Probably the key feature of Toyota's system is to have every step in
the entire process join the creative talents of a specific worker with the
needs of a specific customer, forming a relationship that is not only the
defining feature of a business, but is also the necessary condition to insure its long-run survival (Figure 1–3, upper panel). In a large organization such as Toyota, each worker does not necessarily interact directly
with the final customer who "pays the bill." Instead, hundreds or thousands of individual employees do serve an "internal" customer—the
person in the next operation (Figure 1–3, lower panel). Those hundreds and thousands of internal connections satisfy the overall relationship between the company and the final customer. They do so
because the company links all internal connections in a continuous
flow and because standards that each person sets for his or her work insure that serving the needs of the internal customer ultimately fulfills
the final customer's needs.

The continuous flow of material and work in this system resembles
the metabolic flow of matter and energy that maintains and sustains a
living organism, such as a tree. Analogous to the workers in the above
diagram's continuous flow are the cells in a tree that absorb energy from
the sun's rays, mineral nutrients from Earth and its atmosphere, and
transform them into carbohydrates, cellulose, and other substances that
energize and sustain the tree's existence. Encoded in each cell's DNA
and provided in the constant feedback among the tree's billions of
richly interconnected cells is all the information needed to carry out the
tree's metabolic activities, throughout its life.

In the system depicted in Figure 1–3 it is the customer who provides
energy, in the form of money. This energy enables the company to
transform material into goods and services the customer desires. It also
provides various forms of compensation—such as delight with a job

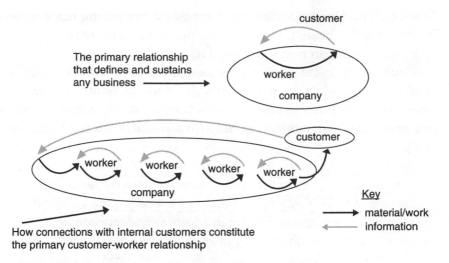

Figure 1–3: Customer-Worker Relationship Defines Every Step of the Work

well done—to those who use their talents and resources to transform material into products that satisfy a customer. Feedback is conveyed through the web of relationships in this system and by standards that are "encoded" in every step of the work, insuring that every person at every point in the web always has all the information he or she needs to do the work.

This was the system that Philip Caldwell observed at Toyota City in 1982. It differed enormously from the decoupled batch-driven systems to which the American Big Three were accustomed by 1980. Those systems were characterized by a high degree of imbalance, large and unavoidable inventory buffers, large machinery, and myriad additional capital and "overhead" resources to transport, expedite, schedule, and rework in every part of the system. Notably, the system Caldwell observed at Toyota did not require the costly "information factory" that was by that time an inescapable part of almost all large-scale American manufacturing systems. This difference is not well understood by most people outside Toyota even today, nearly twenty years later. More will be said about this in the chapter that discusses Toyota's modern U.S. facility in Georgetown, Kentucky. The point to recognize here is that in a balanced continuous flow, as one has in Toyota facilities, *the work itself is the information,* and all *the information needed to direct operations is in the work.* Operations are not driven by external information and controls such as those that have increasingly characterized the typical large-scale American manufacturing facility since the 1950s.

Caldwell witnessed at Toyota a system that conserved resources, including capital, while permitting unprecedented flexibility and variety of output. The system's strength resided in the time, discipline, determination, and ingenuity of each individual worker. Reducing changeovers, for example, took the effort and imagination of everyone on the line. Toyota had discovered that it is more profitable to invest in informed, responsible workers who make decisions on the line than to invest in new capital machinery and other expensive "overhead" resources. Few American or European business leaders have ever recognized that Toyota's strategy of *conserving resources* by incorporating every step into a balanced continuous flow is not the same thing as *cutting costs* by eliminating "nonvalue activity." The latter idea is central to recently popular process improvement initiatives such as "activity-based management," "business process reengineering, " and "lean manufacturing," none of which really captures the essential point of conserving resources by avoiding—not eliminating—waste. More will be said about this in the chapter on Toyota that follows.

By the early 1980s, Toyota's system produced output at just the rate needed to satisfy current demand, as Henry Ford's system had done in 1925, but Toyota now produced that output in varieties. Their continuously linked system featured much smaller machines than those used in American Big Three plants, and each step operated at a slower rate. Indeed, virtually every step operated at just the rate needed to complete the requirements for one customer's order at a time. The steps in Toyota's system were designed "to carry small loads and make frequent trips," like the fabled water beetle in Japanese mythology. And each trip had to matter. Therefore, Toyota's employees always attempted to do things right the first time—a strategy W. Edwards Deming taught in his famous presentations to Japanese manufacturing executives during the summer of 1951. Deming's influence, their own post-World War II circumstance, quiet resolve, willingness to invest long periods of time in the outcome, and their ingenuity are just a few qualities that helped Toyota head in a new direction. The American Big Three, also creatures of their circumstances, featured a compartmentalized system requiring large machines producing output in large batches at high speed that required storage and retrieval.

BEYOND THE ROUGE: LESSONS FOR TWENTY-FIRST CENTURY MANAGERS

The story about Toyota and the American Big Three automakers is background to a much larger issue than the relative performance of two groups of manufacturers. The purpose of the story is not simply to show businesses how certain techniques for organizing work will improve their profitability. Toyota, of course, stands alone among the world's auto makers for having achieved remarkable profits year in and year out for the past forty years (see the Appendix to Chapter 1). Moreover, the American Big Three and most other large auto companies in the world have enjoyed unprecedented profitability in the 1990s, in part because of lessons learned from Toyota. But no company so far has matched Toyota's success.[14] Indeed, most companies have learned little more than how to copy various Toyota methods. None seems to have discovered and mastered the real source of the difference in performance between Toyota and the Big Three from the 1950s to the present. That source is the *different thinking* implicit in Toyota's methods, not just the methods themselves.

The challenge that companies face today—including Toyota itself—is to identify and continually refine that thinking. Virtually all improvement initiatives of the past decade or so—just-in-time, total quality management, business process reengineering, activity-based management, lean manufacturing, enterprise resource planning, scorecard management, and so on—take for granted the quantitative and mechanistic thinking that has shaped business practices for the past fifty years or more. All those initiatives do generate some improvement, but only within narrow limits set by that prevailing mode of thinking. Locked into traditional thinking, adherents to those initiatives invariably ignore, and lose, an opportunity to achieve far greater improvement by adopting new thinking that reframes old questions in new ways that open new doors.

New thinking was implicit in Toyota's perception that variety at mass-production costs requires both continuous flow and a concerted effort to *nurture the pattern of continuous flow in the minute particulars* of every worker's actions. Significantly, that thinking caused Toyota to create a production system with features that resemble those commonly found in living systems. For example, the information system used to guide operations in Toyota is strikingly similar to the information system found in a living organism. It is embodied within, not imposed from outside. Whether or not Toyota consciously designed its system in the light of living-system principles, its pervasive similarities to a natural organic system undoubtedly contribute to the company's legendary prosperity.

The resemblance of Toyota's system to a natural life system may also help explain why no company to date has successfully imitated Toyota's success. Scientists came to understand the principles of self-organizing natural systems and the pervasive influence of those principles throughout the universe just in the last few decades. Only recently have they explained those principles in terms that would enable business leaders to understand what it means to view an organization as a living system, rather than think of it as an inert mechanism. Today this new scientific understanding of the principles that guide the evolution of all natural systems in the universe, gleaned largely from modern physics, enables us to describe the path business leaders must follow to engender those same principles in the activities of their organizations. To help chart that path is the main goal of this book. However, to follow the chart it is necessary to describe, if only briefly, the recent revolution in science that shows how one set of principles explains the emergence and functioning of all systems in the universe—from galaxies, stars, and carbon-based life on Earth to human business organizations.

PRINCIPLES OF NATURE TO INFORM TWENTY-FIRST CENTURY MANAGEMENT

Modern physics tells us that the universe is a self-ordering system that continually transforms a fixed budget of energy and matter according to three principles that have operated since an originating "big bang" some fifteen billion years ago.[15] In essence, the universe is a constantly evolving system that operates according to the same few principles in all its parts, including our Earth and all organic life on it. Human organizations such as the modern global business are themselves systems that self-emerged in the context of the same three principles as all other natural systems in the universe.[16] The thesis of this book is that to survive and prosper in the long run requires a business to follow practices that adhere to those principles.

The three primary principles that scientists consider sufficient to account for all phenomena in the universe are *self-organization, interdependence,* and *diversity*.[17] Self-organization means that everything in the universe has the power to sustain its own unique identity. Just as the universe itself creates its own order and its own identity out of homogeneous, random disorder, so each entity in nature makes real—"actualizes"—an inherent unique potential that defines it as utterly distinctive. By itself, the power to self-organize—to define and sustain the unique self—implies the potential to grow without limit. Indeed, that potential exists everywhere at every moment.

Preventing any single entity in nature from using its self-organizing power to grow without limit is the principle of interdependence. Theoretically, it is possible for any one entity in nature to use all the energy that exists simply to embody its unique self in all the matter that exists. However, nature has not permitted any one phenomenon to fill the entire universe. Instead of only one galaxy, there are billions. Instead of only one type of atom there exist many. This limitation on growth arises from the principle of interdependence. Deeply rooted in the fabric of modern relativistic and quantum physics, this principle holds that everything in the universe interrelates with everything else. Because all things are related, the single self-organizing entity inevitably bumps up against, and is challenged by, other self-organizing identities. This perpetual challenge limits the ability of any single system in the universe to use energy to embody itself into more and more matter.

In fact, the interactions of unique identities transform a propensity for extensive growth into a universal capacity to generate new things—new entities that did not exist before these interactions. Nature combines a cyclical dynamic—the imperative to relate—with a linear dynamic—the imperative to self-organize—in a recursive process that generates endless newness. For example, within galaxies the interaction among hydrogen and helium atoms generates stars; among sexually reproducing organisms on Earth, the interaction of partners generates new offspring; and among humans the interaction that occurs in conversation generates new thinking. Newness continually arises from the constant interaction of unique entities. This remarkable production of new entities occurs because everything is related to everything else, and relationships among self-organizing entities generate diversity, the third principle underlying the unfolding universe.

According to the diversity principle, nature's process never produces the same output the same way twice. Nature never repeats itself because, being a recursive process, it continually acts upon the output of its own operation.[18] In other words, nature self-organizes unique output in a cyclical process that continuously reabsorbs its own output as feedback.[19] Compound interest is an example of a recursive process. Each cycle of the process generates a new amount of money without any input other than "feedback" from the output of the previous cycle. In nature's process, however, newness does not necessarily mean quantitative growth. Instead, it features endless qualitative differentiation among the outputs being produced. In nature, no matter how many billions of recurrences there are of one phenomenon—galaxies, carbon atoms, stars, humans, or whatever—no two are the same. Moreover, the species of phenomena themselves seem to diversify without limit. Indeed, diversification produces constant change—the central discovery modern science has made about the nature of the universe.

Nature's capacity for constant change, constant diversification, insures the survival of the universe and the biosystem on Earth.[20] As systems engineers have long understood, a dynamic open system that clings to one state or condition is destined to collapse. If the surfer riding in the curl of a giant wave clings to one position, he or she will fall. The surfer maintains an upright position—that is, survives—by constantly changing every muscle in harmony with the ever-changing contour of the wave. Similarly, the universe changes continuously through the perpetual flux of a constant budget of matter and energy. The Norwegian ecophilosopher Arne Naess used the phrase "rich ends from simple means" to describe nature's seemingly endless ability to generate newness from the same bundle of matter and energy.[21]

Businesses that emulate the principles of natural systems, as Toyota seems to have done, can achieve the "rich ends from simple means"—

such as variety at mass-production costs—referred to by Naess. Unfortunately, most businesses today are held back from achieving variety at low cost because the thinking that guides their actions is not derived from the principles that shape nature's system. Instead, their thinking derives from principles that are grounded in a mechanistic worldview that has prevailed since the 1700s. The culmination of the work of Copernicus, Galileo, Descartes, Newton, and others, this worldview sees the universe as a machine—a giant "clockwork" as Newton described it. The order a machine manifests is imposed on its parts by an external design. Business leaders holding such a notion regard companies as machines and employees as inanimate cogs in the machine's gears. Guided by unconscious conformity to this mechanistic view, they cannot believe that satisfactory results will emerge simply by following principles implicit in all natural living systems. Indeed, most managers today believe that the best way for an organization to achieve its overall financial goals is to have each of its parts concentrate on achieving local quantitative targets that by design or plan are supposed to add up to the desired company-wide results. Reinforcing that belief is the conviction that what occurs in the organization happens because of external forces and influences that can be expressed quantitatively. The whole is seen as equal to the sum of the parts, and the parts are themselves regarded as independent, not intrinsically related. Such thinking shaped the practices of those manufacturers, like the American Big Three auto makers, that adopted batch-oriented modes of mass production to achieve variety at low costs after World War II.

In contrast to such thinking, modern science now offers a new worldview that has stunning potential to change the way we think about, and conduct, our economic activities. If we were to view a business organization as an evolving, self-organizing system, not as a mechanical collection of parts, we would jettison the misguided notion that order derives exclusively from human intervention. Instead, we would realize that pattern and order emerge spontaneously when an organization conforms to nature's principles. Indeed, the order evidenced by living systems is not externally imposed. Rather, this order emerges from within, from *a process that embodies a self-organizing pattern* in material substance. A living organism can be described, then, as *an embodied pattern*. In other words, its design is not separate from its material substance, which itself evolved from relatively homogeneous "cosmic dust" at the time of the big bang into the diverse manifestations we now perceive in the universe.

Were design separate from and external to matter, one would expect to find identical fingerprints, retinal patterns, and mating calls among different organisms. The fact that individual living organisms are unique suggests that a pattern embodies itself distinctively in the substance of every particular organism. Looking at a business as an embodied pattern—as modern scientists now view a life system—would imply that the *natural* way to manage is *not to impose plans and controls in an effort to shape results.* Rather, the natural way to manage would be to *discover and nurture appropriate relationships and wait for results to emerge spontaneously,* like a skilled gardener who knows that properly caring for the soil is enough. The rest is up to nature.

To emulate nature's system, then, top managers must enable a business to organize its work according to the universal principles of self-organization, interdependence, and diversity. One way to do so is to nurture relationships with customers in every minute particular of the business, as one sees at Toyota. Toyota's system, perhaps unconsciously, appears to adhere to those principles to a very great extent. It does not do so perfectly, of course. But it serves as a useful prototype of what it probably means to organize business activities according to the principles that underlie all natural systems. Thus, work that is organized according to the pattern shown in Figure 1–3 reflects in many ways the three principles that govern the activities of any natural system in the universe. The standards "encoded" in every step of the work—like the instructions encoded in the DNA of living cells—and the constant feedback among the workers reflect the principle of self-organization. The continuous flow that links every part of the system in a web of unbroken, interconnected relationships reflects the principle of interdependence. Finally, the ability of each worker to change his or her steps as part of their normal ongoing work reflects the principle of diversity. In this system, all work responds directly to a particular customer's specific needs and all work consumes only the resources required to meet those particular needs, and no more. Moreover, every worker in the system can vary steps and transform material differently in response to each customer's unique order. Thus, the potential output of the system, if it were designated with alphabetic letters such as A, B, and C, would be ABCDEFGHIJ . . . and so on. The system can transform energy and matter into an unending variety of products and services at very low cost—"rich ends from simple means."

THE RESULTS ARE IN THE DETAILS

A key similarity between natural systems in the universe and the system in Figure 1–3 is that results are not preordained, but emerge from myriad interactions among the parts of the system. In other words, the results are in the details—in the parts of the system and in the relationships that connect those parts. In a natural living system, the result emerges from the ceaseless goings-on in each minute cell of the system and from the billions of relationships and interactions among those cells. So it should be in a business. Results should not be seen as something "out there" to be achieved by having managers, in response to outside information and targets, move parts of the business around as though they were objects on a game board. Instead, results should be seen as emerging from the relationships among every person's work and the needs of internal and external customers. The information that guides such a system—a natural system—must emanate from within. Information from outside the system cannot be used to push the parts around.[22]

Indeed, when its leaders understand that a business should operate according to the principles that guide natural systems, they will recognize that it is futile to impose quantitative targets on workers in an effort to drive bottom-line results. An organic living system, consisting as it does of infinitely interrelated self-identifying entities, is a recursive system that fundamentally defies such external control. The plethora of interactions involving multiple feedback connections make it impossible to anticipate the path that any initiating event will follow. One cannot predict outcomes in living systems because actions (causes) do not generate results (effects) along neatly traceable linear paths. It is not possible to predict quantitative results of activities in a recursive feedback system.

Just as predicting its quantitative results is impossible, so it is impossible to control or regulate the results in a natural living system. Controlling results implies separating the system's parts in order to manipulate or influence the contribution of parts to the whole. In business, examples of attempts to control financial results by manipulating the contribution of parts include laying off employees to achieve cost or profit targets, using market-wide discounts or advertising campaigns to increase revenue, or using performance-based compensation plans to stimulate employees or suppliers to reach targets. Such interventions necessarily rupture or alter relationships among parts of the system. Because results in a natural system are an emergent property of relationships among all parts of the system, altering relationships among the parts changes system's results, but it changes them in unpredictable ways. It is impossible, therefore, to control the consequences of using targets, scorecards, and the like to intervene in any natural system, such as a business.

The conditions that make it impossible to predict and control quantitative results in natural systems vitiate *any* attempts to use quantitative measurement to direct the financial affairs of a business. As the next chapter demonstrates, quantitative measurement implicitly partitions a system into parts. Therefore, efforts to guide, cajole, or drive people's behavior with such measurements necessarily compromise the natural web of relationships that holds together any living system. Quantitative measures can be used to *describe* the state or condition of a natural system. However, using such data to control or regulate the progress of the system only jeopardizes the system's long-term survival. Indeed, the unremarkable financial record of the American Big Three automakers from the 1960s to the 1980s suggests strongly that pursuing quantitative targets, such as financial goals, offers any business an illusory pathway to long-term health.[23] Comparing the Big Three's record with Toyota's suggests that only when a company's practices reflect patterns in nature is its success likely to be remarkable and enduring.

Instead of trying to control or regulate financial results by manipulating parts with quantitative measurements or scorecard targets, the task of management in a business organization should be to nurture relationships and to help people master natural-system principles. That nurturing is the essence of genuine learning, and helping people in an organization discover and implement the principles that govern systems in nature is genuine leadership. If managers focus their attention on adhering to the fundamental principles of natural systems, and if they nurture the disciplines that embody those principles in action, then results—long-term profitability and survival—will take care of themselves.

CONCLUSION

Understanding how businesses might emulate nature's ability to produce "rich ends from simple means" makes it difficult to accept the key tenets of modern strategic management thinking. Strategic management thinking, perhaps the strongest influence on management thought and practice in the past thirty years, teaches that large companies cannot profitably achieve variety and low cost at the same time. It teaches business people that they must choose according to a *strategy*. However, nature does not appear to strategize. It does not choose between rich ends or simple means. It has *both*.

The either/or thinking that says variety (and also quality) cannot be had at low cost, shapes present-day management practices and generates innumerable "problems" caused by those practices. Consultants in the past thirty years or more have generated an entire industry around "problem solving" techniques that are designed to help people cope with these "problems." The surprising truth, however, is that changed thinking, not "problem solving," answers these problems. If businesses adopt the thinking implicit in the living-system worldview, most of the "problems" they struggle to solve today, problems created by acting in conformance with the mechanistic worldview, will suddenly *dis*-solve.[24]

Nature accomplishes what strategic thinkers and most business leaders believe is impossible. Nature does not produce the same "model" of anything twice, from galaxies to fingerprints to mating calls. Nature produces ABCDEFGHIJK etc. in a system where the incremental cost of producing each new variant is zero. If businesses could replicate such a system even slightly, the benefits could be enormous. What prevents companies from applying the principles that seem to enable natural systems to effortlessly produce "rich ends from simple means"? Very likely it is the mechanistic worldview that is so deeply implanted in the modern human mind. As long as that worldview shapes management thinking, managers will use mass-production logic to solve all their problems. Variety at low cost will seem impossible. Only by adopting a natural-system worldview can they hope to build systems that achieve both variety and low cost, like the system articulated in Figure 1–3.

Pursuing this question to a deeper level, what reinforces the prevalence and longevity of the mechanistic worldview in the business world? Undoubtedly the most important influence sustaining that worldview among business leaders is the validity it gives to "managing by results" (MBR), or the use of quantitative targets to run the operations of a business. Because they consider measurement and MBR as inevitable and indispensable, managers see only through the lens of the mechanistic worldview. Therefore, before examining existing models of natural-system behavior, such as the Toyota Production System, it is necessary to explain the insidious influence of MBR and to describe the alternative approach to management that reinforces thinking and practice commensurate with the living-system worldview. With that in mind, the next chapter discusses two contrasting approaches to management—the traditional MBR approach that reinforces mechanistic thinking and the "manage by means" or MBM approach that promises to reinforce natural-system thinking.

2

Relationships (MBM) versus
Quantity (MBR)

> BOTTOM-LINERS BEWARE:
> there's
>   another
> set
> of
> books
>
> —James DePreist[1]

A continuously linked and balanced organization that "works to customer order" (Figure 1–3) reflects a very different management style
than does a decoupled and discontinuous organization that "works to
schedule" (Figure 1–2). Each of these management styles represents a
particular worldview. Working to order involves nurturing patterns and
relationships, the hallmark of the worldview that sees the universe as a
natural system. This worldview informs "management by means," a
management style that features building relationships. Conversely,
working to schedule focuses on quantitative results and unlimited
growth, the main traits of the mechanistic worldview that informs
"managing by results."

Management by results is appropriate to mechanical systems. The
widespread misapplication of management by results practices to businesses—adaptive natural systems—is the source of most problems in
the business world today. The intent of this chapter is to help all managers understand the debilitating long-term consequences of mecha-

nistic MBR practices. It demonstrates why it is essential that business leaders follow the manage-by-means, or MBM, practices alone appropriate to natural systems, such as large-scale companies.

RELATIONSHIPS AND PATTERN VERSUS QUANTITY AND GROWTH

Popular wisdom urges problem solvers to "think out of the box" or to "shift paradigms." Such phrases express an important truth. How we think does define constraints and boundaries—a "box"—that shapes the world we inhabit. To get outside this box requires evaluating the thinking that produced the constraints and boundaries that themselves generated problems. In other words, the solution to problems often demands that we appraise the thinking that gave birth in the first place to the initial situation from which problems arise. Albert Einstein expressed this idea succinctly when he said that "we cannot solve our problems at the same level of thinking that created them."[2]

An example of what it means to "think out of the box" is an "IQ test" that a dog trainer can give to a small puppy.[3] The puppy is placed in a rectangular area that is lined on three sides by a fence separating it from its owner. The puppy's goal is to reach its owner. The problem is how to do that. Many puppies, seeing the fence between themselves and their owner, will try to reach the owner by jumping at the fence and barking. A few, however, will take a moment to survey the situation and will run around the unfenced fourth side of the area to reach their owner. The difference is a matter of perception, of thinking. Thinking that the fence is the "problem" causes some puppies to work hard at trying to overcome the fence. They fail the "puppy IQ test." Puppies that pass the test see an opening in the back that eliminates the fence as a problem.

People in the business world often have difficulty recognizing the opening at the back of the fence because they allow themselves to be guided primarily by quantitative thinking. Quantitative thinking lies at the core of the mechanistic worldview.[4] Thinking quantitatively does have an appropriate place when machines are involved. However, using quantitative measurements to influence interactions among humans or between humans and nature is potentially destructive. The damage arises because quantitative measurements restrict people's perceptions of what is important to only one dimension—the purely quantitative. Consider what the British physicist Henri Bortoft says about the implications of using measurement to deal with natural systems:

> The science of quantity is measurement science. The process of measurement divides whatever it is "measuring" into units which are external to one another, separate but juxtaposed. Whatever is "measured" is thereby spatialized in conception into a string of units juxtaposed along an imagined line which effectively constitutes a scale. In practice, a measurement consists in comparing whatever is to be measured with this scale, and counting the number of units which correspond. This means that wherever science is concerned with measurement, the particular aspect of nature involved has first to be prepared quantitatively. This entails dividing it into a set of homogeneous parts that are intellectually superimposed on nature like a grid or scaffolding. Nature is then seen in the perspective of the framework, *which is not part of nature at all,* but is really an intellectual rearrangement of nature that reduces it to the purely quantitative—i.e., to parts which are external to one another.[5]

Quantitative thinking restricts one's perception to only one artificially imposed dimension, whereas nature consists of many dimensions.

Quantitative thinking originated when Galileo proposed the idea of studying motion as a concept separate from the object moving. Galileo defined motion "quantitatively." He compared it to a scale and "measured" it. He made into objects of study distance traversed in a unit of time and a change in the rate at which distance is traversed. Using such terms as "velocity" and "acceleration," scientists influenced by Galileo related motion to the quantitative measures of other features of a moving object, such as its weight and volume. Isaac Newton eventually showed how to express such quantitative relationships mathematically. Thus he was able to make generalizations about the way any object might move if subjected to a given force. Such quantitative expressions and generalizations led in time to the whole body of modern Newtonian physics and mechanistic technology.

Quantitative generalizations apply to mechanistic systems. In fact, a mechanism is nothing more than a system of parts whose interactions can be defined entirely in quantitative terms. The mechanistic system's operation can be understood completely in terms of its quantitative interactions. Moreover, the connections among the system's parts and the quantitative magnitude of the interactions implied by those connections can all be specified in advance by design and expressed in linear equations. Using such equations to sum up the individual performance of each part makes it possible to understand and explain a machine's overall performance.

The nonmechanical natural world, however, is not separated into parts, one part of which is an object called "quantity." To see natural living systems quantitatively is a fairly recent phenomenon. It was not until the seventeenth century that people began to assume that they should separate objects from each other and systems into parts, specifically in order to quantify them, and also to control them.[6] Today such thinking has become automatic. Economists and business leaders objectify quantity. They treat quantity as a concrete feature of a world separated into parts, and hold that these parts should behave in strict quantitative terms that can be influenced and determined by external controls.

Seeing the world in this light causes business leaders to regard an organization as nothing more than a means to economic ends. As Henri Bortoft says, using quantification, managers attempt "to calculate nature and hence to manipulate it for [their] own ends." By separating our world into external parts, however, the quantifying mind makes nature and our world "lifeless and empty." Indeed, quoting science editor John Davy, Bortoft points out that "the thoughts we embody in measurement are only applicable to dead phenomena—for measurement means dividing up into units which can be counted, and no living thing can be thus fragmented without dying. It is a form of thought entirely appropriate to the inanimate world, but quite inadequate for apprehending life."[7] Obviously, the knowledge one gains by dissecting an embalmed dolphin on the laboratory table hardly equips one to understand the experience of swimming with dolphins. Unfortunately the management thinking that guides most of the world's business and economic activities today is comparable to studying a cadaver when attention should be given to the natural living system.

Studying the cadaver, however, is the prevailing management strategy. Influenced by the mechanistic worldview of the social sciences, late-twentieth-century managers view a business organization exactly this way. They operate businesses by imposing on them an artificial design that connects the organization's parts and then shows its interactions in linear quantitative terms, financial and otherwise. They view the financial performance of the business as the sum of the separate financial performance of each part. Any one of these parts, they believe, can be added to or subtracted from the business with a predictable financial impact on the whole.

The perception that the world is quantitative and that business is therefore mechanistic has for the past fifty years shaped all the variants of strategic planning, financial analysis, budgeting, cost management, and management accounting that have been taught by graduate business schools and practiced in large organizations. Executives versed in such practices and who believe that reality is defined by quantitative measurements are like the puppies who believe that the fence defines reality. Such executives fail the "puppy IQ test."

Executives who use quantitative measurements *without losing sight of the broader reality that lies beyond the mechanistic worldview* will not inevitably fail the "puppy IQ test." The broader reality is that quantity is always sufficient both to *explain* the internal operation and to *describe* the external features (such as performance) of a *mechanistic* system. Quantity cannot *explain,* however, the internal operation of a *natural* system. It can only *describe* the natural system's external features. Measurement instruments can describe, for example, the temperature of an animal's body, the CO_2 content of Earth's atmosphere, the salinity of an ocean, or the red shift of light coming from a distant galaxy. Quantitative measurements give no insight, however, into why, or how, such natural systems function as they do. Measurements never provide understanding of the internal operation of a natural system.[8]

An example of the unfortunate consequences of mistakenly using quantitative thinking to understand and explain the operation of natural systems can be found in the modern passenger airline business. Anyone who flies on commercial airlines today is keenly aware that the safety and reliability of air travel depends primarily on the quality of the jet engines that keep the aircraft aloft. In turn, the quality of those jet engines depends upon the expertise of highly trained engineers. Of course those thousands of engineers who design and build jet engines apply the mechanical principles of quantitative science to their work. Their command of these principles makes all the difference in the world to airline passengers. Managers in the airline industry, however, have for over thirty years applied those same mechanistic principles to running airlines. This misapplication explains why in recent decades the airline industry's earnings are cyclical and unstable, and most major airline companies have an abysmal record for customer satisfaction. Running airlines according to the mechanical principles whose proper application is the design of jet engines leads to serious problems. As in the airline industry, so in all industries problems arise if managers do not restrict the quantitative way of thinking to purely mechanical issues such as designing products and machines. Designing order in mechanical systems often requires quantitative thinking. Running the affairs of a company, a natural system, however, does not.

To run an organization, a living system, entails much more than a quantitative summing up of the separate contributions of each part. The operation and performance of an entity that conforms to the way nature works inherently involves qualitative, nonquantifiable principles. These principles govern relationships and patterns among the system's parts, and it is these relationships and patterns above all that require close attention. Ignoring the qualitative patterns that characterize the internal operation of all organizations results in irrelevant, even harmful, decisions. It is easy for government officials or business leaders to announce a quantitative decision. They can change tax rates or approve investments with the intent of reaching some long-term goal. The imposition of their quantitative target, however, on an organizational system is necessarily ill-fated. Decision makers do not recognize, apparently, that by nature human organizations are living systems and as such do not act according to quantitative imperatives. On the contrary, organizations naturally obey only qualitative patterns expressed in relationships. In natural systems, relationships are reality.

Gregory Bateson compared the consequence of imposing quantitative decisions on a qualitative system to placing tension on a chain.[9] Quantitatively increasing the variable called tension predictably causes the chain to break. Where the chain will break, however, cannot be predicted. So it is when we impose quantitative demands on a natural system that operates according to patterned and qualitative relationships. In Bateson's words, "every quantitative change we impose upon the system is in the end putting stress on the qualitative patterns whose breaking strains and whose evolutions and transformations we do not understand." Speaking of our common habit in the modern world to put the quantitative ahead of the qualitative, Bateson added that "this enormous emphasis upon the quantitative view and the minimal emphasis upon the patterned view is, I believe, the easiest way of descent into hell. The surest."

The descent into hell Bateson referred to emanates, he believed, from the clash between human desires to *maximize* quantities—especially those connected with economic affairs, such as money and property—and nature's inevitable demand on systems to *optimize* whatever they have. Maximizing any object in nature always makes it toxic. A living organism, therefore, optimizes its intake of oxygen, minerals, and other nutrients in order to achieve peak performance. Optimum amounts never exceed boundaries implicit in relationships and patterns. They never accumulate endlessly. Nature optimizes; humankind maximizes. Interestingly, humankind's pursuit of limitless quantitative goals inevitably comes up against what Bateson referred to as "the enormous tyranny of patterns" in natural systems. And the clash is evident on many levels, not just in the sense of a final apocalypse. It occurs whenever our quantitative interventions in natural systems fail to respect the "rigidities and rigors" that patterns and relationships impose. This failure causes tension and stress. We cannot predict where the tension and stress will appear, only that they invariably will appear and invariably will thwart our quantitative decisions and plans.

In this context it is instructive to consider the assumption commonly held by business people that results—that is, a company's "bottom-line" financial performance—can be predictably influenced by using quantitative measures to guide action. That assumption holds true in systems where one can explain a result by saying that it is "determined by" (or "reduced to") summing up the precisely measured contribution of each part of the system to the whole. One way to define such a system is to say that all effects, or results, are linear and repetitive consequences of uniquely identifiable and measurable causes.

But that definition fits precisely what we mean by a mechanistic system. Thus, if one wants to increase the output of a machine one knows how much extra input, and where, it will take to do the job. An analogy is shooting a rifle at a target. If the bullet misses the target the first time, the gun sight tells you how much to adjust the position of the barrel to make the mark the next time.

The situation with a natural system is entirely different. Outcomes in the natural system are produced by relationships among parts, not by the parts themselves. In a mechanistic system composed of separate, unrelated parts, influencing outcomes, or results, is regarded as a matter of moving parts. In a living system, satisfactory results emanate when parts are harmonized in patterns of relationships. Harmonious relationships produce satisfying results. To develop harmonious, patterned relationships requires practice and mastery of discipline, not just moving parts according to the dictates of a quantitative measure or set of measures. The dancer who merely memorizes a choreographed routine—the target—will never rival the dancer who patiently masters every skill that contributes to an inspired performance.

In business, results can be measured in myriad ways, both financial and nonfinancial. The problem is that MBR-oriented managers do not distinguish between results and the actions one takes to get the results. Generations of managers have assumed, following the mechanistic worldview, that the actions they take to improve or sustain business results can be articulated in quantitative terms, as can results. If profits are not quite where these managers think they should be one month, then they assume they can move costs or move revenue ("adjust the sight") in the next month by the amount of the deviation, and all will be well.

Dr. W. Edwards Deming observed that such "managing by results only makes things worse."[10] The task of managers, then, is to stop treating business results as a target one reaches by aiming better. Instead, business results are an outcome that emerges spontaneously from mastering practices that harmonize with the patterns inherent in the system itself. In other words, *manage the means*, not the results.

To appreciate how differently managers must think who "manage by means," it is necessary to understand fully the methods and consequences of what has been done for the past fifty years or so to "manage by results." The following survey of MBR spells out background essential to understanding the discussion of MBM that fills the remainder of the book.

MANAGING BY RESULTS: "AMPLIFYING OUR GRASP BY LOSING TOUCH"

Historian Eric Lampard once noted that "as [civilization] matures, [humans] come to depend less on direct or immediate perceptions and more on abstract or conceptual understandings." He commented wryly that we thereby attempt to "*amplify our grasp of the world* by losing touch with it."[11] Separating systems into parts to study, analyze, and manipulate results is not a practice that originated, of course, with quantification, or with Galileo's efforts to study motion quantitatively. Humans had learned to use the power of analysis to examine complex problems long before they discovered the idea of quantification. To abstract from, to generalize about, and to conceptualize are distinctively human abilities. People long ago applied the ability to think abstractly to technology, hoping to *control* the concrete reality that the abstractions represent.

The use of abstract quantitative targets in the practice of "managing by results" entails "losing touch" with the natural reality of the organizations we manage. These quantitative abstractions cause us to see the organization as a mechanistic system. We thereby believe that these abstractions can be used as tools to "amplify our grasp of the world." Unfortunately this belief ignores the reality that a human organization is a living system which can be understood and acted in only as a web of relationships, not as a mechanical collection of quantifiable parts. By ignoring that reality, MBR managers erroneously attempt to control financial results by focusing people's attention on quantitative targets. They fail to see that good results in a living system are achieved only by nurturing relationships.

The immediate root of the tendency to see business mechanistically is the meteoric rise after World War II of techniques for using quantitative financial information from accounting sources to plan and control financial results. This is the phenomenon we know as management accounting, about which more is said in the next section. However, that phenomenon itself had still deeper roots that help explain why the tendency to treat every political, social, educational, and economic issue quantitatively is so deeply imbedded and so pervasive today. Probably the ultimate root of the modern habit of using quantitative abstractions to represent, or stand in place of, concrete things is language, "the mode of behavioral coordination through which humans bring forth the world they create with each other."[12] By using words, human beings give abstract shape to the real world they occupy. Language lets human beings separate a particular thing from its context. Formulated in a phrase, a tangible thing can then be analyzed intellectually, as if it existed apart from its physical context in the real world. Because of language, "there is no limit to what we can describe, imagine, and relate [as mental abstractions]."[13]

Since language allows humans to objectify and depersonalize particular things, its power is formidable. When we use language to create abstractions and to generalize, we remove and separate particular things from their context and treat them as if they were not part of a pattern in a living system. Thus, the first use of a simple word such as "tree" begins to separate us from the natural habitat we share with other living beings. Once we objectify "tree" with a word we stop living among the "lungs of the earth" in the wild and begin to see trees as the source of results such as fruit, shelter, tools, transportation, shade, decoration, wind barrier, writing surfaces, and toilet paper. By the twentieth century, trees, now almost extinct as a wild species, had become a harvestable crop grown on "tree farms" where the primary result is to maximize the production of "fiber" for industrial and commercial purposes. Thus, managing by result—managing to secure a "sustainable" supply of fiber—subjects the web of relationships in the natural forest system to the stresses and strains of clear cutting and managed forestry, thereby threatening the long-term viability of that natural system.[14]

In the same way that language lets us think abstractly about fiber and trees, language also allows us to treat the abstract concept of a business result as if it were an actual object that existed separately from the messy, organizational context that gives rise to it. Viewed as an independent entity, this abstraction, the quantitative business result that we entertain only in our minds, seems to be more real and concrete than does the real-world situation from which it emanated in the first place. It is not a great leap, then, from seeing abstract results as concrete realities to trying to manage them by arbitrarily manipulating the relationships from which they emanate. Such manipulation involves separating ends from means, or goals from the acts that achieve them.[15] In Western culture, the separation of means (the way, or *how* a goal is achieved) from ends (the goal, or *what* is achieved) has often been accompanied by a belief that the end, or goal, is immutable and permanent and the means are ephemeral and changing. Therefore, ends seem more "real" and more "valuable" than means. This perception has led to a willingness to resolve moral anguish over a clash between worthy ends and despicable means by turning a blind eye to the means and condoning acts that in themselves, apart from the goal, would never be tolerated. In other words, "the end justifies the means."

Management by results has so influenced thinking that managers today seldom address moral issues. When government and business leaders discuss means, they invariably refer to them as if they were merely amoral instruments used to achieve such abstract ends as economic growth or shareholder wealth maximization. Exacerbating this tendency to manipulate means to achieve preordained ends has been the sharp increase after World War II in quantitative thinking in all realms of society—political, educational, and business. Executives throughout North America and Western Europe in the past fifty years have increasingly used quantitative—especially financial—targets to shape, guide, and control activities in government and in business.

For example, government officials, using economists' abstract quantitative notions of the general good, provide targets to define, plan, and control government programs. Economists explain that what matters in society are such things as national product, employment levels, price indexes, and money supply. Using abstract mathematical models of "the economy," economists identify quantitative targets and interpret results. Moreover, economists increasingly run branches of government responsible for implementing results-oriented economic policies. Seldom do those economists or their abstract models of the economy consider the impact of those policies on the web of relationships that connects humans to each other and to nature.

Business managers use similar abstract mathematical models—usually designed in the first place by academic economists—to identify financial targets that derive from abstract financial notions of what constitutes the good of the company. More often than not accountants, rather than economists, have shown managers how to use quantitative financial abstractions to run companies. The resulting use of accounting abstractions to guide business affairs is what we know as management accounting. Tracing the history and major practices of modern management accounting reveals how management accounting encouraged mechanistic thinking to dominate management practice in today's business world.

A BRIEF HISTORY OF MODERN MANAGEMENT ACCOUNTING

Most people think of accounting as a familiar and universal practice that has always been used as it is in organizations today. Accounting consists of the record-keeping and reporting systems that a business uses to keep track of what it owns and owes and how well it performs financially. The best-known output of such systems, apart from payroll checks and invoices, are periodic financial reports called balance sheets and income statements. Accounting in this sense is embedded in the fabric of all business organizations the world over. Its roots are ancient, coming most immediately in the Western world from double-entry bookkeeping techniques developed in northern Italy around the beginning of the thirteenth century.

Almost anyone in a present-day business organization, when asked whether it is proper to use financial information from the accounting system to plan, direct, and control the operations of the business, would return an incredulous stare. Of course it is! In fact, accounting information is used to manage business activity every minute of every day in almost every business in the world. What is not generally understood, however, even by most accountants and financial executives, is that the practice of using information from financial accounting systems to run a business—what we know today as management accounting or cost management—does not date much farther back than the era of World War II. Management accounting did not become widely prac-

ticed in the business world until the decade of the 1950s. Once introduced, however, it took off quickly and spread rapidly throughout all
businesses. Today management accounting is as common to business
people as rising in the morning and going to work.

The history of management accounting's rise out of financial accounting was not well understood until H. Thomas Johnson's work beginning in the 1970s.[16] His articles, inspired and assisted by the
business historian Alfred D. Chandler, Jr., traced the uses people made
of quantitative information, financial and otherwise, to run the operations of managed organizations from New England textile mills in the
early nineteenth century to giant industrial organizations such as
DuPont and General Motors in the early twentieth century. These
studies show that double-entry financial accounting records were seldom the source of the numbers, financial or otherwise, that managers
used to plan and control activities of large-scale companies in the nineteenth and early twentieth centuries. Those companies usually developed product cost, process cost, gross margin, and other managerial
decision-making information from data about market prices and from
data about the underlying operations that transformed raw materials,
building space, and machinery into saleable products or services.

For example, the directly traceable cost of a bolt of woven cotton
was based on information about quantities of raw cotton consumed,
market prices of cotton, hours of labor time consumed, wages paid to
workers, and costs of miscellaneous supplies consumed in the manufacturing operations. The type of cost that accountants today would
refer to as "indirect" or "joint" cost was seldom large enough to warrant
special attention. Nevertheless, by the end of the nineteenth century
many manufacturers were making surprisingly sophisticated calculations, using information about the *work that causes* such cost, to trace
even that cost to products and other cost objects.

In effect, companies compiled information about costs and profitability in order to know how a managed organization's results compared with those one could achieve if its activities were performed,
instead, in the marketplace. After all, people built these organizations
believing that the "visible hand" of management could perform its activities at lower cost, and more profitably, than if they were performed
by the "invisible hand" of the marketplace. But moving activities from

the market to the managed enterprise caused one to lose the price information that automatically enabled one to gauge the economic sense of those activities in the market. How could one know if it was cost-effective to hire workers and purchase machines if one *managed* all the activities that went into, say transforming raw cotton into yarn and finished fabric? The answer was to compile the cost of the managed activity and compare it to what it would cost to outsource the work to an independent weaver in the market.

Managers' compilations of information used to judge product margins, process efficiencies, departmental profits, or divisional returns on investment were made almost always outside the double-entry financial accounting system itself, at least before the 1920s. In fact, the people who compiled and used such information in the nineteenth and early twentieth centuries seldom were accountants, and the accountants themselves were seldom involved in gathering or using such data. Information for evaluating or running managed operations—even financial figures about cost, profitability, and returns—came primarily from nonaccounting sources, and was used largely by nonaccounting operating managers.

By the 1940s, the financial information managers used to plan and control operating activities came increasingly from accounting sources. In additional studies published in the 1980s, Johnson showed how this development caused management accounting to cease being an instrument used to assist the growth of robust managed organizations and became, instead, an instrument that contributed, especially in the United States, to the stagnation and decline of businesses during the 1960s and 1970s.[17] A full explanation for this development may never be possible. Certainly it parallels the rise of the accounting profession from relative obscurity before World War I to a position of enormous prominence and power in the business world by the 1950s. But it is too simplistic to trace the growing managerial uses of accounting information after 1950 to the growing presence of accountants, whose numbers probably would have increased rapidly simply because of the rise of securities regulations and complex corporate income tax legislation after the 1930s. It is more reasonable to say that the demand for accountants themselves was even further increased by the rising use of accounting information for management decision making after 1950.

Managerial uses of accounting information after World War II probably emanate from one primary underlying cause—namely, the growing use of quantitative economic abstractions in national government planning during the 1940s. A wartime fascination with using economic statistics in national planning carried over and influenced the use of accounting information in business decision making. The perception that national income accounting statistics and Keynesian economic ideas could do much to end the tyranny of the business cycle and prevent the recurrence of economic depression cast a glow of invincibility over the new economics profession, most of whose members held academic positions in universities. It is not surprising, perhaps, that accounting professors in graduate business schools quickly saw an opportunity to capitalize on this belief in the merit of using economic statistics to run the national economy. After World War II, professors of accounting and finance in graduate business schools such as Harvard, Chicago, and Columbia started to show corporate executives how to use their accounting information to plan and control business activities in the same way that economists were showing governmental administrators how to use national accounting statistics to plan and control the affairs of a national economy. In part this idea emanated from accounting professors who had received doctoral training in economics, which was about the only way a university accounting professor could receive a Ph.D. before 1950. But the idea also received impetus from accounting instructors whose experience with wartime agencies had introduced them to advanced uses of operations research and mathematical economics to solve strategic and tactical military problems. Small wonder that immediately after World War II graduate business schools became immersed in research on ways to apply neoclassical economic models to accounting information to formulate a basis for decision making in business.

The subject of management accounting largely evolved from the research and writing of academic accountants striving to show how business operations can be planned and controlled with accounting targets and feedback from accounting information systems. Textbooks in management accounting that began to appear in the late 1950s and early 1960s wedded accounting information with economic theory to show business decision makers how to use variable costs as economists would use marginal costs, how to "cover" fixed costs and profit with variable contribution margin by relating output to "break-even" points, how to keep managers' attention focused on bottom-line financial targets with "feedback" from standard-cost budget variances, and more.

Unwittingly, perhaps, the writers of such textbooks were teaching a new generation of managers to *put aside understanding the concrete particulars of how a business organizes work.* They taught them, instead, to focus exclusively on abstract quantitative generalizations about financial results. In time, this teaching contributed to the modern obsession in business with "looking good" by the numbers, no matter what damage MBR does to the underlying system of relationships that sustains any human organization.

Giving further impetus after World War II to the idea of running the operations of a business with accounting information was the development of the multidivisional approach to organizing administrative activity in large, diversified companies.[18] The multidivisional form of enterprise originated in the United States in a small handful of companies in the 1920s, but only after World War II did it become a popular model for organizing businesses. Beginning in the early 1950s, the innovation spread rapidly, quickly becoming one of the most common modes of delegating management tasks in large-scale businesses.

The unique feature of the multidivisional organization was the introduction of a level of managers that had not existed before. Managers at this level ran what appeared to be self-standing, fully articulated multifunctional companies known as divisions. The manager of a division, however, reported to a top management group that represented, in effect, the market for capital and the market for managers. Historically, multidivisional companies emerged first in manufacturing organizations that for one reason or another found themselves selling products across a diverse range of markets or geographies. Today such organizations might cope with this diversity by incorporating the activities of each homogeneous product line into a separate company and selling it to a similar company in the mergers and acquisitions market. However, before 1980 an efficient market for such transactions did not really exist. In the absence of such a market, companies like DuPont just after World War I or General Motors in the early 1920s learned to capture opportunities created by diverse patents or brand names by creating and managing a diverse array of single-market or single-product divisions. Each division was an independent organization except for two constraints. A division did not have the right to raise capital in the outside market, and it could neither hire nor fire the division's top managers. Those rights resided in the corporate top management group that owned and oversaw the affairs of all divisions.

Top management supervised divisions in large part through a process that transformed management accounting into "manage by results." Corporate top managers used accounting reports—literally the balance sheet and the income statement—to drive the activities of divisional top managers. This practice introduced the idea that parts of a company could be transformed into profit centers or investment centers whose top managers were *judged by other managers* (not yet by capital markets) on the basis of financial results. Given this circumstance, successful managers believed they could make decisions without knowing the company's products, technologies, or customers. They had only to understand the intricacies of financial reporting. Small wonder that by the 1970s managers came primarily from the ranks of accountants and controllers, rather than from the ranks of engineers, designers, and marketers. Managers who succeeded at "getting results" defined by financial targets were increasingly in demand. They moved frequently among companies without regard to the industry or markets they served. Aiding and abetting the divisional managers' efforts to "look good" in terms of financial results were the university accounting professors who showed them how to control business operations with accounting targets and with feedback from accounting systems. Indeed, a synergistic relationship developed between the management accounting taught in MBA programs and the practices emanating from corporate controllers' offices, imparting to management accounting a life of its own and shaping the way managers run businesses.

A pioneering exemplar of managing by results, of driving human organizations with quantitative abstractions is Robert McNamara whose career spanned six decades in academia, big business, and government. An accounting instructor at Harvard Business School before World War II, and a specialist in operations research projects with the U.S. government during the war, McNamara was one of the so-called Whiz Kids recruited by Henry Ford II and his mentor Ernest Breech, a former General Motors executive, to resurrect Ford Motor Company's diminished fortunes in the late 1940s. McNamara left the presidency of Ford in 1961 to join the new Kennedy administration as U.S. secretary of defense, a position he held until 1968 when he resigned to become president of The World Bank (also known as the International Bank for Reconstruction and Development).

McNamara's career vividly illustrates the tendency of modern business and government leaders to view circumstances in techno-oriented mechanistic terms rather than in natural systemic terms.[19] Moreover, his record in business and government reveals the destructive consequences of applying mechanistic thinking and manage-by-results strategies to human organizations.

As corporate controller and as president of Ford, McNamara played a large role in helping move the postwar Ford organization toward the decoupled, discontinuous, and mechanistic way of organizing work discussed in chapter 1. He also instituted the practice of using transfer prices to control Ford's ostensibly decentralized "GM-style" management structure.[20] Despite their apparent success at turning Ford around in the 1950s, the policies and management techniques promoted by McNamara during his career at Ford arguably placed that company squarely on the track that virtually guaranteed its inability to compete effectively with Japanese auto makers in the 1970s and nearly led to its bankruptcy in the early 1980s.

During his tenure as U.S. secretary of defense McNamara was one of the chief architects of America's Vietnam war strategy. For the disastrous consequences of that ill-conceived application of manage-by-results thinking he belatedly apologized in his 1995 autobiography. The appalling nature of the behavior triggered by McNamara's insistence on using quantitative abstractions and operations research modeling to run the Vietnam war was chillingly captured by journalist George Leonard in an essay in which he referred to "highly trained young abstractionists sitting at the controls of giant bombers, many miles removed in height and psychic distance from the consequences of their acts. They address themselves to grid coordinates which first were expressed abstractly on pieces of paper, then encoded in electronic-inertial devices. At a certain point in the sky, the abstractionists actuate the devices, which then release hundreds of tons of high explosives.

Neither the abstractionists sitting in their orderly, antiseptic surroundings in the sky nor those on the ground who conceived the operation are motivated by personal malice. They are concerned only with clearing out specified rectangular areas of jungles. The planes wheel in the sky and fly away, and that's all there is to it."[21]

Several people who witnessed his work at The World Bank say that McNamara's policy of managing by results at Ford and at the U.S. Department of Defense continued during his reign at The World Bank. During his tenure there, McNamara drew on economic theory and quantitative modes of analysis to recast the particular, local problems of people in underdeveloped countries into the mold of abstract generalizations about poverty, income distribution, economic specialization, and global trade. Johns Hopkins historians David Milobsky and Louis Galambos explain that McNamara in 1968 quickly applied his expertise in quantitative communication and control to the "goal of creating a better world through publicly guided economic development. He shortly had the Bank marching to the new drum of operations research and systems control."[22]

Notably, McNamara shifted the Bank's focus from giving technical assistance to *individual lending projects* in the third world to accelerating sharply the absolute levels of lending to *underdeveloped countries* themselves, all with the intent of eliminating "absolute poverty—utter degradation" in the third world. This shift placed greater attention on national-level economic analysis and downplayed attention that Bank officials previously placed on technical knowledge of specific projects. With this change, according to Milobsky and Galambos, "higher levels of abstraction and aggregation made technical work and technical values seem less important."[23]

Not surprisingly, McNamara's record at The World Bank has not escaped harsh criticism from colleagues and historians. Just as McNamara and his colleagues at Ford Motor Company had done in the 1950s, and as McNamara and his Defense Department colleagues had done in Vietnam in the 1960s, so at the World Bank after 1968, McNamara seemed to follow the practice of basing decisions on abstract quantitative models. Because he downplayed the concrete relationships that shaped people's lives in the systems his policies affected, McNamara's policies tended to sacrifice minute particulars in those systems for the "general good." The "general good" was defined by abstract quantitative results, as measured by accountants and economists. As one recent observer of The World Bank's record explains, McNamara's lending policies forced third world countries to march down development paths taken previously by the developed industrial nations of the world, without regard for environmental and human consequences. The results have been predictable. "No longer 'destroying villages to save them,' McNamara [destroyed] whole economies. Today, the countries that went along with him are saddled with silted-up megadams, useless crumbling roads to nowhere, empty high-rise office buildings, ravaged forests and fields, and the overwhelming, unpayable debt to Western bankers that makes up much of the legacy of World Bank policy from McNamara to now. Whatever harm this man caused in Vietnam, he did more during his tenure at the World Bank."[24]

The long train of unfortunate consequences flowing from McNamara's strategies did not emanate from malice or indifference to the fate of human beings affected by his policies. It is extremely important to understand that. The same consequences will almost inevitably befall any organization—in business, in government, or in education—that is led by people who subscribe to this type of management thinking. McNamara espoused the application of mechanistic thinking and MBR practices to natural systems. People who embrace such thinking do see the problems caused by their mechanistic approach to management. They often believe, however, that the solution to these problems is more diligent, more assiduous attention to the same approach. They fail to see that the behavior generated by their mechanistic thinking causes disappointing results in natural systems—results that become worse each time they repeat the same behavior. This leads into a reinforcing "vicious" cycle.

The "causal loop" diagrams in the next three figures present a map of the type of behavioral structure that exists in most organizations led by mechanistic MBR thinking. The diagrams show how behavior in complex, interconnected, interrelated, cybernetic systems—that is, natural systems—can generate unintended side effects that feed back, or influence, final outcomes in unexpected, often dramatic, ways. The point of the diagrams is to show that the unfortunate consequences of MBR behavior are counterintuitive and, therefore, not easily recognized as being caused by the very thinking and behavior that generate the consequences.[25]

In the diagrams, the plus or minus sign by an arrow indicates a change between two variables in, respectively, the same or the opposite direction. Thus, the plus sign next to the arrow labeled "Gap" indicates that if all else remains the same, an increase in "Desired Result" (the target) will cause an increase in the gap between desired and actual results. The loop in the diagram in Figure 2–1 shows the first phase in a sequence of events that occurs when managers are encouraged to "wrench the system" (i.e., manage by results) in order to close a gap between desired target results and its actual results. Thus, an increase in the gap between desired and actual results causes an increase in the variable labeled "manage by results." In most cases this implies that managers will attempt to improve results by "cutting costs" or "raising revenue."

In the style characteristic of "manage by results," no one discusses *how* cost or revenue are to be changed. That decision is left up to individual managers, who in most cases are expected to "just do it." Examples of steps managers will take to manage bottom-line targets include: increasing output and building inventory (to defer fixed costs); deferring discretionary expenditures for research and development; postponing maintenance programs; encouraging employee turnover as a way of holding down direct labor costs; cutting back employee benefit

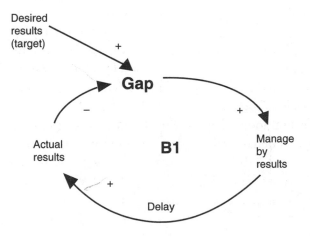

Figure 2–1: Short-Term Self-Balancing Phase of MBR

programs; purchasing materials and supplies only from vendors who bid the lowest prices; cutting employee training programs; and postponing capital investments in expensive new technologies (that is, scraping by as long as possible on old, fully depreciated assets).

The initial steps that managers take to cut costs or to raise revenue will in fact improve actual results and close the gap for a short time— long enough, managers hope, for them to get a favorable performance review, a bonus, or promotion. Consequently, the loop labeled B1 is referred to as a *balancing* (i.e., deviation-dampening) feedback loop because, like the thermostat that controls a household furnace, the action that managers take ostensibly achieves the desired result and "turns off" the need for further action until some later time when the gap between desired and actual results reopens and starts the process all over again.

What is usually not recognized is that the actions taken to improve results in balancing loop B1 will eventually set in motion *long-term* forces—and probably sooner than later—that reduce the short-term improvement in results, reopen the gap, and reinforce the need for

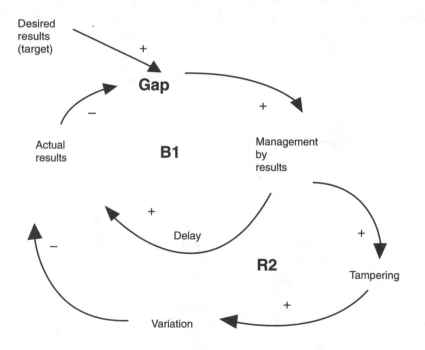

Figure 2–2: Long-Term Destabilizing Impact of Tampering

more managing by results. Indeed, the usual steps managers take to close the gap between desired and actual results have two unintended side effects, depicted in *reinforcing* (i.e., deviation-amplifying) feedback loops R2 and R3, shown in Figures 2–2 and 2–3.

The reinforcing loop labeled R2 in Figure 2–2 indicates that many of the initial steps managers usually take to close the gap in Figure 2–1— steps such as employee layoffs and skimping on things such as research, training, maintenance, customer service, supplier development, and community building—amount to *tampering* with and weakening long-term fundamentals of systemic health. That weakening of long-term health is reflected in increased variation (+) of results, the long-term consequence of which is a reduction (–) in average actual results over the long haul. But a reduction in actual results produces an increase (or double negative) in the gap between desired and actual results.

The same pattern emerges when one considers the second long-term consequence of the steps taken in B1 to manage by results. In addition to the *tampering* which weakens systemic fundamentals (R2), those steps eventually *demoralize* the company's work force, customers, and investors by showing management's indifference to investing in the future. As shown by the reinforcing loop labeled R3 in Figure 2–3, demoralization also tends to increase variation in results, thereby diminishing actual results, and thus creating pressure for more short-term manage-by-results interventions.

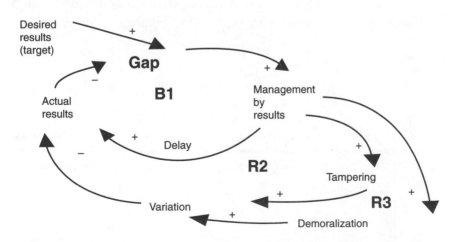

Figure 2–3: Long-Term Destabilizing Impact of Demoralization

Short-term efforts to manage by results set in motion, then, a number of unintended long-term consequences that reinforce a demand for more and more short-term results-oriented steps—like a cat chasing its tail. As suggested by the stories in figures 2–1, 2–2, and 2–3, the net long-term result of repeated efforts to improve financial results through short-run MBR interventions is increased variation, or instability, in long-run financial results. This is the situation that faced McNamara, and faces all MBR practitioners like him. They do not perceive the long-term destabilizing and destructive consequences (Figures 2–2 and 2–3) of their short-term efforts to reach quantitative targets (Figure 2–1). They do not desire those consequences. And yet, as the structure of the behavioral patterns in the figures indicates, attempts to drive quantitative results of natural systems with quantitative mechanistic targets generates behavior that invariably weakens and destabilizes the natural system.

The long-term impact of this self-destructive management behavior on the financial results of a business is depicted by the widely oscillating, increasingly variable time series marked by the letter A in Figure 2–4. Increasingly unstable earnings is one of two virtually certain long-term consequences of "managing by results." The other consequence, covered in chapter 1, is the tendency for MBR companies to incur added costs because they decouple their operations and then attempt to plan and coordinate activities with increasingly elaborate information technology—what is referred to in chapter 1 as the "information factory." Both consequences—increased long-term instability of earnings and higher operating costs—are captured in Figure 2–4 by "A."

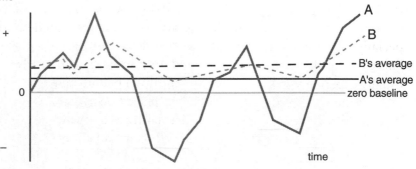

Figure 2–4: MBR Destabilizes and Diminishes Results

The time series labeled A depicts the long-term earnings of a company being managed as a mechanistic system using MBR practices. Its leaders are trying to fulfill only the universal desire to grow, without being mindful of the universal imperative to relate to other entities. The disappointing level and instability of long-term earnings are consequences of trying to grow without limit. The time series labeled B tracks the earnings of an MBM company that is being managed as if it were a living system. Its earnings record suggests leaders who balance the need to grow and the need to connect with others. Earnings on the B time series show a higher average level with less variation than on the A time series. Some variability occurs on the B time series, but almost never, if ever, does it reach the peaks or the troughs reached by the earnings on the A time series.

As discussed in chapter 1, a company operating according to the principles that guide living systems would limit work and resource consumption in every operation at all times to what is expressly needed to fill the next customer order. Companies whose practices adhere to such principles will produce continuously linked and balanced flows of work, leading to earnings records like that depicted in time series B. By contrast, the practices followed by an MBR company will lead to a long-term earnings record such as that depicted in time series A. Chapter 1 also showed how the demand for financial results and limitless growth in such companies often translates into decoupled, disjointed, batch flows of work that generate higher costs and relatively unstable results.

The pattern of operating earnings shown by the time series A in Figure 2–4 resembles the pattern of many manufacturing companies in the United States over the past four or five decades. The variation of operating income is higher and the average level is lower than desired. Especially irksome is the fact that performance during upswings often fails to offset the sharp and prolonged drop in earnings that companies usually experience in downturns. Ironically, a major cause of this instability is the widespread pressure always placed on managers to steadily increase profit. Although nothing in nature ever grows infinitely, financial markets and business experts all seem to believe it is "normal" and "necessary" for companies always to grow unceasingly in size and total profitability. Of the millions of companies that existed since 1900, only a handful have achieved unbroken growth for two decades, and most have failed in less than five years. This fact does not seem to diminish a belief in the need for unbroken growth.[26] Only a few people—W. Edwards Deming being a notable example—have had the courage to stake their careers on challenging that belief.

At the core of Dr. Deming's message is the assumption that variation in nature is normal. To everything there is a season. No trend in a cycle persists indefinitely. Nothing in nature grows infinitely. Limits are inevitable. Indeed, all variation in nature seems always to occur within rather well-defined boundaries. Nature's operations, in other words, generate controlled variation and cyclical change, rather than stasis and sameness.

Oblivious of, or indifferent to, principles at work in nature, most modern managers seek for their companies unlimited growth and consistently rising profits. To stamp out variation in results, companies inexorably press everyone to produce more in every succeeding period. The unanticipated upshot of these efforts to "control" variation is even more variation than would occur if the system were left to its own natural devices. In other words, efforts to suppress variation by pushing the system relentlessly to grow inevitably generate increased variation in results. Over the long haul this amplified variation decreases a system's effectiveness, thereby reducing average results. Moreover, such variation implies increased risk, which undoubtedly depresses the market's valuation of individual companies.

Were managers in most organizations surveyed, they probably would say that unwanted variation in bottom-line results, as shown by the time series A in Figure 2–4, emanates from causes such as flawed tools of analysis, inaccurate forecasting, or poor communication between planners and doers. Most respondents would call for better measurements and measurement tools, or an increase in performance-based incentive systems. Unfortunately, such relentless steps only tend to make matters worse. Just as in nature nothing is more likely to amplify variation than stimulating a system repeatedly and with increasing intensity, so it is in a company when repeated stimulation occurs in the hope that if results fall short of a target in one period, a more forceful stimulus will bring results up to expectations in the next period. Such behavior reflects the mechanistic premise that applying twice as much force to an object for the same period of time will double its velocity. It does not recognize, unfortunately, that when one applies increased force to a living system, unexpected results will surely occur.[27] Indeed, everyone has experienced at some time or another how differently a person responds to a sharp rebuke than to a soft tone. Despite this experience, managers today tend to regard employees as cogs in a machine, not as living parts of a natural system. Therefore, when results are not on target, managers conclude that people are just not trying hard enough.

Particularly lethal to human organizations is the belief that a change of measured outcomes in one part of the business will register the same amount of change in overall results. In other words, to raise profit by $1 million in the next period, simply reduce payroll $1 million by laying off employees. The desired result, of course, never happens. Some unexpected variance develops. Moreover, this variance is inevitably explained away as the result of poor measurement or poor communication. Almost never is failure to achieve a result traced to the flawed initial assumption that a business should aim at targets. The unacknowledged assumption in support of aiming at targets is that a business is a mechanistic system, not a natural living system. Managers attempt to drive work with quantitative targets, blissfully unaware that a business is a living system and therefore any changes in any of its parts will reverberate throughout it in what Dr. Deming called "unknown and unknowable" ways. These ways will lead to unexpected and even counterintuitive overall results. Unconsciously locked into a mechanistic thought pattern, frustrated managers react to their evident failure to "control" results by expanding and sharpening their use of measurement tools, unconsciously making things worse in the long run.

Dr. Deming observed that over 97 percent of the circumstances that affect a company's results are unmeasureable, while less than 3 percent of what influences final results can be measured. Nevertheless, American managers, according to Deming, tend to spend over 97 percent of their time analyzing measures. Less than 3 percent of their time is spent on what really matters—the unmeasureable.[28] Given management's skewed emphasis on measurement issues, it is perhaps not surprising to see how often the management literature and executive education of the last forty or so years has been dominated by attention to standard-cost budgeting, performance evaluation, cost management, balanced scorecards, and other measurement-focused unsystemic panaceas inspired by unquestioned faith in our ability to "control results."

The comparison of the two time series in Figure 2–4 is not meant to portray the actual performance of two real-life companies. It merely offers a hypothesis concerning the performance that we would expect to observe whenever we compare the long-run records of two companies that are managed in two very different ways—one as a mechanistic system (company A) and the other as a natural system (company B). The long-run earnings record of one unarguably MBM-oriented company—Toyota—clearly resembles the pattern of company B. Toyota has reported positive, albeit variable, operating profits every year since 1960. Moreover, the company's long-term profitability is among the highest in its industry, with less variation in results from year to year than that shown by competitors. Toyota appears, in other words, to have achieved the long-term performance trend shown above in track B. But it has done so, as will be shown in the next chapter, with a management style that embodies principles of natural-system behavior. Other companies yet to be studied in this context, but which seem to observe natural-system principles, that also have long-run earnings records like that of company B include Southwest Airlines, a commercial airline company in the United States, Hewlett-Packard, the world-renowned pioneer in electronics and computer technology, and Mayekawa, a medium-sized Japanese manufacturer of industrial refrigeration equipment.

The story told in Figure 2–4 should provide a cautionary signal to companies enjoying robust earnings in today's brisk economic environment. The sustained yearly increases of corporate revenue and profits that have accompanied the longest economic boom in history and the unprecedented rise of stock prices in Europe and North America since the early 1990s are fueled in large part by one of the most dramatic consumer spending booms in history. Although the comparison is seldom made, the impact of the current spending boom is not unlike the impact of the postwar consumer spending boom of the late 1940s and early 1950s. In both periods, almost any company doing business in consumer-related markets could sell everything it was able to produce at a price certain to earn ample profits.

Furthermore, the thinking that shapes management practice in most large companies today resembles that of the 1950s. Both periods take for granted a mechanistic worldview. Both intuitively rely on mechanistic management practices and are oblivious to patterns of relationships that connect a company's people to each other, to the customer, to the community, and to the ecosystem. The likelihood is that given these similarities, the crises faced by large American companies in the 1960s, 1970s, and 1980s will befall the current crop of manage-by-results companies. A business cycle downturn would perhaps awaken the average large company to the long-term dangers of MBR thinking and practice, as those have been discussed so far in this book. One hopes that before a downturn can happen, people running large companies will replace mechanistic MBR thinking with MBM thinking. Management by means rests on fundamental principles that guide the operation of systems in the universe. Pursuing practices based on those principles not only will assure the long-term health and viability of organizations, it may also dampen and mitigate the eventual impact of future economic downturns.

CONCLUSION

A shift in management thinking from the prevailing mechanistic worldview to the new worldview underpinning MBM will bring a change in thinking for the next generation of managers more revolutionary than that which any previous generation has ever experienced. If the present generation of managers and management scholars understands completely the nature and the consequences of the thought and practice that has dominated management practice for the past fifty years or so, change is possible.

The story of the relationships between quantitative science, modern management accounting, and our power to abstract demonstrates that measurement science and management accounting warp and ultimately destroy the concrete web of relationships that should link members of human organizations with the evolutionary changes that occur constantly in all natural systems in the universe. People who truly understand that story are equipped to reverse and mitigate the effects of traditional MBR thought and practices.

Undoubtedly the best way to reverse and mitigate those effects is to adopt a mode of thinking and management practice more in line with the principles that scientists now say are guiding the operation of all living systems. That practice has been referred to above as "manage by means," or MBM. MBM companies will pull *all* work, eventually, according to customer order. MBR companies, by contrast, push all work according to target-driven schedules. The remaining chapters of the book will discuss in more detail the specific ways that certain organizations work according to MBM principles.

Chapters which follow describe and discuss the thinking and practices that Toyota uses to *produce and deliver* products to customer order, that Scania, a Swedish truck maker, follows to *design* products to customer order, and that practitioners of order-line profitability analysis use to *assess* results to customer order. The thinking and practices in each case—Toyota producing to order, Scania designing to order, and order-line practitioners assessing to order—embody principles found in natural living systems, not principles found in mechanistic systems. Each of these three situations opens a unique and penetrating window onto future practices that business must adopt if they are to support and sustain a viable human presence on this planet. The following examples indicate how dramatically different from current business practices are those that will evolve from MBM thinking.

Means and Ends

The mechanistic world of MBR considers means to be ephemeral and incidental passages on the way to abiding and sought-after ends. In natural living systems, however, means and ends co-evolve simultaneously. In such a scheme, *"means are not subordinate to ends* so much as creative of them—*they are ends-in-the-making."*[29] Modern scientific understanding of natural systems reinforces the notion that means are not incidental paths leading to eternal ends. They are abiding pathways no less important than the ends to which they lead. Interestingly enough, Buddhism, Taoism, and Eastern and Western religions also see the end in the beginning. Even they support the suggestion that disciplined mastery of management practices that seamlessly connect means and ends—practices whereby every one of a company's parts links a customer's need to the company's ability to serve that need—will naturally and spontaneously yield satisfactory results.

Parts and Wholes

In MBM companies, in contrast to MBR organizations, everyone's attention will focus on doing work, not on manipulating quantitative abstractions about work. There will be no distinction between "knowers" and "doers" or "thinkers" and "actors." Every person's activity will embody that most fundamental condition of natural life systems—namely, that "all knowing is doing and all doing is knowing."[30] Thus, the MBM organization will manifest the deepest trait of a natural system: each part reflects the whole in its entirety ("holographically"), no part simply adds to the whole in a mere quantitative sense.[31] Specifically, this means that every person's work focuses on the *union* between customer and company which is the rationale for the whole organization.

The "Information Factory"

In MBM companies no one will use quantitative financial information from the accounting system (or elsewhere) to set operating targets to drive or control work. Quite simply, the "information factory" that guides and controls operations in MBR companies will cease to exist. There will still be accounting and information systems and all the computer technology that goes with them. But they will focus entirely on financial reporting and traditional record-keeping. Management accounting will be gone and there will be no positions comparable to those occupied in MBR companies by accounting and finance personnel known as "controllers." Persons in those positions today will be employed in MBM companies to assess how well company practices abide by natural-system principles, not to assess how closely financial results come to pre-ordained targets.

Profit Beyond Measure

In both MBM organizations and MBR organizations profit is considered necessary. But there the similarity ends. Whereas the MBR manager will consider profit as the overall goal and purpose of the organization, to be maximized "at any cost," the MBM manager will perceive profit as necessary for the company's survival, but not the company's reason for existing.[32] Indeed, profit to the MBM manager will be seen as breathing is to a human organism: necessary, but not what life is about. Thus, quantitative measurement has a quite different meaning for MBM managers than it has for MBR managers. For MBR managers measurement is the indispensable tool for understanding what mechanistic steps one must take to maximize results—profit and shareholder value. MBR managers perceive measurement as marking the pathway to profit simply because they view the organization quantitatively—as separated parts (one of which is the financial results) that contribute independently and linearly to the result. MBM managers, on the other hand, view the organization in terms of patterns and relationships that connect people in the organization with each other, with customers, with the community, and with the ecosystem. Their concern is to nurture the development of practices and disciplines that instill in the organization principles resembling those found in natural living systems, content that satisfactory results will follow. While measurement can be used in important ways to describe and track the course of the system's external features, one of which is its financial results, measurement never can explain or motivate interventions into the internal web of relationships that shapes the company's work and assures it of satisfactory results. In that sense, the MBM organization achieves "profit beyond measure."

3

....

Produce to Order

Nature uses only the longest threads to weave her
patterns, so each small piece of her fabric reveals the
organization of the entire tapestry.

—Richard Feynman[1]

For at least twenty years, Toyota Motor Corporation has produced the
highest quality product and service in its industry, at the lowest cost.
For nearly forty years Toyota has had an unbroken record of annual
profits, without layoffs. Moreover, Toyota designs and markets new varieties of product faster, and at less cost, than any of its competitors.
Regularly it tops the industry in overall productivity. Attempts to understand and replicate the exceptional performance of Toyota have inspired countless studies.[2] Those who have studied Toyota extensively
discover that this company has outpaced the competition for decades
not because of management fads, but rather because of its own "home-
grown" methods.

Toyota's legendary ability to achieve high quality and variety at low
costs arises not from "managing by results," but rather from mastering
practices that maintain and reinforce a balanced, continuous flow of
work from order to delivery, and beyond. Those practices—as observed
at one of the company's newest and largest facilities in the world, Toyota Motor Manufacturing, USA–Kentucky (known by the acronym
TMM-K)—do not call for reaching targets for profit, costs, or growth,
nor do they rely on running operations with sophisticated computer-

driven information systems. However, mastery of these practices, as this chapter shall note, has enabled Toyota, more than any auto maker in the world, to achieve satisfactory financial performance decade after decade.

To appreciate these practices, it is essential to consider the thinking that has prevailed at Toyota Motor Corporation since the 1960s, and in predecessor companies owned by the Toyoda family since at least the 1920s.[3] As the following section shows, TMM-K's particular ability to achieve quality and variety at exceptionally low costs emanates from the distinctive thinking and practices found in the Toyota Production System. This system operates according to principles resembling those guiding the operation of natural living systems on Earth. It offers clear proof that when an organization emulates living systems, it will excel. Having examined the thinking that distinguishes Toyota, this chapter will explore in detail the disciplined mastery of work evident in the Toyota Production System (hereafter referred to as TPS). It will indicate how TPS enables Toyota's facilities around the world to survive and excel without relying on traditional "management by results" practices.

TMM-K[4]

Toyota Motor Manufacturing–Kentucky (TMM-K) opened in 1988, producing its first car in May of that year. It is the first integrated auto-making and assembly plant built by Toyota outside Japan. Situated on 1,300 acres on the outskirts of Georgetown, Kentucky, twenty miles north of Lexington, the plant originally consisted of 3.7 million square feet of space dedicated to producing about 200,000 Camry sedans per year. Today the plant, divided into several adjoining sections, occupies approximately 8 million square feet and annually produces about 500,000 autos, including Camry and Avalon sedans and the Sienna mini-van, as well as more than 500,000 engines, including both 4-cylinder and V-6. The plant employs about 7,500 people in stamping, die-making, body weld, paint, plastics fabrication, engine making, power train manufacture, and final assembly operations. The seats installed in every vehicle produced at TMM-K are manufactured two miles from the TMM-K site in a facility owned by Johnson Controls Company.

Anxious to replicate Toyota's legendary success, business leaders constantly stream to TMM-K. Most of these people come away exhilarated because they know they have witnessed something remarkable. Nevertheless, their tour leaves them essentially unenlightened. These visitors do spot the uniqueness of individual elements in the Toyota Production System and many of them strive to introduce these elements into their own companies. As a consequence of new practices borrowed from Toyota, often they see performance improve, sometimes considerably. No company, however, has actually duplicated Toyota's performance.[5] They have not replicated Toyota's success because visitors have not grasped the principles informing the separate elements of Toyota's system. Just as one cannot understand the properties of water merely by analyzing the properties of oxygen and hydrogen, so one cannot understand the source of Toyota's performance by analyzing distinct parts of the system.

Ken Kreafle, employed by General Motors for sixteen years before joining TMM-K in September 1987, emphasizes the systemic nature of the Toyota Production System when he describes his encounters with guests from other companies. After touring the Toyota facility, invariably they say, "You have shown us A, B, C, D, E, and F. Our own plants have these already. Now please show us G, the secret ingredient that makes you different." Ken tells them there is no magic G. Toyota's superior performance rests not on magic, but rather on its entire production process and the thinking that gives rise to it. The disciplined mastery of numerous practices at TMM-K sustains a balanced, system-wide continuous flow of work. These disciplined practices also permit rapid change at every step in that continuous flow. Although these practices are not easy for outsiders to identify and grasp, knowing them well is the only pathway toward truly understanding the thinking that informs TPS. To see these practices is to realize that the principles characteristic of TMM-K are identical to those sustaining natural systems. Before we consider these subtler practices in detail, first let us examine some of the distinctive elements of Toyota's system that are immediately apparent to astute visitors to TMM-K.

A number of conditions at TMM-K strike the first-time visitor as being markedly different from those one observes in most large manufacturing plants in North America. Such things as reduced noise levels, steady pace of work, and the use of the "andon cord" especially command the visitor's attention. Recognizing these differences between Toyota and other automobile manufacturers is the first step toward understanding fully the unique nature of Toyota's production system.

The relative quiet of all parts of the TMM-K complex, except for the stamping area, is perhaps the most obvious difference a visitor notices between Toyota and any other American plant. Even stamping, for all its noise, is quieter than are similar operations in other companies. Equally impressive are the cleanliness and orderliness everywhere. A place has been designated for everything, and everything seems to be in its place. Work moves, furthermore, in a balanced manner. There is a surprising lack of either hurriedness or idleness among workers. Everyone is busy, but busy in an almost relaxed, rhythmic way. The only sign of hurriedness in the plant is that of the quiet, yet inexorable, coming and going of steady lines of electric-powered tow-motor trains that transfer parts and components from one work area to another. So essential is it for these vehicles promptly to make their appointed rounds that they have right-of-way over pedestrians in the long, broad aisles that criss-cross the entire plant complex.

At TMM-K, as at any Toyota facility in the world, even a preoccupied visitor must notice the flashing lights and musical sounds coming from overhead boards which resemble electronic scoreboards in a sports arena. Located near every work area in the plant, these overhead boards, called "andons," the Japanese word for lantern, signal that a team member (line worker) has identified a problem possibly needing supervisory attention. The flashing lights and distinctive musical sounds identify a specific area, the nature of the problem, and the status of the alert.

The lights and sounds are triggered by the "andon sensor system," a distinctive feature of Toyota plants that appears in every work area in various guises. Probably the best known example of the andon concept is the "andon cord," an overhead cord located within arm's reach of each team member that runs like an old-fashioned clothesline throughout every assembly area. A team member knows that it is his or her responsibility to pull that cord at the first sign of any problem.

Pulling the andon cord does not, as has been rumored, immediately stop the flow of work on the line. Pulling it merely alerts supervisory personnel—team or group leaders—to be prepared to assist the team member who has identified an abnormality. While the team member addresses the problem, the line continues to flow without interruption until it reaches the end of the standard interval, or "takt time," at which cars leave production—usually about 55 to 60 seconds. The line stops only when a team member, team leader, or supervisor is unable to solve a problem within the remaining current takt-time interval and does not release the andon alert.

Even when stopping becomes necessary, work does not stop in the entire plant. On the contrary, it ceases only in the segment of work stations immediately surrounding the affected work station. At TMM-K, each production line, from the paint shop to the end of the line, contains about twelve segments, each segment consisting of about thirty work stations. Each segment is separated from the rest by a buffer of about five vehicles. Because team members and supervisors remedy most problems in less than a minute, pulling the andon cord seldom causes the line to stop even in one segment, and rarely in the entire plant.[6]

The andon cord system enables team members promptly to identify and signal the time, place, and condition of an abnormality, no matter how slight. In so doing, the andon cord system contributes to yet another difference between TMM-K and other North American auto assembly plants. In TMM-K, rework areas are sparse. Whereas North American auto plants often allocate several hundred spaces for cars temporarily parked to await rework, at TMM-K only a few dozen rework bays exist.

TMM-K also differs from other automotive plants in North America in the high degree to which it fabricates and assembles an automobile's major components on one site. In the typical North American decoupled automotive manufacturing organization depicted in Figure 1–2, the various parts tend to be made in widely different geographical locations, separated from final assembly. No other North American auto assembly plant brings together stamping, welding, a power train department that machines and assembles engines and axle components, and plastics fabrication all under one roof. Although such a high degree of integration under one roof is not absolutely necessary to achieve continuous flow of work, it is consistent with Toyota's long-standing strategy to achieve an unbroken continuous flow in as many operations as possible, from component making through final assembly.[7]

Visitors to the TMM-K plant are likely to notice these obvious differences between Toyota and typical North American car manufacturers. Less obvious is the significant truth that the distinctive features of Toyota's system are the consequence of deeply ingrained habits of thought. Only by grasping that unique thinking can managers hope to attain the success experienced by Toyota. This thinking, integral to the MBM (manage-by-means) philosophy, is explored below.

THE THINKING THAT SHAPES THE WORK THAT PRODUCES TO ORDER AT LOW COST[8]

The most striking feature of Toyota's success is surely its achievement of "rich ends from simple means." Since the 1970s, Toyota has had a capacity greater than that of any of its competitors to profitably produce and sell increasing varieties of high quality vehicles at low cost. This remarkable achievement rests on Toyota's distinctive approach to organizing work. This approach, as discussed in chapter 1, is much closer in spirit to the processes observed in natural living systems than it is to the traditional techniques of mass-production manufacturing. Efforts to copy Toyota's way of organizing work usually fail. Would-be imitators often end up dismissing Toyota's variety as overstated, or they search for hidden financial stratagems they believe Toyota uses to manage the costs of complexity (see box). These imitators simply do not seem to realize that Toyota achieves variety with high quality and low cost not so much by managing the costs of complexity as by avoiding complexity in the first place.

A System for Winning Every Bet

In late 1992 Toyota was able to produce over 1 million variants of its vehicles, including all physical differences such as color, trim, body style, and options. In September 1992 they actually used about 40,000 of those variants in the 200,000 or so vehicles they sold, for an average of 5 vehicles per variant. Moreover, about 80 percent of the vehicles sold used only 20 percent of those 40,000 variants; the other 20 percent of sales accounted for 80 percent of the variants.

Toyota obviously ranked as both a high volume and high variety producer. Yet, they achieved the lowest cost per unit and highest profitability of any maker in the industry. How did they do this?

While not referring explicitly to Toyota, modern strategic cost management thinkers argue that a company with Toyota's 80/20 sales pattern can increase profitability by focusing attention on the 80 percent of sales that touched only 20 percent of the variants actually produced (low cost of complexity) and dropping the 20 percent of sales that called on the other 80 percent of variants (high cost of complexity). The problem with this reasoning, however, is that customers, with over 1 million possible variants to draw from each month, will not settle on the same mix of variants from month to month. Each month's volume, drawn each time from the 1 million possible variants, is likely to be distributed in a similar 80/20 ratio. If so, then coping with variety by cutting away the small-volume/high variant tail of that distribution each month will only lead in a downward spiral to bankruptcy. Clearly, Toyota does not manage the costs of variety by doing what strategic cost management experts advocate.

Indeed Toyota's legendary manufacturing guru Taiichi Ohno once explained their remarkable success by comparing what they do to betting on horse races. He explained Toyota's production system by comparing it to *a system for winning every bet*. In effect, Toyota, referring to the 1992 data, picks a winner from 1 million possible outcomes approximately 200,000 times a month! The company does this, however, not by trying to forecast and build to plan, but by organizing work so that it can "place bets one-hundredth of a second before the horses cross the finish line." What Ohno meant is that Toyota's system enables it to produce only when customers order and pay. Although that would be illegal at a horse track, it is eminently sensible in business.

Source: Kazuhiro Mishina, "The Logic of the Toyota Production System," unpublished working paper, April 1994, pp. 10–12.

As indicated in chapter 1, most large-scale companies view complexity as an inevitable concomitant of variety. They attempt to control its costs by pursuing economies of scale. However, their efforts to control the costs of complexity by increasing the scale and speed of output, that is, by "being efficient," often harm quality. By contrast, the way work is organized at TMM-K (Figure 3–1) makes it possible to increase variety without additional costs, without increasing scale or speed, and without jeopardizing quality. Indeed, Toyota views increased variety as an *opportunity* to sharpen disciplined work practices that reduce costs and improve quality—*not* a source of complexity and cost that workers must control by continually producing more output in less time.

This system, portrayed conceptually in Figure 1–3, is depicted in more concrete terms in Figure 3–1. A key feature of the system is the use of customer order information to pull material through the plant. Reflecting differences in history and culture, Toyota's plants in Japan produce most vehicles literally to order for the final customer, while their American plants produce almost all vehicles to order for individual dealers. Thus, starting with the receipt of orders from dealers—the plant's external customers—work at TMM-K proceeds along a continuously flowing line from the stamping and welding of body parts to final assembly. At hundreds of work stations situated along both sides of that line, team members attach and install parts which they pull from line-side conveyance racks that are replenished every hour or so by kanban, a process described more fully below. Some of these work stations receive continuously replenished flows of major component

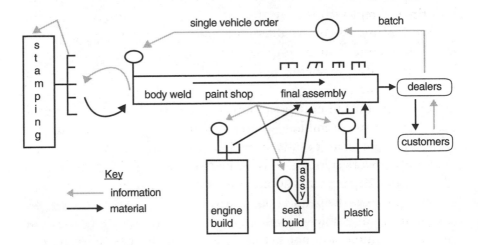

Figure 3–1: Toyota Production System at TMM-K in the 1990s

subassemblies such as engines, transmissions and axles, seats, and plastic bumpers and dashboards. Throughout the entire plant, the flow of information from both external and internal customers initiates and directs how material flows from worker to worker.

The flow of material for each individual vehicle is initiated and guided by information contained in the individual dealer's initial order.[9] This initial order starts the flow of material. From the point at which material flow begins, workers respond to information from the next work station which tells them when their internal customer is ready to receive material. An especially important point about the flow of material and the flow of information as shown in Figure 3–1 is that information from the customer (external or internal) always initiates work on material, and worked-on material always flows toward the source of customer information. In a pattern that resembles the one seen earlier in Figure 1–3, *customer order information and material transformation are joined at every step of the process.*

At TMM-K, an "external" customer order is the only information introduced from outside the work process, from start to finish. Anything that any worker does on an order after the process begins is initiated and directed by information arising from within the work process itself. For the most part, this information is a pull signal that is triggered by the next station, the "internal" customer, to indicate it is ready to be replenished. The nature of the signal depends on how long the lead time to replenish is in relation to the order lead time. When the time to replenish is comparable to the order lead time, that signal can be nothing more than an outstretched hand or the nod of a head saying, "I am ready." When the replenishment lead time is longer than the order time, the pull signal can be an empty place in a prearranged buffer, where the buffer in effect serves as the next "customer."[10] In the case of major subassemblies, where a department requires a long lead time to prepare what it sends to the line, the information can be a signal from any work station that is located early enough in the process to allow for that department's appropriate lead time. For example, when a vehicle body exits the paint booth a signal can be sent to the off-site department that assembles the vehicle's seats. Sending the signal once the vehicle is painted, and not before, minimizes the chance of error in matching body type with seat type. Moreover, the time it takes the vehicle to travel from the paint shop to the seat insertion station is within the lead time it takes the seat assembly department to complete and deliver its work to line side.[11]

The two associated flows, customer information and material transformation, are always linked, never separated, in every step of the process shown in Figure 3–1. This linked pairing of information and material referred to in chapter 1 unites customer and company—and this union is the fundamental reason any business organization exists. The work depicted in Figure 3–1 is organized so that each task and each step in the system transforms material in response to a customer's express order for a product or service. This way of organizing work creates the union between the company and the customer that was depicted in very general terms in Figure 1–3. Similarly at TMM-K, the continuous connection between company and customer, that is, between customer information and material flow, is basic to everything that goes on in the plant (Figure 3–1). That unbroken connection is one of the main differences between a natural production system (Figure 1–3) and a mechanistic, batch-oriented production system (Figure 1–2).

Several other important details also distinguish Toyota's system at TMM-K (Figure 3–1) from the traditional batch-oriented mass production system (Figure 1–2). Besides making each individual customer's order visible in the flow of work one by one, the system at TMM-K releases orders as far upstream in the work process as possible. At TMM-K that point is at the beginning (head) of the body weld area, immediately following the stamping area. At no other point does information from an external customer order directly initiate the release of material in the production process. To reiterate what was said before, all subsequent work from body weld on through final assembly is triggered *by the work itself* in one of three ways: (1) From body weld, work flows downstream by moving one station at a time into the next station as soon as it becomes empty. (2) Off-line work to make large, difficult-to-ship items such as engines, plastic bumpers, instrument panels, and seats is triggered by a signal from a work station sufficiently far upstream to allow time to make and deliver the item to the line—usually just as a vehicle body leaves the paint area. (3) Parts and components added to the vehicle in each work station, including stamped body parts used in the body weld area, are on line-side storage racks in standard containers that go back to the appropriate supplier when empty.

Contrast how this system triggers work with the way work is scheduled in traditional, computer-oriented Material Requirements Planning (MRP) systems of the sort that underlie the work shown in Figure 1–2. MRP systems do not release individual customer orders into a continuous production flow. Instead, they batch orders for a week or a month and release batch production instructions to *myriad* shops all at once. The work in different shops is not connected with the work in other shops. It is connected with instructions from a computer and it flows into final assembly from inventory stocks stored in warehouses. Thus, instead of costlessly using the work itself to transmit all the information that is needed to process the work, MRP systems create a costly "information factory"—shown by the dotted lines and arrows in Figure 1–2—that continually cycles and churns masses of data that flow separately from the work.

An important issue at Toyota Motor Manufacturing–Kentucky is where in the production process the customer order should enter the work stream. Unlike systems designed to achieve variety at low cost through "mass customization," the Toyota Production System tends to locate this point far upstream, as close as possible to the point where work begins.[10] That choice tends to increase an order's lead time (time from receipt of customer order to delivery), but it also improves the system's ability to accommodate product variety. Technically speaking, order-fulfillment lead time is shorter the closer the customer-order entry point is to the downstream shipping point. However, the parts and work that embody an order's unique variety must necessarily occur at or after the point where the customer order enters the work stream. When the customer-order entry point is close to the shipping point, as it is in mass-customization systems, order-fulfillment lead time is shortened. However, variety is then limited to largely cosmetic, surface differences. It is obviously very difficult and costly when entry and shipping points virtually converge to vary components or systems that are deeply imbedded in the product. Moreover, allowing for a great deal of even cosmetic variety near the shipping point implies having enormous numbers of stored parts and lots of extra manpower at that end of the work stream. Thus, by distancing the work needed to provide variety from the upstream work required to make the basic vehicle, mass customization does nothing to eliminate the mass-production trade-off between variety and low cost.

Ideally, the work required to create variety will flow together with the basic work performed to make the product. Introducing a customer order at the start of the production cycle causes work and variety to flow together at every stage. Placing the order entry point near the start of the production process, as shown in Figure 3–1, insures that the *steps to provide variety will be an integral part of the work in virtually all work stations* from start to finish. In fact, Toyota in Georgetown is able to introduce the customer order as early as the body-weld station. It can do so because in its pursuit of continuous flow, it has located under one roof material transformation, machining, and assembly. By contrast, most other auto makers, driven by a desire to achieve economies of scale, have centralized material transformation and machining in a few very large facilities, and they have decentralized final assembly in many smaller dedicated plants. These arrangements were made with the intention of mass producing variety efficiently. Ironically, instead it results in a decoupled, discontinuous production flow held together by a costly "information factory" (Figure 1–2) that *virtually prohibits efforts to make variety an intrinsic part of every stage of the work.*[13]

Permitting variety to be an intrinsic part of everyone's work does more, however, than simply reduce the cost of offering increased varieties. *It also enables greater variety itself to act as a source of improved productivity and efficiency*, rather than a source of additional cost, because workers *in every work station* are able to perform different work for each different variant. These different kinds of work encompass both the steps that workers perform on each vehicle and the parts which they add to each vehicle that passes through a work station. For example, workers are equipped when necessary to perform steps and add parts on both left-hand drive and right-hand drive vehicles, on both manual- and automatic-geared vehicles, on both sedan and van styles, and so forth. The more different things that individual workers can do in a takt-time interval, the more efficiently they can do all work, including the work needed to accommodate different varieties and the work needed to accomplish new model changeovers.

Traditional manufacturers, by attempting to increase variety in a mass-production context, end up creating conditions in which variety conflicts with efficiency (Figure 1–2). Consequently, their efforts to increase variety only generate increased amounts of indirect cost.[14] Then, to control those costs, they design production facilities to minimize variety, not to maximize opportunities for creating it. Their facilities tend to separate material transformation and machining work from assembly work, concentrating material transformation and machining into fewer large plants, and dispersing final assembly into more smaller plants—each designed to assemble one platform. This overall system of plants is intended to produce variety at low cost through scale and speed (Figure 1–2). But a key to each plant's success is to design every individual work station so as to *minimize the amount of variety that any worker must handle* at any time. In those plants they follow management practices that maximize the quantity of output produced by each plant and by each worker in a given period. In effect, the traditional manufacturer acts as if low *average* cost per unit were the answer to low costs in all settings, from zero variety to maximum variety.

By contrast, Toyota creates an entirely new type of cost structure in which *increased product variety*, far from impeding efficiency, in fact *generates improved efficiency and profitability*. Toyota does this by insuring that the work needed to create variety occurs with the work done to make each unit. To accommodate variety in all its work, Toyota's TMM-K production facility is designed to provide economies of proximity, not economies of scale, by integrating material transformation and machining with final assembly in the same plant. Equally important are the steps Toyota takes to build management practices—such as those that enable smooth handling of different build sequences from unit to unit—to meet the challenges of handling variety. Management practices at TMM-K accommodate the handling of increasing amounts of variety by enabling the amount and type of work to vary as efficiently as possible in each and every step of the production system. Toyota's management practices focus attention on the minute particulars of how workers in each station address each customer order. They do not have general policies meant to push output through every part of the system in an effort to reduce average unit costs. Toyota's unique management practices constitute a system that reduces costs by continually increasing the amount of variety any worker can handle at any time.[15]

TOYOTA PRODUCTION SYSTEM[16]

TMM-K's management practices comprise what is referred to as the Toyota Production System, or TPS. These practices help Toyota avoid the so-called indirect costs which tend, in a batch-schedule, mass-production system, to rise exponentially as variety increases. Traditional manufacturing practices endeavor to hold such costs in check by increasing the scale of facilities and by driving people to produce more and more output. Toyota's unique management practices enable the company to sustain high quality and increase variety while maintaining steady or falling costs. TPS achieves this without having to increase the scale of facilities or the volume of output.

Discussed below are five practices essential to the Toyota Production System: takt time, standardization of work, jidoka (error detection), just-in-time (including kanban), and heijunka (leveled production).[17]

Takt Time

Perhaps the most fundamental TPS practice—arguably the one that makes continuous flow possible—is to flow work through each part of the entire system at a uniform "pulse rate" or *takt time.* This steady rate is the result of meticulous attention to the process layout and the work flow. These are so designed that in every work station a properly trained worker can complete the necessary steps in a time interval that equals the rate at which vehicles are released to customers. That takt time, like the rate at which a heart's beat sends blood pulsing through an animal's system, will be the same for every work station in the entire plant. The rate is specific to an individual plant's condition and maturity. In a new plant with a relatively inexperienced work force, or when an established operation produces a new vehicle model, as in the case of TMM-K when it first produced the Avalon model in 1995, work will be paced at a fairly slow takt time such as 75 to 80 seconds per vehicle. A seasoned work force producing familiar models, however, will work at a takt time as fast as 54 or 55 seconds per vehicle.

Depending on the takt time (line speed), the difference in potential output during a shift of 450 minutes (8 hours less two 15 minute breaks) can be considerable. Whereas 337 units per shift can be produced at a takt time of 80 seconds, 490 units can be produced when a

takt time of 55 seconds is maintained for the entire shift. It is striking
to note that a Toyota plant never changes the takt time abruptly or arbitrarily to achieve plant-wide cost or output targets (say near the end
of an accounting period). Takt time is changed to adjust output only in
response to a change in market demand. The adjustment is staged in
steps according to a well-honed planning process.

Takt time establishes a rhythm to the line. Workers become accustomed to it as one becomes accustomed to the beat in a musical performance. Experienced workers in Toyota's older plants are skilled
enough to change takt times frequently with great ease. At the present
time takt times do not change nearly as frequently in Toyota's overseas
facilities such as TMM-K as they do in its Japanese facilities. As workers become more seasoned, however, they all will possess the same abilities to vary takt times to meet changing customer demands.

Standardized Work

To insure that work flows continuously according to a uniform
rhythm, Toyota people take care to *standardize work* in each and every
work station throughout a plant. Work standards at Toyota are designed jointly by team members and engineering supervisors. Toyota
assumes that workers have sound, informed ideas, and it encourages
them to develop and share their ideas. Workers describe and time
every step performed in a work station, and they document the steps
and times on a standardized work sheet that is posted conveniently in
the work area. In developing standards, they give attention, in descending order, to worker safety (especially ergonomics), customer
quality, productivity, and cost. Work standards change often, as team
members and supervisors perceive safer, better ways to do things.

By imposing agreed-on work patterns, standards insure that a team
member can see quickly and easily when something abnormal occurs.
Abnormalities encompass not just product quality defects, but also de-
ficient tooling, unsafe practices, and departure from productivity
norms. Standardization provides benchmarks for "normal" that enable
one to see whether or not the same work is done differently each time
it occurs. Because benchmarks make abnormal outcomes visible the
moment they occur, team members are able to stop work and correct

errors on the spot. Errors do not go undetected; they are not left to be remedied later by "troubleshooters" or, worst of all, identified by customers. Standardization creates a discipline that improves quality and holds costs in check not because work is done repetitively, but because work passes from hand to hand free of errors.

An unfortunate aspect of assembly work in any setting, even Toyota's, is its potential for boredom and stress, both of which can contribute to injury on the job. Therefore, to improve safety by minimizing and alleviating monotony, team members at TMM-K may move every two hours to a different work station. Such movement not only reduces boredom, stress, and injury, but also it assures that everyone always understands and performs according to the current standard. Thus, error is minimized, costs are maintained, and the frequent changes required to produce high variety are facilitated.

Standardization contributes to stable costs and higher quality by insuring that work is done safely and comfortably in the necessary takt time. Work is not standardized in Toyota plants by having industrial engineers dictate from above the "one best way" that a worker must perform a task, repetitively, as fast as possible. This image, a throwback to the early days of "scientific management" inspired by the ideas of mass-production expert Frederick W. Taylor in the early 1900s, does not fit the Toyota concept of standardization. In contrast to Taylor's often inhumane and always cost-oriented practices, work standards at TMM-K make certain that all steps performed are *ergonomically* appropriate. Team members on the TMM-K line receive training and advice on how to do work in ways that reduce bodily stress and injury. Moreover, while Taylor advocated having every work step documented, timed, and improved over and over again, he put industrial engineers, not the line workers themselves, in charge of such activities. And standard work, for Taylor, was not geared to stable takt times or standardized kanban-style material flows.[18]

Jidoka

Another distinctive TPS practice originated in the early Toyoda family enterprises that manufactured automatic textile-weaving machinery. Nearly a century ago, Sakichi Toyoda, founder of the Toyoda family business, discovered the advantage of machines that could stop automatically when something went wrong in a process, such as when a thread broke on an automatic loom weaving a bolt of fabric. After automatic stops were placed on looms, a worker no longer had to sit monotonously watching a single machine for errors. Freed from such dull attention, the worker could tend more looms than before, using a wider range of skills than were needed simply to watch the output of an individual machine. The automatic-stop device had the effect, in other words, of reducing worker boredom while increasing labor productivity to generate higher quality output. Today the Toyota enterprise uses the Japanese term *jidoka* to mean a machine that has been invested with human-like intelligence.

In post-1950 Toyota the concept of jidoka was expanded to include, in addition to automatic-stop devices on machines, any stop process, whether initiated automatically by a machine or manually by a worker. Instrumental in making manual work stoppage a reality was, of course, the development of the andon cord, an innovation that reputedly was inspired by the cord trolley passengers pull to signal the driver to stop. Combined with uniform takt times and standardized work processes in every work station, automatic and manual stop devices enable team members to take prompt action to remove and remedy abnormalities as soon as they become visible.

Sophisticated students of TPS realize that the ability to detect and remedy abnormality increases a worker's understanding of how the overall system functions. This ability may also lead to unexpected insights because an abnormality may signify not error, but rather that the system is doing some unexpected thing worth learning and repeating. Thus, jidoka may appropriately be referred to as a learning exercise, as well as a process for detecting error.

Just in Time

Another TPS practice undoubtedly originating in the Toyodas' early textile machinery company was firmly in place by the 1930s in the small automobile-making operation that Kiichiro Toyoda, Sakichi's son, developed within the textile machine company. This practice reflects the conviction that waste must be avoided and flexibility increased. To achieve these goals, workers in an assembly operation are supplied only with the kinds and amounts of items they need, and only as they need them. To this idea Kiichiro applied the phrase "just in time". Kiichiro had visited Henry Ford's River Rouge facility before World War II. He returned home convinced that Ford's continuous flow system could be adapted to small-volume production in Japan by using the *just-in-time* concept.

Taiichi Ohno, co-architect of TPS with Kiichiro, arrived at the same conclusion when, just after World War II, he studied operations in a modern supermarket in the United States. The practice that particularly impressed Ohno on his visit to an American supermarket was that of the store clerk replenishing a bin or shelf almost as soon as a customer removed something. Presumably this sight influenced Ohno to expand the concept of just-in-time to mean "make only what a customer has ordered, when the customer orders it and not beforehand."

Ohno's thinking eventually generated *kanban*, Toyota's withdrawal and replenishment system. In that system, an "upstream" work station commences work on something only after it has received a card, a kanban, from the next door downstream work station calling for specific material or parts. In effect, the downstream card-delivering work station is a customer, and the upstream work station is the supplier. The kanban principle is fully in place throughout every Toyota plant. Because of it, every worker views himself or herself as both customer and supplier.

Where producing varieties of output affects stations further and further upstream (not just at the end of the line), as at TMM-K, wide assortments of parts are needed at each work station. To achieve such assortments without either excess inventories of parts or stockouts that stop the line is difficult. Kanban creates a discipline that reduces chances for either problem to occur. The key to kanban is its power to match information flow with material flow throughout the system. In other words, information about replenishment flows directly with the material, at no cost, and not through a costly off-line control system. The presence of a well-functioning kanban process also can help reduce the space needed to store parts at line side. Thus, kanban helps keep in check, or reduce, parts supply costs and space costs that otherwise would grow, probably exponentially, with increasing variety.

The withdrawal and replenishment kanban cards may have inspired Dr. Edwards Deming's idea of a "living process map," which he often described in his four-day seminars. Dr. Deming said that to incorporate his ideas, an organization first should create a living map of its system by having every employee join hands with the person upstream, whose work supplies him or her, and with the person downstream, to whom he or she supplies work. The continuous flow of kanban in a Toyota plant implicitly generates such a map every minute of every operating shift.

Heijunka

Heijunka, the leveled sequencing of variants in production, helps enable the manufacture of endless varieties at the cost of mass-producing only one variety of a thing all the time.[19] Perhaps the least intuitive of Toyota's distinctive practices, heijunka helps deal with the problem that producing varieties of product on the same line means that the cycle times of work in individual work stations will differ from variant to variant. Indeed, a work station can have no work at all for some variants and an abundance of work for other variants, as when an auto maker assembles two or more different platforms on the same line. This causes variation in cycle times that impedes line balancing and creates bottlenecks that move unpredictably among work stations as the mix of varieties changes.

Toyota mitigates these balancing and bottleneck problems by sequencing production so that variants occur as evenly as possible. This is heijunka. Thus, if half of the day's units are vans and half of those are equipped with air-conditioning, then work is scheduled so that every fourth unit coming down the line will be an air-conditioned van. This prevents accumulation of cycle time imbalances that could stop the line, or worse. For example, if one station requires 40 seconds to do its work on a non-air-conditioned van and 65 seconds on an air-conditioned van, heijunka sequencing avoids having the 65-second work occur two or more times in a row and improves chances of maintaining a 60-second pace without interruption.

Alternatives to heijunka include costly steps such as adding work stations or creating off-line stations, both of which lengthen the line and probably add people. For heijunka to work, however, there must be close integration of assembly with upstream material transformation stations and very flexible workers. In fact, workers accustomed to heijunka are better equipped to rebalance a line when unanticipated changes occur. This makes it easier to handle unexpected disruptions and to introduce new models.

To see how heijunka works, imagine two companies—Toyota and another manufacturer with a decoupled batch-oriented system (e.g., Figure 1–2)—that must fill identical orders for seven units of two models of final product, A and B. The orders are for three As and four Bs. The manager of the decoupled operation would undoubtedly hold that the optimal production schedule for producing these seven vehicles called for two batches: AAA and then BBBB. The manager's rationale would be that producing the seven vehicles in two batches calls for changing over only once, thus minimizing the time and resources lost in changing over between models. A Toyota plant manager, however, would say that the optimal production schedule is BABABAB, a schedule calling for changing over six times. The time and resources it takes to make six changeovers at Toyota are no greater than, and could be less, than the time and resources the decoupled company requires to make one changeover. Imagining this scenario is to imagine reality. Changing over at Toyota became such a science after the 1950s that differences by a factor of six or more separated Toyota from almost all its competitors in the world by the late 1970s. This separation continues.

The BABABAB "leveled" schedule reminds one of the ABCDEFGHIJ. . . schedule that chapter 1 indicated is characteristic of nature's systems. Because changeover times are markedly reduced, leveled production costs Toyota less than its competitors spend producing the same output in all-or-nothing batches. That is one of heijunka's chief virtues; it largely explains why Toyota pays so much attention to leveling the mix of varieties scheduled each day. For example, assuming a 60-second takt time, if 480 vehicles are to be produced on a given day and 8 have sunroofs, then TMM-K will save resources by scheduling one sunroof on every 60th vehicle. By doing so, it is possible to scale the unique capital, machinery, or other resources needed to make and install sunroofs to the demands of one sunroof per hour. If work on the sunroofs is batched, however, and all are done in one 8-minute interval, then any unique capital or other sunroof-specific resources will have to be scaled to the demands of 8 sunroofs per hour. In other words, the sunroof-specific resources required to batch would be 8 times greater than the resources demanded to handle 1 sunroof per hour. Faster and probably bigger equipment would be needed to stamp or form sunroofs, bigger racks would be required to hold them, and more space would be occupied by sunroofs when they were being made, and so forth.

Toyota strives to achieve a leveled heijunka sequence not only in final assembly but also in *every subassembly and component fabricating process leading up to final assembly*.[20] In other words, they work assiduously to develop the capacity to do heijunka as far upstream as possible. The importance of developing this capacity was remarked on in the 1970s by Taiichi Ohno when he was asked to compare the system developed by Toyota after 1960 with the system developed after that date by the major American auto makers. Ohno said that the Americans understood the work flow established by Henry Ford at his River Rouge plant by the 1920s, but they failed to carry it to its logical conclusion. That conclusion, according to Ohno, was to extend the continuous work flow from the final assembly line to all other upstream processes. But while American producers maintain a continuous flow in final assembly, "they *force* the work to flow" in upstream areas. Consequently, "*America's system of mass production,*" said Ohno, "*generates unnecessary losses in pursuit of quantity and speed.*"[21]

Ohno indicates that a customer's order, ideally, should initiate work *not just* in final assembly, but in *all* preceding processes back to engine build, power train, and, in many cases, closely linked suppliers. Consequently, if the shift that is scheduled to produce three As and four Bs learns, just as they finish BAB, that customers have canceled the orders for the next two Bs, they do not have to make *any part* of those two vehicles. They can proceed in the next two cycles to make AA, the two vehicles remaining from the original order, and then move on to new orders.

The situation is quite different, of course, for the decoupled batch producer whose schedule for the shift is AAABBBB. Assume that they learn about the two canceled Bs just as they start making the first B. Undoubtedly they have processed all parts in batches from start to finish. Therefore, they will have everything made and ready to assemble for *all four* Bs at the time they *begin* to assemble the first one. What can they do about the two canceled orders? At best, they might assemble the vehicles and try to sell them for the sunk cost of the parts plus a little more than their out-of-pocket assembly costs. At worst, they may have to scrap the already made and now unsaleable parts. The high-cost inflexibility inherent in this system (Figure 1–2) contrasts sharply with the low-cost flexibility Toyota achieves in its production system calling for continuous flow and rapid changeover (Figures 1–3 and 3–1).

Quite apart from its economic ramifications, heijunka also mitigates the peculiar monotony and pressure workers feel when they do things in batches. When steps associated with one particular model are repeated inexorably during one time of the day and not done at all at other times, workers have less opportunity to learn or feel challenged. However, Toyota's leveled schedules, by spacing *different* models evenly over the day and by mixing model production, enable all workers on a shift to engage in all the steps involved in making all models. In time, everyone becomes capable in all varieties of vehicle produced. Therefore, no matter how many variations occur, each and every vehicle that is made is attended to with the same level of expertise.

Heijunka does not occur overnight. It takes time, perhaps many years, for an organization to become skilled at heijunka. Toyota developed leveled production by proceeding in small steps. In the early days of the postwar era, for instance, if annual plans called for 20 percent A and 80 percent B, Toyota began by producing all the required As in one month out of every five; then the company moved to producing As one week out of every five; then one day out of five; then one hour out of five; finally, one vehicle out of five. Of course, each step along the way entailed faster and faster changeovers. However, moving production from month-size batches to a lot size of one unit reduced planning lead times and also reduced unique requirements for capital and other resources. Resources were needed to produce only one unit at a time, not one month's worth of units at a time.[22]

TPS RESEMBLES A NATURAL LIVING SYSTEM

The thinking and related practices known as TPS enable TMM-K and other units of Toyota to achieve variety and quality at competitive costs with activities intrinsic to, not separate from and in addition to, the main work of manufacturing vehicles to fill specific customer orders. Variety at high quality and low cost is a spontaneous result of the careful attention Toyota pays to the way work is organized. It seems profoundly significant, then, that Toyota's system unconsciously organizes work according to principles identical to those modern science observes in living systems on Earth. You will recall that three principles pertain in every living system: self-organization of a unique identity, inherent interrelationship of all things, and continual change of state. These three principles of living systems can be seen at work in TPS.

TPS sustains the system's own identity and insures its continued well-being under all conditions. TPS practices help create constant feedback mechanisms of the sort that interrelate all parts of a living system and maintain a coherent relationship between the system and its ever-changing environment. A living organism's internal feedback mechanisms enable the organism to preserve its unique identity and to survive by constantly altering its state. This process is reminiscent of a trapeze artist who stays upright on the wire by continually adjusting a balance pole in order to maintain a coherent position on the contour of the constantly changing wire. Notably, the trapeze artist's internal feedback system prompts behavior that insures his or her survival by maintaining a coherent relationship with the wire.[23]

An example of how specific elements of TPS insure the organization's survival as a distinctive entity living in relationship with its environment is how jidoka and standardized work resemble the operation of a living organism's immune system. An immune system constantly detects and transforms or rejects abnormalities that enter the organism's continuously flowing metabolic system. The organism does not have to wait for a delayed "report" from an "information system" to learn about and act upon such abnormalities. Jidoka and standardized work each contribute to detecting abnormalities instantaneously in the flow of work, thereby easing the task of handling inevitable human errors and enabling the system to generate great variety at low cost. They are effective and efficient primarily because they enable each team member to detect visually and make immediate adjustments for any deviation from normal conditions at any place in the work flow. Far better than having an information system that reports defects with delay, jidoka and standardized work give Toyota employees the capacity to detect and act upon abnormalities as they happen.

Feedback processes at work in living systems are evident in more than jidoka and standardized work. The kanban replenishment and withdrawal system essential to just-in-time is also analogous to the functions of the nervous system in an animal. Just as the elements of an animal's nervous system create a network that interconnects sensory cells and motor cells, so kanbans connect workers, thereby providing the essential link uniting company with customer. By responding as they do to replenishment kanbans, upstream workers resemble motor cells acting in response to sensory stimuli from downstream internal customers. By efficiently providing for instantaneous motor response to sensory stimuli, kanban enables a continuous flow system to conserve resources while it flexibly produces variety and high quality.

Recent research in neurophysiology reinforces the idea of comparing TPS to the working of an animal's nervous system. The biologists Humberto Maturana and Francisco Varela describe the nervous system, including the brain, as an "eminently simple mechanism" that dramatically increases the "realm of interactions" among parts of an organism. Like that nervous system, continuous flow and the disciplines of TPS create a web that connects Toyota's parts in a "dance of internal relations" that generates increasing variety and high quality at low cost.[24] Moreover, this dance, like the dance of relations in an animal's nervous system, is self-directed. It is not run by a central control system. Although scientists once thought of the brain as an isolated control center that receives information from and transmits instructions to other parts of the organism by means of the nervous system, today they see the brain as one distinctive part of the nervous system, not as the organism's central control system. The organism's control resides in the intricate pattern of relationships connecting all the parts, not in any particular parts themselves.

The Toyota Production System has a remarkable similarity to the nervous system as biologists now depict it. It increases the range of interactions among the company's parts, such as employees, customers, and suppliers. The pattern and scope of those interactions, not central instructions or targets, create the results that one observes at Toyota. Because of those interactions, information flows with the work and the work itself is the information linking company and customer in a profitable bond. The relationships supported by those interactions, not top-down instructions or targets, determine the pace and the outcome of work at Toyota. Every worker performs standardized work at the appropriate rhythm because of the traits inherent in the TPS, not because "expert" handlers of abstract quantitative information instruct and cajole everyone to hurry along and meet "the targets."

Without continuous flow, however, the TPS disciplines—all or in part—could not accomplish the results that Toyota has achieved over the years. Companies that implement one or more of the TPS disciplines often fail to achieve long-term results like those observed at Toyota because their system does not proceed in a continuous flow. This is especially evident when conventional, "decoupled" organizations (e.g., Figure 1–2) intently pursue "lean manufacturing," "demand pull technology," "time compression management," or some other TPS-inspired "performance improvement" initiatives while also reinforcing the discontinuity of their work flow with competitive local-level performance incentives. Such organizations can improve lead times and productivity in the short run, but without continuous flow they will not enjoy the results that the TPS disciplines generate at Toyota. Instead, they will increasingly improve a great deal of work that should not be done in the first place.

Continuous flow is not achieved simply by physically linking all steps in an operation. That more is required than a change in physical appearances is illustrated by a feature often observed in final assembly plants of auto companies that aspire to emulate TPS concepts such as the andon system. In such plants, the chain in the floor that pulls cars through final assembly is often installed *without a break* from beginning to end. Therefore, anyone who pulls the andon cord will necessarily stop work in the entire plant. It is not surprising that andon cords are seldom used in such plants. What the designers of those plants apparently fail to realize is that Toyota segments the chain in final assembly into several sections, usually ten or twelve, with each section separated by buffers of five or six cars, so that interruptions of up to ten minutes or so are confined to a limited area. Only interruptions that last longer will cause stoppages in an adjacent section of the plant. The entire plant will stop only if an interruption in one area lasts two hours or more. Since most of the problems that prompt workers to pull the andon cord in a Toyota plant are resolved in a few minutes or less, it is rare for more than one section of the plant to be stopped at any one time.

This story suggests that designers of automobile final assembly plants often view the andon system in the context of traditional batch-oriented mass production thinking which says "get output through the system to hold down costs; mistakes we fix later." Indeed, the prevalence of this old thinking became apparent during a conversation one of the authors (Johnson) once had with a training executive from an American Big Three auto company. When this executive was asked how her company presents the andon system in employee training courses, she said, "Employees are told that the andon system is very important to achieving high quality, but they are told that they must use the cord responsibly. That means, don't pull it unless it is absolutely necessary, because pulling the cord and stopping the line is very costly." Her remark suggests the chasm between other auto makers' thinking and Toyota's. The point, of course, of an andon system is to avoid costs by enabling employees to stop their work at will, to correct errors and deal with anomalies.[25]

A company can, of course, achieve variety without continuous flow by decoupling work processes and assembling finished vehicles from parts stored in warehouses, as the case of most batch-oriented manufacturers after World War II illustrates (Figure 1–2). That strategy does not lead to flexibility, however, nor does it yield costs nearly as low as those Toyota has been able to achieve for approximately thirty years. The decoupled batch-flow type of system can effectively vary the mix and volume of finished output only within the constraints established by the economic lot size of batches for key components such as body panels, interior trim, seats, and so forth. If the lot size of batches is equivalent to two months or more of finished output, then it is possible to change the original plans for mix and volume without scrapping excess parts inventories only a few times a year at best. Producing, however, in a continuous flow according to customer order and with the help of those who have mastered decentralized TPS practices, it is possible efficiently to vary mix and volume far more frequently. Theoretically, this system allows stopping after finishing any unit being worked on and changing over to something else. Nothing has to be scrapped, because nothing has been made in advance of an order. That flexibility is unattainable in the decoupled system of Figure 1–2, but it is a condition of TPS that Toyota's people drive relentlessly to perfect.[26]

TPS, PRODUCTIVITY, AND JOB SECURITY: "LEAN" VERSUS "LIMITED"

The pattern of work one observes at TMM-K and other Toyota plants is often described with the word "lean." Toyota uses resources sparingly, particularly in comparison with the resource requirements of non-Toyota, conventional production systems. Taiichi Ohno avoided using the term "lean" to discuss TPS. Instead, he used the term "limited." "Limited production" meant, to Ohno, achieving continuous flow in lot sizes of one throughout the *entire* manufacturing flow, from raw material to finished product. Contrasting this with "lean" production, Ohno said that "the idea [of 'limited' rather than 'lean' management] is to produce only what can be sold and no more. The idea is to *limit,* not necessarily to *reduce* the quantity. The important thing is to . . . produce what can be sold at the lowest possible cost."[27]

The emphasis of many of today's "lean" management initiatives, especially those associated with concepts such as "reengineering" or "activity-based management," run counter to the thinking of Toyota's managers as articulated by Ohno. Today's "lean" manufacturing initiatives too often emphasize *eliminating* waste or "nonvalue" activity. These programs promote campaigns to downsize, flatten, and trim. Nothing is further from the spirit of Toyota thinking. For Ohno, and for all mature practitioners of TPS to this day, the goal is to *avoid,* not eliminate, waste.

Avoiding waste is a *design imperative* that requires creating flexible conditions that make it *economically feasible* to provide only what customers want, when they want it, and then to stop. Such flexible conditions are the essence of Toyota's ability to produce variety at high quality and low cost. Ohno believed, as do his followers, that such conditions are created by mastering practices that systematically avoid waste. In that context, if Toyota discovers symptoms of waste or overinvestment, the reaction is to look for, and remedy, departures from TPS practices, not to embark on schemes to lay off workers or eliminate resources.[28] To reduce costs by cutting resources, as "lean" programs often advocate, manifests traditional thinking like that which in Chapter 2 was associated with puppies that fail the "puppy IQ test." Holding costs in check by limiting resource consumption to what is needed to meet each customer's needs, one by one, manifests new thinking.

A balanced, cyclical pattern of continuous flow in the work of every person in the organization, not driving people to meet quantitative targets, explains Toyota's long-term success. TPS practices have enabled Toyota decade after decade to achieve much more than any other auto maker while using fewer resources. Disciplined mastery of the TPS practices, not repeated aiming at targets defined by bottom-line financial results, produces high performance for the company.

Toyota's system succeeds largely because each person's work, at the ideal limit, uses only the minimum resources needed to produce one order at a time. Another reason is that employees diligently pursue the spirit of continuous improvement known as *kaizen*. Kaizen generally refers to the sustained endeavor of all employees to search for ways to improve the standard for work in each process. In other words, kaizen entails finding a better way to do things, not just removing problems that prevent one from reaching the current standard. One crucial result of kaizen activity is seen in employees' efforts to eliminate an entire task. For example, employees may make a task redundant by redesigning the layout of work so as to eliminate unused takt time—that is, the difference between the actual time spent on a task (cycle time) and the total takt time that is available. Should four adjoining tasks—stamping and spot-welding tasks, for instance, that make a piece of the underbody frame—each require 45 seconds of a 60-second takt time, it may be possible to combine those four into three tasks, each with 60 seconds of actual work, and eliminate one task.

Toyota's strategy continuously to improve productivity focuses always on doing work in less time without disrupting established rhythms. It does not entail doing work faster by stepping up the pace.[29] TMM-K employees know that this improvement strategy will reward them for discovering ways to conserve time. For example, they will be promoted or assigned to coveted positions on full-time "kaizen teams" if they come up with important ideas for saving time. They never have to fear, however, that their success at discovering ways to do more with less will prompt the company to lay them off.[30] On the contrary, Toyota continually creates new jobs by insourcing work from the outside (e.g., engines, axles, die making) and by creating teams that are assigned to help suppliers themselves learn more about the Toyota Production System. These teams benefit Toyota because they outsource expertise rather than jobs, the latter kind of outsourcing being prevalent in companies today.

TPS AND INFORMATION SYSTEMS

Because TPS stimulates constant change as part of everyone's normal work, it achieves variety and quality at as low a cost as can be imagined. Handling change apart from the normal work is the main cause of the complexity that bedevils batch-oriented mass producers' attempts to achieve quality and variety at all, much less at low cost. The principal manifestation of that complexity is the "information factory" discussed in chapter 1. The absence of complex computer systems to coordinate and control work at TMM-K emphatically demonstrates the difference between TPS and traditional batch-oriented modes of mass production.

Like the processes that comprise a living system, TPS practices create an inherent capacity for awareness of order and disorder. The processes which sustain a living system involve constant feedback of the output from one cycle of interactions into the input of the next cycle. Recurring feedback helps the living organism maintain its essential identity while simultaneously undergoing the subtle changes needed to maintain a coherent relationship with its environment. In other words, recurrent feedback makes the entity self-referencing and at the same time self-sustaining. At Toyota, TPS practices have the same effect of enabling the system to identify both order and disruption.

The self-referencing feedback mechanisms present in any living organism enable it to be aware of both disruption and harmony in its own

Management Accounting: TMM-K vs. Japan

When Toyota created its TMM-K facility in the United States it took advantage of that opportunity to design a management information system that would fit the spirit of TPS. Historically, Toyota in Japan had always maintained cost accounting and standard-cost budgeting systems resembling those used for decades in most American and British manufacturing companies. The truth is the early Toyoda company had copied those Western systems and they were carried over into the Toyota auto company after World War II. Those systems were anathema to Taiichi Ohno, who is alleged to have said that he succeeded with TPS only because Mr. Toyoda kept the cost accountants out of his hair.

In effect, those cost and management accounting systems have existed, since Ohno's time, in form only. Information from those systems does not drive operations at Toyota. This fact is poorly understood by some American accounting professors who, upon being shown these ancient systems at Toyota in Japan, conclude that they are used just as management accounting control systems are used in American companies. They are not, and Toyota in 1988 took care not to duplicate such systems at TMM-K.

Glenn Uminger, hired by TMM-K as a financial controller in 1988, was told by Toyota to install the internal accounting system he thought appropriate for TPS. He was told pointedly not to study or copy the internal accounting system in place in Toyota's Japanese plants. Instead, he was sent to Japan to learn TPS. The system he helped install at TMM-K is discussed below.

function. This is an important point. As Gregory Bateson noted, that a system may have such awareness provides an answer to two fundamental questions: "'What is man that he may recognize disease or disruption or ugliness?' and 'What is disease or disruption or ugliness that a man may know it?'"[31]

When viewed as analogous to the processes inherent in living systems, the remarkable achievement that is the Toyota Production System becomes evident. TPS instills in every person in the organization an awareness both of disruption and of harmony. Everyone recognizes disruption when it occurs, and everyone knows how to set it right. No "expert" with an after-the-fact information system is needed to explain that something is, or is not, right. At TMM-K, as in a natural living system, the information is implicit in the work, because the work is itself the information.

People resist hearing that TMM-K does not need computer information systems to provide instructions or targets to guide work. People do not accept the idea that Toyota must supply to workers very little information other than that which flows automatically with the work, "real time." The reality is, however, that TMM-K does not compile and use the kinds of information used by virtually all other manufacturing companies. TMM-K does not have the standard-cost systems (see box), the MRP scheduling systems, or the shopfloor computer systems that almost every manufacturing organization in the world, especially in the United States and Europe, considers to be indispensable. These systems are not necessary in Toyota's continuous flow setting because *every employee's mastery of TPS practices insures that results are immanent in the work.* Results are not seen as independent objects to be managed by manipulating parts of the work system in response to "bits" transmitted via an external information system.[32] Toyota's view of information is extremely difficult for outsiders to comprehend, as one observes while escorting American and European executives on tours through TMM-K.

These knowledgeable outsiders often understand that Toyota does not rely on external shopfloor control systems, such as MRP, to manage the flow of work in production. Somehow they cannot see or will not grant, however, that Toyota also does not rely on accounting-based systems to monitor and control operating costs in production. They resist the truth that Toyota does not drive operations with statistical controls, standard cost variances, or any similar information from accounting or production control sources to achieve its renowned high quality or its low costs.[33] Results at Toyota are embodied in the details of the company's particular operations. They are not viewed in terms of generalized abstractions imposed from above.

Comparing the relationship between the parts and the whole in Toyota's production system with the relationship between parts and whole in life systems sheds additional light on how Toyota embodies results in the particulars of everyone's work. In a living system, each cell performs its own specialized function. At the same time, each cell performs some or all of the additional functions required for the entire organism's survival. In other words, while some cells perform particular functions associated with the brain, the heart, or the lungs, each of these cells also metabolizes, communicates, and self-replicates. The organism, therefore, is a seamless web of distinctive parts that embody, fractally, the pattern of the whole. Because of the rich pattern of mutual interactions among those parts, the organism accomplishes its purposes without any need for a separate information and control system.

Similarly, at TMM-K each person embodies—is a fractal of—the pattern of the whole production system. Therefore, each person is able to respond autonomously, and contribute capably, to a customer's needs. This responsiveness and flexibility insures that variety and quality can emerge at the lowest possible cost. By contrast, traditional management systems, such as those described in chapters 1 and 2, incur much higher costs because they ask management to view each person and each work unit as an independent object capable only of responding to outside instructions.

Because managers of firms that employ traditional manufacturing practices tend to regard their companies as machines, not as living systems, these business leaders fail to understand the Toyota principle—a principle of nature—that results are immanent in the details. On the contrary, conventional thinkers believe their company's results must be defined by an abstract quantitative model that managers impose on the workplace. Instead of seeing carefully nurtured details—the means—as "results in the making," they see the details as expendable steps to be twisted and shaped in any way necessary to achieve a preordained result. These thinkers do not understand, of course, the principles of natural living systems that inhere in, and give vigor to, the TPS.

None of these comments is meant to imply that Toyota does not have accounting and production planning information systems. Of course it does. Toyota has a comprehensive array of information systems, accounting and otherwise, with which to *plan*, in advance of operations, and to *report* results of operations after the fact. But information from such systems is *not allowed to influence operational decisions*. Toyota operations are guided by the discipline of TPS, mastered through constant practice, in the context of continuous flow. Toyota operations are never guided by arbitrary commands to meet disembodied targets.

Glenn Uminger, a financial controller when he came to TMM-K in 1988, shows (see Figure 3–2 and the box above) how Toyota isolates the operations in its plants from the influence of accounting information.[34] The "black box" in the center of the diagram refers to a plant operation, such as the operation at TMM-K. The accounting system calculates the cost of what is made inside the "black box"—in the plant—by tracking the items designated with arrows *outside* the box, such as the material going into vehicles, the number of people working in the plant, the machinery and equipment installed in the plant, and the number of vehicles produced. Underlying the magnitudes of those items, but beyond the purview of the accounting system, are the design of vehicles and components made in the plant and the thinking that guides the basic layout of machines and equipment inside the plant. The accounting system that monitors the cost of the items designated with arrows, however, does not enter the black box! In other words, no cost system traces or calculates the flow of those items inside the plant. As Uminger puts it, "TMM-K has never had a standard cost system to track operating costs, and we probably never will."[35]

Readers of this chapter will understand why Toyota does not use its accounting system to track the flow of costs through the plant. To cre-

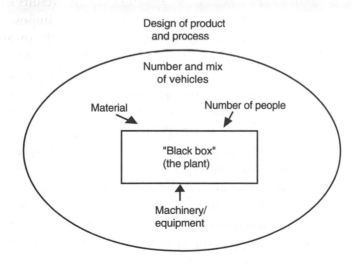

Figure 3–2: No Cost Accounting in the Black Box

ate such a system would use resources to no good end. Indeed, everything that decides how efficiently and effectively material, people, and other resources are consumed inside the plant is determined by how well everyone inside the plant masters and applies the practices of TPS in a continuous flow setting. If in any period the plant makes the planned number and mix of vehicles, using the requisite material and work force, then the cost of the finished vehicles will be as planned. No accounting information compiled during the period can help the managers and workers in the plant achieve, or improve, that outcome. The only things that will insure proper costs are mastery and maintenance of TPS: perform every step according to the established takt time; follow standard work procedures; recognize abnormal conditions and stop to correct them when they occur; work only in response to a customer order; space varieties over the shift as evenly as possible, and so forth. Do those things properly, and cost takes care of itself.

A minor exception to the statement that accounting information does not enter the plant is a monthly report the accounting department sends to group leaders on the shop floor, showing three items: scrap, supplies, and overtime. This report sends information to the "point of action" concerning costs that are controllable in the plant. However, plant personnel rely on this accounting feedback only to track long-term trends, never to become mindful of the costs in the first place. As consumption occurs, employees invariably see the consumption of resources giving rise to these controllable costs. Although scrap occurs rarely, team members know immediately when material is damaged and must be scrapped, and they take appropriate action. They respond similarly in the case of miscellaneous supplies and overtime cost.

Toyota's uniqueness extends to its handling of overtime. Overtime is a vital buffer that makes it possible to have a uniform takt time, while simultaneously encouraging workers to stop the line and make corrections whenever abnormal conditions arise. Obviously, something has to give if it takes every minute of a shift to fill all customer orders in the uniform takt time and if stopping the line to remedy errors consumes some of that time. The "lost" time caused by line stoppages is made up by overtime. For this reason, among others, Toyota plants are scheduled to work only two eight-hour shifts per day, with four hours of open time between shifts. That open time is available for overtime, as well as for scheduled maintenance. No one disputes the policy, because everyone recognizes that the trade-off for overtime is the power Toyota's line stops give workers to make the highest quality vehicles in the industry.

The alternative to overtime, common throughout the rest of the automobile industry, is for management to "speed up the line" in order to produce additional vehicles whenever necessary, for whatever reason.[36] Conversely, workers on the Toyota line focus their attention on the rhythm and discipline of work, not on the speed and quantity of throughput in the plant. Toyota is the only company that sets uniform takt times. By setting takt times as it does, Toyota acknowledges and honors human capacities to produce what customers need. As people in Toyota say, responsibility for safety and quality rests with the employees in the plant. Responsibility for quantity and cost of output rests with the top management in the plant and in the company. If output falls behind schedule, managers swing into action helping workers solve problems that might be slowing things down. Toyota managers *never* "speed up" the line in order to control costs or quantity of output. Top managers at Toyota will never jeopardize safety or quality by issuing an order to speed up the line. On the other hand, in conventional firms, top management, in pursuit of quantity and cost, does speed up the line, with adverse effects on quality and safety. Speeding the line to manipulate cost also defeats the primary purposes of attaining a standard rhythm—to preserve quality and safety while consuming as few re sources as possible. By assigning responsibility for costs and quality as it does, Toyota continuously improves its ability to produce exactly what customers want, precisely when they want it, at the lowest possible cost.

Toyota management discharges its responsibility for costs not by taking arbitrary steps to manipulate operations, but largely in the vehicle planning stage. During the design stage, long before the first penny has been committed to making a vehicle, Toyota has always placed enormous importance on setting and achieving cost targets. To do so, over the years Toyota has developed a famous technique for target costing. Simply stated, target cost is the maximum cost the company can afford to incur to produce and sell a vehicle and still earn a required profit at the price customers are expected to pay. A key element of target cost is, of course, the expected cost of the operations involved in manufacturing and assembling the vehicle—the costs to be incurred inside the "black box" shown in Figure 3–2. To estimate this cost, planners use up-to-date data—"cost tables"—about standardized work methods and cycle times for every step in the continuous flow, from start to finish. Preparing these data implies that all operating processes are planned simultaneously with the product itself, and in as much detail—down to every spot weld and every wire connection.[37] Thus, the completed target cost data provide the most detailed and most reliable product cost information any manufacturer has ever had. Almost none of this information emanates from the accounting system itself. Nor is the accounting system an important source of the information used to periodically update target costs.

CONCLUSION

Toyota set out over forty years ago to bridge the apparent trade-off between meeting individual customer demands for variety and achieving satisfactory company profitability. They focused attention on mastering a disciplined pattern of work that is known as the Toyota Production System (TPS). TPS has enabled Toyota to produce greater varieties of higher quality cars at lower cost than any other auto maker in the world. Using this system, Toyota has become the world benchmark for low cost—yet it does not use cost information to drive operations. As a TMM-K financial executive says, the company never had, nor does it ever intend to have, a standard-cost accounting system that provides cost and variance information for controlling operations.

Certainly, however, Toyota is concerned about costs. Toyota people often refer to TPS as a cost reduction strategy—a pathway to lower costs. TPS aims everyone's energies at avoiding waste—whether in the form of time, resources, space, energy, human potential, or customer dissatisfaction. Toyota's strategy for avoiding waste—thus reducing cost—is to instill in everyone in the organization (including suppliers) a deep dedication to mastering a disciplined approach to work. That discipline aims at *maintaining*, and then improving, what already works; it does not condone arbitrary wrenching of the system in the

hope of improving results. Toyota managers do not capriciously manipulate the system whenever results fall short of targets. Instead, they
recommit everyone to mastering and pursuing the practices of TPS and
the logic of continuous flow. Indeed, they act as though results are immanent in the way each and every employee pursues his or her work.
They act as if adequate results will follow if and only if everyone nurtures "the way."

A particular strength of Toyota's system is its ability to integrate
problem solving and the creation of variety with the basic work every
person performs to fill each customer's order. For all practical purposes
quality and variety are not achieved by having off-line workers respond
to off-line information systems. Problem identification, problem solving, and changes required to provide customers with variety are all handled real-time by line workers as part of the direct work that is done to
make every vehicle. Quality and variety are achieved with no added resources, then, and no additional complexity beyond what is required to
perform that direct work. Moreover, handling quality and variety this
way not only does not add costs, it stimulates the development of
human capabilities that normally stagnate in routinized mass-production settings. Thus, problem solving and attending to variety, by em-
bedding constant change into direct work on the line, become a
positive force for improving productivity and efficiency. They are not
seen as a damper on efficiency, not as a source of "indirect" cost to be
eliminated as "nonvalue activity."

Batch producers, on the other hand, routinize direct work on the
line in order to separate it from the creation of variety and the solving
of problems. Such routinization insures that the handling of variety and
the solving of problems will require a layer of indirect cost that is separate from, and added to, the work of production itself. So different is
the approach at Toyota that one sees them even introducing *model
changes* (not just order variety) more frequently than other auto makers, simply to stimulate line workers to review and improve processes,
thereby to improve profitability and efficiency. Frequent changes in the
location and timing of work in line stations occasioned by model
changes reinforces habits of thought and disciplines that feed back into
and reinforce the efficient handling of varieties during regular production. Toyota's system thereby stretches the capabilities of workers in a

way never possible in a system that accomplishes variety by batch-production methods, and with infrequent model changes.

Toyota's approach to organizing work solves the perennial problem of how to produce variety and high quality at low cost for large markets. With their production system, Toyota can produce in response to a customer's paid order exactly what the customer wants, when the customer wants it, and consume only the resources it takes to produce the item ordered, no more. Toyota does this with management practices that focus on having each particular person's work respond as well as possible to each customer's order. In this way, every cycle of work can differ from the last cycle—by enough to meet each customer's unique needs—with costs no higher (perhaps lower!) than they would be if every item were mass-produced identically, one after another.[38]

Manufacturers that attempt to control the costs of producing variety by fragmenting work and scheduling it in batches focus on average costs per unit, *not* on each particular person's work. But by decoupling and batching work so as to reduce average unit costs they incur many costs above and beyond the minimum needed just to make units that customers would actually order and pay for. Batch scheduling and high-speed production cause producers to incur costs making what customers often do not want, and failing to make what they do want. Those costs, incurred in an effort to minimize average unit costs, are what accountants refer to as "indirect" or "fixed" costs. Ironically, it is the presence of such costs that first triggers the belief that the answer to profitability is efficiency—reducing costs per unit by increasing scale and speed. While efficiency and profitability are one and the same to mass producers when variety is absent (e.g., Henry Ford's making of Model-Ts, as in Figure 1–1), efforts to provide variety at low cost by pursuing batch-production principles cause indirect costs to accelerate, thus hampering efficiency and profitability (Figure 1–2).

Toyota organizes work so as to avoid such indirect costs and incur only costs needed to fill orders as they arise, no more. Toyota's system does this by shifting from the batch-oriented mass-production way of organizing work, according to general principles of scale and speed, toward the natural way of organizing work, where each minute particular reflects the patterns that shape the whole. Thus, Toyota achieves low costs by integrating flexibility and problem solving into the flow of direct work itself, not by striving to achieve scale economies. To avoid having variety and quality cause indirect activities separate from the direct work itself, Toyota organizes work so that variety-producing and quality-producing activities become an integral part of the direct work that is done to fill each order. Moreover, the system achieves low costs by managing the *quantities* of resources used—material and labor hours—not by haggling with suppliers and workers over prices and wages. The system produces to order only vehicles that customers have ordered and paid for, consuming only the resources needed to make each vehicle.

4

....

Design to Order

Nature . . . doth not that by many things, which
may be done by few.

—Galileo Galilei[1]

Scania, a Swedish-based multinational manufacturer of heavy trucks, buses, and diesel engines, provides another example of how adherence to the principles implicit in living systems leads to financial stability and longevity in the face of stiff competition. After 1950, Scania faced the same challenge that Toyota had to overcome—that of producing variety and high quality at low cost. To accomplish this feat, Scania created a distinctive strategy to meet its own unique goal. Unlike Toyota, which refined a process for manufacturing at mass-production costs at least as many different kinds of cars as any competitor makes, Scania created a process for designing trucks individually tailored to meet any particular customer's specific needs. Although no two trucks are necessarily alike, this design process helps insure costs as low as any in the industry. Scania achieved variety at low cost by focusing on product design.

Scania focused its attention on product design after World War II primarily because it wanted to grow by exporting trucks to as many parts of the world as possible. To market all over the world meant designing trucks to meet an enormous range of climate, terrain, and road conditions, as well as a wide range of specialized transportation purposes. To meet the unique requirements of each customer in widely varying circumstances, and to do so at low cost, Scania after the 1950s devised an innovative modular design system.

The initial impetus for modularization came from Carl-Bertel Nathorst, a brilliant mechanical engineer and industrial economist who led Scania from 1940 to 1951.[2] Under Nathorst's leadership, Scania committed itself in the 1940s to an ambitious plan for expansion that would entail exporting heavy trucks abroad. To accommodate the anticipated growth of output, Nathorst transformed Scania's workshops from the individualistic craft-oriented mode of production typical of early industrial enterprises to the standardized mass-production method that had become the general practice among automotive manufacturers before World War II. More than this, Nathorst recognized the great potential of Scania's existing "component philosophy." This philosophy promoted "the aim of minimising the number of vehicle components by far-reaching standardisation." Nathorst advocated that "engines and chassis for both buses and trucks were, as far as possible, to be built from a limited number of components, using the *maximum number of common parts.*"[3] Nathorst's approach to parts commonality led eventually to a design strategy that is known today as modularization.

Its modular design system was identified by Scania's senior executives in a 1994 survey as the main reason for the company's sustained profitability.[4] Scania's executives believe that this unique design system has enabled the company to achieve higher margins on revenue and more stable profitability for a longer period than any other truck maker in the world. Indeed, despite a very cyclical market for heavy trucks, Scania has been profitable in every year since 1934. Moreover, since the 1950s Scania has increased greatly the multinational scope of its activities. The company today employs around 23,000 people worldwide, has production facilities in eight countries—Sweden, Denmark, the Netherlands, France, Poland, Brazil, Mexico, and Argentina—and assembly plants in more than a dozen additional countries. Scania trucks, buses, and engines are sold on all continents and in over one hundred countries, but not in the United States. Over 97 percent of Scania's output is sold outside Sweden, approximately 60 percent of this output going elsewhere in Europe. In the 1990s, Brazil has been Scania's largest single national market for all its products.

In all of these diverse markets, Scania, like most European truck builders, manufactures all the critical components that go into its products, including cabs, chassis, engines, and transmissions. Scania also attends carefully to the design of every part that goes into every component. In concentrating on product design, Scania's disciplined attention to how it fills each customer's order emulates those practices found in natural living systems. How those design practices have enabled Scania to achieve uninterrupted profitability and superior margins on revenue for seven decades is the subject of this chapter.

MODULAR PRODUCT DESIGN[5]

Modularization is a principle of design that divides a mechanical system or structure into standardized elements—modules—which can be interchanged.[6] Simply by making modules interchangeable as a result of designing common interfaces between them, one can make different versions of any machine or other structure with relative ease and at low cost. Modularization reduces the cost of accommodating change because it permits one to make a change by varying only the minimum number of components that affect the condition being changed. All other components remain the same. For example, the memory capacity of a desktop computer can be increased simply by unplugging the existing memory chip and replacing it with another identically interfaced chip that contains additional memory circuits. Nothing else is changed.

Another example of modularization is seen in the blocks created by the Danish toy company known as Lego. Using these modular, interchangeable blocks, an inventive child can build a remarkable variety of distinctive structures. From a small number of modular parts come a wide variety of unique designs. Similarly, the peripheral equipment made for personal computers and the rolling stock used on national railway systems are modular. They can be used interchangeably for many purposes.

Presumably one can alter the performance or the properties of a modularly designed system by changing the design of only one or a few specific parts of the system and it will continue to work flawlessly, despite the changed parts. Adhering to the principles of modular design simplifies methods of producing variety in any system, thereby reducing the cost of achieving variety.

To modularize its trucks, Scania identifies four elements that fulfill distinctive purposes necessary for the truck to operate: *engine* (used to generate power); *transmission* (the gearbox, transmission shaft, and final gears used to transmit power to the wheels); *cab* (used to house and connect the driver with the rest of the vehicle); and *chassis* (axles—front and rear—and frame used to carry loads). Today, Scania's truck modules consist of three cab types, four engine types, four transmission types, and fifteen chassis types. The challenge is to standardize these modules so that any size of one module is capable of fitting together with all sizes of the other modules. For example, each of the three cabs will take any size engine.[7] Cab designers put attachment mounts in identical places in all three cab designs to hold all the varieties of engine sizes. Engine designers know the precise locations of these mounts in each cab and how much space each cab affords.

Just as the whole truck consists of four self-contained modules, so also each of those modules contains smaller, self-contained modules. In a new modular diesel engine currently under development at Scania, for example, the combustion chamber is itself a module. One can construct different sizes of engine—say nine liter (5 cylinder), twelve liter (6 cylinder), and sixteen liter (V-8)—by combining modular combustion chambers that contain identical two-liter cylinders, pistons, and cylinder heads. Similarly, varieties of the chassis module can be constructed with different combinations of identical axles transmitting power to the wheels. For example, a 6 × 4 chassis has three axles with power transmitted to two of them and a 4 × 2 chassis has two axles with power transmitted to one of them. In these cases, different combinations of identical submodules inside the engine or chassis modules produce very different performance in the truck as a whole.

When the modular design principle is extended to smaller and smaller parts within a system, the effect is significant. It becomes possible by making only a very small change at the local level to effect a desired difference in the character or the performance of the whole. This ability to change the whole repeatedly and endlessly by making small changes in the parts is perhaps the most important trait of Scania's modular design strategy. It enables Scania sales personnel to configure each customer's truck *to order* with benefits similar to those Toyota enjoys by being able to produce automobiles to order. The modular design system makes change a regular part of the normal work that transforms a customer's wants into a delivered product, not an exceptional event brought about by activities separate from that work. In this way, changes for every difference that customers might desire do not have to be specified by designers ahead of time, before customers appear. Sales personnel can configure a different truck for each customer and the company incurs no more design cost than if all customers ordered exactly the same vehicle.

To develop its modular design capability, Scania's design engineers spent decades creating a unique design system, just as Toyota's manufacturing engineers spent decades creating a unique production system. The modular strategy grew out of the company's decision after World War II to specialize its efforts on the heavy range of trucks. They believed that this range offered excellent opportunities for growth and profitability. However, heavy trucks, concentrated in construction and in long-distance (interurban) hauling, faced an enormous range of loads, road conditions, and climates. The key to success with the heavy range seemed to be an ability to make trucks to meet each individual customer's specific demands. Scania believed that excellent opportunities existed in the heavy range for producers that could efficiently meet great varieties of customer demands. They saw modular product architecture as the key to supplying high-quality variety at the lowest possible cost. Moreover, choosing a modular architecture made it all the more advantageous to focus on the heavy range, as opportunities to share common components among heavy, medium, and light trucks are extremely limited. Perhaps the most important example of a shared component in the heavy range is the exclusive use heavy trucks make of the diesel engine, because of its reliability, durability, overall transportation efficiency, and ease of maintenance.

Having chosen modular design as the best way to profitably make great varieties of heavy trucks, Scania's engineers set out in the 1950s to identify and measure all the various demands that heavy trucks could face around the world. In a sense, they set out to measure the range of environmental demands to which each distinct module in a truck would have to adapt. They weren't attempting to precisely design each and every truck in advance; instead, they identified the main factors influencing each function of a truck, and then they assessed the range of conditions for those factors in the various parts of the world where Scania trucks might operate. Specifications such as torsion, torque, weight, and stress received careful attention.

For example, with fatigue strength identified as the critical performance factor for load-carrying components, stress tests were conducted to determine the optimal number and sizes of components needed to meet the range of stress-inducing conditions Scania trucks would meet in the world. In this way they hoped to design components that would meet but not exceed the requirements for durability and performance under any customer's specific conditions. Similar steps were taken in designing the engine and power-transmission modules where, instead of fatigue strength, factors such as fuel consumption, speed, and grade handling were identified as critical to performance.

To rationally select components that would efficiently meet worldwide customer demands, Scania focused its primary attention on studying the durability of each module, and its components, under varying operational loads in different worldwide applications. Operational load took into account combinations of road resistance (grade and surface) and truck weight. Over a period of many years, durability tests were conducted in the field and in laboratories to study the impact of operational loads on modules and components. These tests led, eventually, to specifying a range of component sizes that could satisfy the requirements of all conceivable operational loads with a minimal number of different sizes.

Eventually, Scania's design engineers extended their exhaustive field testing and laboratory simulation to include all the purposes performed by each of the truck's four basic modules—generate power, carry load, comfortably house and protect the driver, and transmit power. They defined the detailed specifications that each submodule, component, and part must meet for a module to perform adequately over the range of all possible customer conditions. The result of this effort is a continually evolving *matrix* showing the specifications of each and every part that a truck requires to meet any condition a driver might face in the world.

Scania's modular design matrix shows part by part and module by module the specifications needed to meet any need under all possible conditions. Once identified, a specification is entered into the matrix just once and is not modified until someone discerns a way to improve it. The presence of the matrix insures that no designer's time is spent "reinventing old wheels." Instead, design resources are expended either on addressing new, previously unidentified customer needs or on improving old solutions to existing needs.

Meeting new needs, the company recognized long ago, requires keeping ahead of the customer. As Sverker Sjöström, former head of development at Scania, once said: "The company always must be looking around the corner and be ahead of the customer with new developments. By the time the customer sees a new idea it is too late for the company to react." In this spirit Scania for many years led in developing new technologies associated with turbocharging and turbocompounding, with synchromesh gearboxes, and with environmentally responsive improvements in fuel economy, engine emissions, exterior noise levels, and vehicle safety (better structural design and electronic braking and gear changing).

Notably, Scania's design engineers do not create blueprints or bills of material for finished trucks in anticipation of a sale. Scania creates bills of material only in response to customer orders. Indeed, Scania does not design trucks in advance of customer orders any more than Toyota builds cars ahead of customer orders. A customer's order ultimately "pulls" the design of a specific truck from data in the matrix. Sales and dealer personnel, without having to call on design engineers, work with a prospective customer to specify a truck's bill of material that meets the individual customer's needs with the minimum number of unique parts. Scania's design engineers, like the designers of Lego blocks, do not have to attend to the configuration of each particular customer's specific vehicle. Their job is to create the pattern of specifications in the modular design matrix.

Scania's superior financial performance certainly owes a great deal to the precision with which its design system can identify and specify the minimum changes needed to meet any individual customer's specific needs. This precision benefits discriminating customers and thereby generates added revenue and increased long-term loyalty. It also benefits the company by enabling it to fill even the most demanding and unique orders at the lowest possible design cost. These benefits help create a positive reinforcement between the continual improvements Scania's design engineers make to their modular design matrix and the increasing variety and complexity of needs that customers present to Scania each year.[8] Obviously, neither Scania nor its customers see the advantage of their relationship in terms of *independent* benefits gained in a one-time transaction. Instead, they see the advantage in terms of *mutual* benefits arising from an ongoing *interaction.*[9] Largely because of this mutually reinforcing interaction, Scania's executives claim it enjoys a higher customer retention rate—between 70 and 80 percent in most markets—than any of its European rivals, whose rates range between 50 and 70 percent.

Some Scania people believe that the modular design system's power to create a mutual interaction between company and customer has the potential to infuse everything the company does, producing what they refer to as a "spirit in the walls." Implicit in this vision is the idea that communication linking company expertise with specific customer needs should extend far beyond the design department itself. Every person and activity in the company, not just the design engineering group, should see how the modular design matrix connects their own work, the customer, and the company's long-term welfare simultaneously. The ultimate goal, perhaps, is to have everyone aware that Scania's long-term profitability rests on having customers pleased not just with the physical features of a truck at the moment of sale, but with everything that using the truck does to make the customer's business more enjoyable and more profitable. That awareness marks the difference between a results-oriented company that sees profitability extend no farther than making a sale and a process-oriented company that focuses on building profitable lifetime relationships with customers.

An indication that managers in Scania are means-oriented and focused on process is the degree to which many of them possess extensive knowledge of various areas in the company. In addition to having at least some formal training in engineering, many managers with ten years or more experience have worked in at least two areas of the company. As a result of this broad experience, such executives are able to draw upon a deep familiarity with design engineering and manufacturing engineering issues and, in many cases, a working knowledge of problems encountered in marketing, distribution, and after-sales service. This wide-ranging knowledge enables managers to create subtle linkages that undoubtedly contribute to efficiency, flexibility, responsiveness to customers, and robust profitability.

Scania's top managers who possess broad familiarity with the company's operations also show, in many cases, a desire to walk directly in the customer's shoes. To that end many members of the top executive team are licensed to drive all the company's products. Moreover, these individuals frequently make overnight trips driving trucks with their own and competitors' customers to experience firsthand the customer's point of view. This direct contact with customers and their particular expertise enables many Scania executives to understand and knowledgeably discuss the broadest possible implications of any problem that may arise. These managers communicate and interact as if they were a cross-functional team continuously designing and improving, never disbanding at the end of a project. When executives understand product development, production, and customer awareness, they see these as forming an organic whole and recognize how one member affects the others. Thus, sharing of modular design principles potentially creates a unique web of relationships that can enable Scania to achieve quite naturally and without upheaval the responsiveness and flexibility that countless corporations around the world today are trying to achieve by artificially reengineering themselves into "flat" or "horizontal" organizations.

An obvious advantage of its unique modular system is that Scania thereby requires a much smaller number of different parts than any of its competitors does to make an equivalent variety of trucks. Scania's many different varieties of trucks share a surprisingly high percentage of parts in common. Indeed, commonality of parts is the major source of Scania's ability to deliver large varieties of trucks at very low cost. In the same way that Toyota's production system succeeds by avoiding waste, not by eliminating it, so also does Scania's design system avoid waste. By achieving high commonality of parts among its great varieties of trucks Scania makes it easier to *avoid* the costs and complexity attendant on making changes in designs.

Scania's reliance on commonality of parts is, remarkably enough, consistent with the way nature works. All systems in the universe use very few different parts to achieve astounding diversity. For example, all the complexity found in the human brain results from combinations of very few different neural-system parts, all the elements in the universe are made from a very small number of distinctive sub atomic parts, and living organisms contain only a limited number of different genes. Different as they are, all humans share over 99.5 percent of the genes in their DNA. In other words, less than one-half of one percent of those genes account for all the differences among humans. Nature clearly generates rich ends from simple means.

EXAMPLES OF MODULARIZATION AT SCANIA

Scania's focus on modularizing components—from the smallest to the largest—explains why their designers say that they design not trucks, but rather high quality components poised to become trucks. A few examples of the modular design system evident in Scania's engines, chassis, and cabs illustrate its many advantages.

Since the early 1990s, governmental mandates to control engine emissions have greatly influenced Scania's thinking about engine design. Historically, engines had always been the least modularized part of Scania's trucks. In fact, three basic engine designs had evolved more or less independently since the 1950s, and these three designs effectively satisfied the diverse needs of all customers until the end of the 1980s. Then in the early 1990s, prompted mainly by demands for emissions control, Scania's designers inaugurated an extensive program to modularize their diesel engine.

By designing standardized interfaces and modularizing parts of the engine such as the combustion chamber, fuel pumps, and injectors, Scania will be able rapidly and expeditiously to meet all foreseeable government emission requirements. They will do so, moreover, without having to design an entirely new engine each time emission standards change. Indeed, each change can be met by optimizing only the one combustion chamber module. Furthermore, the new modularized engine will meet each customer's unique need for power more effectively and efficiently than ever before.

Scania's designers also use modular principles to provide the chassis that each customer requires. The customer traversing unusually rough, back-country roads in less-developed regions of the world, for instance, needs a truck with a frame that handles a great deal of torsion and bending. The usual way to accommodate this requirement is to use higher-gauge steel—in effect, a new part number—than is called for on trucks traveling on interurban highways. Scania, however, simply "nests" two of the L-shaped sidebars that it already uses in frames designed for medium and heavy service on normal highways. Two existing parts are combined to provide the extra-heavy frame suitable for rough back-country conditions.

The versatility of Scania's modular design system is also evident in the three cab designs of the recently retired Series 3 as well as the new Series 4 truck models. Each cab design accommodates a variety of engine sizes, engine configurations, sleeping facilities, and doorway configurations. Nevertheless, every cab in each series shares the same front windshield and driver compartment. Although they differ between the two series, one windshield and one driver compartment serve in each of the three cab types in both series.

The driver compartment offers an example of how designers achieve variety in performance without adding new part numbers. All three Scania cab types contain the same driver compartment, which is assigned only one part number. Different drivers prefer different sleeping accommodations in their cabs, of course. Some prefer one bed, while others prefer two. Scania's design engineers easily meet both needs with one driver compartment by specifying that bracket holes for two bunk beds be put in all driver compartments. If a particular driver's purpose calls for just one bed, it is a simple matter to fill in the unused bracket holes intended for a second bed. By overspecifying in this way the uses of one part, designers satisfy two distinct customer needs with only one part number.

Within the driver compartment, other modularized parts are standardized and interchangeable. In particular, the dashboard is designed to change easily between left-hand drive and right-hand drive trucks. On Scania trucks the dashboard consists of three parts. One part is a panel that contains space to accommodate the dials and gauges that must be in front of the driver. Another part is a panel that contains space to accommodate additional instruments and storage compartments. The third part is a small wedge-shaped section located between the two panels, to hold them in place. By having two variants of the middle wedge, Scania designers allow the driver-side and passenger-side dashboard panels to be swapped to suit the placement of the steering wheel. Thus, dashboards on all Scania trucks can be configured for either a left-hand drive or a right-hand drive with only four different part numbers—driver-side panel, passenger-side panel, and two variants of the middle wedge.

A less carefully conceived dashboard design might require two entirely different driver-side and passenger-side panels, making it necessary to build five different dashboard parts (including a common middle section) for the two varieties of truck. At first glance, it may seem there is little difference between using four and five part numbers for these two varieties of truck. However, systematic attention to reducing the number of different part numbers can eliminate an enormous amount of complexity in the long run. It is no accident that Scania in the early 1990s could sell as many units as its closest competitor, in many more varieties, and yet require only half as many different part numbers to make those units. This ability to produce far more varieties of end product with a fraction of the part numbers is a major reason for Scania's superior profitability among European truck makers in recent decades.

The example of dashboard parts needed to make left-hand or right-hand drive vehicles prompts one to ask why Scania does not design just *two* dashboards, one outfitted for left-hand drive vehicles and a mirror image of that one outfitted for right-hand drive vehicles. In fact, that would be an optimal solution to dashboard design if choosing between left-hand and right-hand drive were the *only reason* customers would ever have for a different dash design. Making two dashboards under that condition is an example of an *integrated* design, the antithesis of modularization.

When a condition that shapes customer needs is essentially the same for all customers, and not likely to change, certainly it is optimal to integrate into one piece everything that is needed to meet that condition. Scania integrates the design of windshields and driver compartments on its cabs. They also design an integrated front axle to fit all new Series 4 trucks, because road surface conditions today, unlike conditions twenty or thirty years ago, are much the same for all customers in the world. The modular axle found on old Series 3 trucks has been replaced by an integrated axle that uses twelve fewer components, weighs 31 kilograms less, and can carry an extra ton of weight.

The conditions affecting dashboards, however, are much less uniform than are those affecting windshields, driver compartments, or front axles. Drivers have many needs for different dashboards other than different locations of the steering wheel. Different needs for instrumentation, communication equipment, and navigational devices, for instance, make it impractical to cast the dashboard with one single mold for each steering-wheel location. The modular design permits one to meet customers' varying demands for optional equipment by varying the configuration of dashboards with minimal part number complexity.

Even where differences in customer needs make it necessary to produce different parts, Scania's designers take care to design those parts so that the different varieties can be manufactured as much as possible with the same tooling. Thus, different cab designs make it necessary to vary the height of the outside panel on the back of the cab. Specifically, the outside back panel comes in two different sizes. However, the two sizes are designed so that they can be stamped with the same press die. When that die is in use, stamping press operators simply have to know when to insert a longer or a shorter piece of sheet metal in the press.

From decades of disciplined practice, Scania's design engineers have developed an intuitive "sixth sense" for spotting ingenious ways to make small changes in modules with few, if any, additional part numbers. Always, of course, Scania's designers give first consideration to meeting each customer's unique needs—to achieving variety. But their basic design rule is to strive continually to meet any need with fewer different part numbers, not more.

MODULARIZATION, PART NUMBER PROLIFERATION, AND COSTS

It is widely understood that when variety in end products is desired, modular designs reduce substantially the costs of achieving that variety.

Management experts usually give two reasons for this result. First, modularization decreases costs, they say, by reducing the number of different part numbers required to meet a given variety of customer needs. Second, using fewer part numbers allows mass-producing parts in longer runs and larger batches, thus capturing scale economies. Both reasons are true as far as they go. Neither reason, however, reflects a thorough understanding of why modularization improves a company's long-run financial performance by affecting revenue and profitability. The next two sections consider further financial implications of modular design.

Part Numbers, Commonality, and Costs

The proposition that fewer part numbers reduces costs usually is considered to be unarguable. Commonsense observations certainly support the idea that reducing the number of part numbers *by itself* saves money. Fewer part numbers mean, for one thing, a need for less design work and fewer designers. Moreover, fewer part numbers make for less work and less confusion in manufacturing. They also mean less work and fewer resources required to ship, store, and keep track of parts in the after-sales market. Finally, all things being equal, a product made with fewer different part numbers will be easier to service and probably more dependable to operate.

But reducing part numbers in itself is not sufficient to guarantee improved profitability and decreased costs. It is the *way* numbers are reduced that affects overall profitability. Scania's particular way of decreasing part numbers enhances opportunities to earn revenue because it maintains and even increases the variety of end products. Moreover, it increases profitability because the added revenue from increased varieties of product comes with little, if any, increase in cost.

Reducing the number of part numbers by attending carefully to the degree of parts commonality among end products increases revenue because it does nothing to reduce the variety of end products that a company makes and sells. If a reduction in part-number count curtails the variety of a company's end products, revenue probably will decline. Such is the predicament of many companies with activity-based accounting systems that use "part numbers" as a cost driver to motivate design decisions. In such companies, the average design and handling cost may be $1,000 per part number if annual parts design and handling costs are $100,000 per year and 100 different part numbers are in use. In that case, the activity-based cost of a part number used 10 times in the year—for example, the middle wedge used only in right-hand drive dashboards in the example above—is $100 per part ($1,000 ÷ 10), while the cost of another part number used 10,000 times in the year—say the middle wedge used only in left-hand drive dashboards—is $0.10 per part ($1,000 ÷ 10,000). Companies that use such activity-based cost driver information to motivate people to hold down costs are likely to discourage developing and marketing products that use unique and, therefore, costlier part numbers. In the example discussed above, such thinking would prompt avoiding seldom-sold right-hand drive vehicles and concentrating exclusively on the much larger market for left-hand drive trucks.[10]

If companies use cost targets to make marketing and production decisions, probably they will move away from the pattern of endless diversity. Instead, they are likely to engage in the homogeneous mass production of "global" products. Many auto and truck manufacturers in recent years have, for example, in an effort to profit from scale economies, mass-produced high volumes of standardized products that they often refer to as "world cars" or "world trucks."[11] In effect, companies that build such products passively respond to their cost system by pushing for higher volumes of homogeneous output. Sacrificing any capability they might have had to satisfy the unique demands of individual customers, such companies allow pursuit of cost targets to make them hostage to the "world" product.

The idea of sacrificing customers and revenue to reduce part-number complexity is not likely to occur at Scania. Scania does not drive its engineers to monitor and eliminate "high cost" part numbers, that is, part numbers used in small quantities. To do so implicitly eliminates customers, an outcome Scania does not tolerate if at all possible. For the same reasons, moreover, Scania does not monitor and eliminate so-called 80/20 customers, the 20 percent of customers whose orders consume 80 percent or more of all unique part numbers used in a period. Instead of trying to reduce *high cost* or *low use* part numbers by eliminating particular varieties of truck (and customers), Scania design engineers are motivated to think of increasing the *commonality* of parts *in all* trucks. By having the same parts function in many contexts, commonality in fact streamlines the creation of new varieties of product. The more that each part number serves—is common to—many purposes, the easier it is to identify and modify *only* the parts one must change to meet any new customer need.

Consider how Scania's designers meet a customer's need for more power. They change only the engine module and the *input* torque capacity of the gearbox where it interfaces with the engine. By contrast, most truck designers have believed for years that increasing the engine's power, because it increases the *output* torque of the gearbox, also makes it necessary to increase the torque capacity of the final gear that connects the gearbox to the rear drive axles. However, when years ago Scania's engineers researched the influence of operational loads on each truck module, they discovered that the torque capacity of the final gear varies with road resistance, not with engine horsepower—at least within a very wide range of conditions that covers most truck operations in the world today. Since road resistance is determined by the surface quality of roads, not by engine power, Scania's engineers realized that they could leave the torque capacity of final gears untouched while meeting customer demands for increased horsepower. In fact, since road quality in most of the world was improving dramatically in the 1960s and 1970s, they actually *decreased* final gear torque capacities while raising engine power. By scientifically modularizing truck design, Scania's engineers in recent decades have met customers' demands for more horsepower with far more commonality of parts than its competitors achieved, and at less cost.

To measure their progress achieving commonality—using the same part for many purposes and in the same context—Scania's design engineers use a metric they refer to as the "density index."[12] This index ranges from a value of zero, indicating that every part in each different truck variety is unique, to a value of one, indicating that every part in each truck is the same. A density of one indicates that each and every customer's need is met with the same design—like Henry Ford's Model-T automobiles in the early 1920s. When conditions facing every customer are identical, modularization holds no advantage. In such a case, probably it would be optimal to "cast" the design into one integrated mold that delivers the same product with unerring precision to every customer. If, however, different customers face different conditions, then it is desirable to vary the design. Each variation should affect the existing design as little as necessary, to keep costs in line. The density index indicates how efficiently each truck variation is achieved.

Ordinarily, each design variation that adds a part number moves the density index away from one and toward zero, implying less commonality and, presumably, higher costs. On the other hand, if a design change alters the part number count but does not change the density index, then it is assumed that commonality and costs have not changed. Thus, Scania's design engineering "density index" enables one to see what no accounting information system—activity-based or otherwise—can possibly reveal; namely, that reducing the number of part numbers without attending carefully to modular design principles can actually increase costs if it reduces parts commonality.[13]

Generally speaking, for any variation in design, the closer the index moves toward one, the better. An exception to that rule occurs if a company engages in the currently popular practice of outsourcing the design and manufacture of its products' major modules or modular subsystems. Such outsourcing causes a company to replace several part numbers in its design and production system with, conceivably, just one part number—the part number of the externally sourced module or subsystem. All other things being equal, this substitution of one part number for many—especially where variants of the outsourced item contain many different parts that no longer appear on the books of the outsourcing company—will move the density index closer to a value of one. Although this outsourcing of entire modules or component subsystems supposedly will reduce costs, it probably will do so only in the short term. In the longer term, the loss of design competency and the potential loss of control over product performance caused by outsourcing major components may diminish overall financial performance.

Part Numbers, Scale Economies, and Costs to Manufacture, Distribute, and Service

Originally Scania attributed the cost savings from modular design to the scale economies ostensibly achieved by mass-producing components and parts. In fact, many top executives in the company still hold this belief today. By reducing the number of different parts needed to produce any given variety of trucks, the company supposedly can mass-produce each part in large batches and long production runs. The low cost achieved by mass-producing components presumably explains how Scania profitably sells customized trucks at competitive prices, even though it sells fewer trucks than the industry leaders.[14]

Whether or not Scania achieves scale economies and low costs in this way is arguable. Lower manufacturing costs are more likely to result not from batch-producing in long production runs, but rather from a balanced, continuous flow of work—the principle at work in Toyota. Indeed, a number of Scania executives in the late 1990s began to study how Toyota achieves low costs in its manufacturing operations. Already able to "design to order," these executives hoped to emulate Toyota's ability to "produce to order" in its component making, sub-assembly, and final assembly operations. However, pilot projects in Scania plants had not shown conclusive results by late 1999.

Quite apart from any programs Scania may pursue to reduce costs in the manufacturing area, its modular design strategy itself already has the effect of reducing manufacturing costs. For many reasons, simply reducing the number of different parts puts Scania's manufacturing costs below those of other truck makers. For instance, the care taken by Scania's designers to reduce the varieties of parts needed for their range of products cuts back on complications with ordering and storing material, and it curtails confusion. It also reduces the need for tool changes and die changes. A Japanese authority on "lean" manufacturing techniques once expressed surprise at how few stamping presses Scania's Oskarshamn cab plant used, considering the rather ordinary changeover times and the variety of cabs produced in the plant. What he did not see, at first, was that the small number of different parts used to make the variety of cabs reduced the demand for presses by reducing the need for changeovers.

The cost impact of modularization extends, of course, beyond manufacturing itself to the distribution function and to after-sales service. Obviously, if fewer different parts are needed to make the range of trucks sold, then fewer parts must be stored in company warehouses and in dealers' inventories. The extensive ramifications of reducing part numbers generates savings not only in design, but also in production, distribution, and servicing. According to Scania's own estimates, product design and development costs fall more or less in direct proportion to the reduction of part numbers; production costs of a component that is made in a traditional manufacturing setting fall about 10 percent with every doubling of the quantity of the component produced; and distribution costs, caused by parts ordering and storage, fall about 30 percent when the number of part numbers is cut in half.

Using these estimates, Scania once calculated the bottom-line financial impact of its modularization and component standardization program by comparing its European operations during the 1980s with a competitor that produced and sold approximately the same number of trucks, but required about twice as many part numbers. Thus, the competitor's product development costs, averaging about 1.3 billion Swedish kroner (SEK) per year, were nearly double the .7 billion SEK that Scania on average spent on product development each year. In addition, Scania's more parsimonious parts selection generated average annual savings in production and in distribution amounting to about .4 billion SEK. In total, then, during a decade when its annual net operating profit before tax ranged between 1.3 billion SEK and 3.8 billion SEK,[15] Scania enjoyed around 1 billion SEK more operating income per year on account of its attention to modularization and component standardization.

SCANIA AND THE NORTH AMERICAN MARKET

Scania's use of modular design and its integrated manufacturing strategy are important reasons why its long-term earnings are higher and more stable than they are for other truck companies. Its particular approach to design standardization enables Scania to address a larger number of unique customer needs with no more resources than are used by any other truck company. Just as Toyota values its production system as the means to achieving its financial goals, so Scania perceives its disciplined mastery of design practices to be the means to satisfactory financial ends. Scania never sacrifices its design principles to achieve short-term financial targets.

To continue a decades-long history of higher and more stable earnings than its competitors, Scania believes it must continually rededicate itself to the modular design and integrated manufacturing practices that have been its particular alternative to "managing by results." Those practices differentiate Scania even from its relatively integrated competitors in Europe. But they differentiate Scania even more sharply from the heavy truck makers in North America, where Scania does not market trucks.

After suffering severe financial losses in the 1970s and early 1980s, virtually all North American makers of heavy trucks were acquired by European makers in the late 1980s. The Europeans intended to restore the American truck makers to profitability by introducing them to their own more integrated manufacturing practices. For the most part, these North American operations earned respectable profits during the late 1990s.[16] However, recent financial success did not occur because European truck makers succeeded in transplanting their unique manufacturing practices into North America. The success simply reflects an unprecedented boom in North American truck sales. The Europeans' North American heavy-truck divisions still follow more or less the same practices that they employed as free-standing companies during the less prosperous 1970s and 1980s.

Indeed, the North American truck-making industry, driven by the extremely short-term cost focus of its major customers, is a collection of independent component makers and final assemblers. Unlike a highly integrated producer such as Scania, the major North American truck makers for decades have done little more than assemble on their own chassis a cab, engine, transmission, and axles that the truck buyer has purchased from outside suppliers. This strategy reflects the historic market power of North American truck buyers, about two-thirds of whom operate very large fleets. Unlike small owner-operators (about one-third of the North American market) who look for image and good residual value, large fleet buyers are concerned mainly to minimize the purchase price of the trucks they buy.[17] Thus, large American truck buyers—not truck makers—purchase key truck components from suppliers who specialize in making engines, transmissions, axles and the like. The truckers purchase in large quantities from the lowest-price bidders, including the truck assembler who bids on and makes the chassis, and often the cab.

In effect, a truck buyer's purchasing department, not a truck maker's engineering department, designs most heavy trucks built in North America. Cost-driven outsourcing, demanded by the largest truck buyers, is as close as the North American truck industry comes to thoughtful design. Scania's modular design and integrated manufacturing strategy is alien to their thinking. The North American truck buyers' overriding emphasis on minimizing immediate purchase and assembly costs reflects, of course, the traditional cost focus that has dominated American business thinking since World War II. However, trucks designed with this cost focus in mind often cause service problems, especially for small and medium-sized haulers.

Such problems were referred to in a recent published interview with Ulf Grevesmühl, head of Scania's business in Mexico where truckers, until recently, bought only American-made models. In the past few years, however, Mexican truckers have been able to purchase Scania models. Scania trucks are the only make on the Mexican market for which all the main components are manufactured in-house. Because they do not manufacture as many components in-house as Scania does, American truck makers, as Grevesmühl noted, "can never provide the total service back-up that we can. If the owner of a US truck has engine problems, he turns initially to the dealer who sold him the truck. [The dealer] sends him to the engine manufacturer[, who] is likely to tell him that the gearbox is the cause. The gearbox supplier, in turn, may claim that the fault is in the rear axle and send him to the final gear manufacturer."[18]

By designing and manufacturing all critical modules of a truck, Scania elects to concentrate on building long-term customer loyalty with very dependable products. The company is not interested in catering to short-term purchasers, no matter how large their orders, whose demands for cost cutting outweigh the long-term economic consequences of systemic product design. Sensing an enormous gap between its own more systemic design-oriented strategy and the typical American heavy-truck buyer's short-term focus on cost minimization, Scania has chosen, until recently, to stay out of the North American market for heavy trucks. Its new venture into the Mexican market is based on the belief that a large number of North American buyers are ready to appreciate the Scania difference.[19] It is not based on a decision to sacrifice its long-standing design and manufacturing strategy in an effort to capture a share of the giant North American heavy truck market.

MANAGING BY MEANS VERSUS MANAGING BY RESULTS

The wisdom of Scania's holding to its time-tested strategies can be assessed in the context of the principles that guide the operation of all living systems on Earth. Living systems produce "rich ends from simple means," as does Scania. Because Scania's design system emulates key features of living systems, Scania is able to sustain higher and more stable long-term earnings than do other makers of heavy trucks. The Scania design system connects company with customer in a web of interdependent relationships in which every design decision unites an individual customer's need with the company's capacity to serve that need. Scania's system links customer with company as long-term partners focused on the same objective—mutually sustainable profitability. Customers purchase Scania products with an eye to much more than the "deal" made at the time of sale. As noted earlier, Scania's customers do not define their relationship with the company as a one-time transaction between independent entities. Instead, they look to Scania for superb design, manufacturing, and transport-industry expertise, trusting that Scania sells products and services that will optimize both partners' returns over the life of a vehicle.

Meeting the particular needs of each customer in the most economical way is the challenge that justifies Scania's existence. The company never attempts to meet any customer's need simply by "throwing metal over the wall." They believe that making products that precisely address each specific customer's needs is the best way to produce satisfactory financial returns year in and year out.

The long-term consequences for Scania could be disastrous if it were to replace its long-standing modularization and integrated manufacturing policies with currently faddish results-driven strategies that focus on indiscriminate cost cutting, economies of global scale, financial performance incentives, and the like. Nevertheless, financial analysts and the business press since late 1997 have pressured Scania's top management to take such steps.

This pressure arose because Scania traded its shares for the first time on the Stockholm and New York stock exchanges in late 1996. In 1995, the year preceding the listing of its shares, Scania had earned a record 15.9 percent return on sales. Financial writers and analysts now stridently insist that "the market requires" Scania's top management to achieve a minimum 15 percent annual return on sales. Disappointed that Scania's 1997 return on sales of 7.6 percent was less than half of 1995's return, business journalists in early 1998 asked if it were not time for Scania to change its way of doing business.

These journalists reflect, of course, the recent fascination of the global finance community with American manage-by-results thinking that is so antithetical to the disciplined focus on means practiced by Scania in the past few generations. Thus, they consider it irrelevant to the company's year-to-year financial returns that the introduction of a new truck model moved Scania from the top of one learning curve in 1995 and 1996 to the bottom of a new learning curve in 1997. In 1995 and through the third quarter of 1996, Scania sold only the Series 3 line of vehicles that it had produced since the early 1980s, whereas in 1997 it sold in Europe only the new Series 4 line that was introduced in late 1996.

Oblivious to this issue, Swedish business writers in early 1998 discussed rumors that Scania should be sold to another company whose managers would "know what to do" to quickly restore Scania's earnings to 1995's record levels. Ironically, one such article that compared recent years' returns at Scania with those at other European truck makers portrayed Scania at the top, Volvo in second place (breaking even), and Mercedes in third place (with negative returns).[20] Presumably the writer of that article did not imply that executives of those other European truck companies should replace Scania's top management. Probably he had in mind the typical American mutual fund watchdog's image of an ideal top manager, such as the infamous "Chainsaw" Al Dunlap. If so, then he undoubtedly is concerned with something besides Scania sustaining the unbroken string of profits it has earned in every year since 1934.

Indeed, truly long-term profitability does not seem to be a major concern among shareholder interests that today are pressuring companies such as Scania to abandon their means-oriented management practices in favor of a results orientation that will focus the company's attention on short-term targets imposed by financial markets. European business people often speak of "the American virus" when they refer to the manage-by-results (MBR) practices that such shareholder interests invariably espouse. "Virus" is an apt term to describe the results-at-any-cost management practices that have dominated American management thought for the past two generations. Such mechanistic practices, used in the singleminded pursuit of financial gains for a single group, the shareholders, will drain the life out of any business.

In effect, "the American virus" thrives by killing the host through layoffs, divestitures, outsourcing, and other desperate moves aimed simply at cutting costs, and at selling indiscriminately to anonymous purchasers whose only interest also is cutting costs. During periods of overwhelming prosperity, such as the last half of the 1990s, when the tide is in and all ships are floating, virtually all companies can profit, of course, as they pursue such strategies. Seldom, however, do companies recognize during those periods that such manage-by-results (MBR) strategies carry the potential for severe long-term financial losses. MBR thinking causes companies during periods of prosperity to sacrifice system and discipline to the pursuit of financial targets. In the inevitable economic slump that follows, advocates of such thinking can then be depended upon to have many new MBR strategies—such as activity-based management, reengineering, restoring core competencies, and so forth—to pick up the pieces.

The MBR virus that infuses the work in most American companies today has engendered a "just do it" spirit that contrasts starkly with the disciplined mastery of practices that one observes in companies such as Scania and Toyota. In both Scania and Toyota the management system cultivates a strategic discipline that transmits throughout the entire company a focus on resource-conserving practices that cause people to consume at every moment only the minimum resources required to fill one customer's needs at a time. In contrast to such management discipline, American businesses substitute an obsession with meeting scorecard targets without regard for the means used to do it. We can hope that a better understanding of how companies such as Scania and Toyota have operated over the past few generations will convince business people everywhere that there is a better way.

CONCLUSION

In the 1950s, Scania elected to pursue a strategy that mimics one of nature's most ubiquitous patterns: to produce variety at low cost, without at the same time sacrificing high quality. The modular design system Scania created to reach this goal embodies the three principles implicit in the operation of all living systems: namely, self-organization, interrelatedness, and diversity. Using the modular design matrix, the company unites with each individual customer in a relationship that satisfies the needs of both by creating an endlessly diverse array of vehicles at very low cost.

Every design decision at Scania focuses on uniting and resolving the two forces that generate profit—revenue and cost. In this simultaneous union of revenue and cost, a specific customer need triggers design decisions that resolve the need with the fewest possible changes to an existing product module. The system continually unites every new need with the capacity to do exactly what has to be done, and no more, to fill that new need. The system's purpose is to continually meet new customer needs as expeditiously as possible—not to pursue financial, part number, or other scorecard targets. By focusing all design activities on that purpose, the system enhances profitability year in and year out.

For the past thirty or more years, Scania, like Toyota, developed a simpler way than did any of its major competitors to achieve variety with lower cost. However, the modular design process that enabled Scania to achieve variety at low cost was the consequence of years of trial and error. Everyone in the company maintains mastery of this distinct process only by continual, relentless practice.

Although Scania has achieved favorable financial results for a much longer period than any competitor, they never set out to achieve those results by acquiring outside companies,[21] by selling off pieces of the company, or by consistently laying off employees.[22] Whereas such identity-destroying practices are common in companies that attempt to achieve financial targets by manipulating people and resources, Scania seems to achieve far better long-term financial results by focusing operations not on quantitative targets, but on mastering practices that maintain and enrich the quality of relationships among existing employees, suppliers, and customers. Their superior long-term financial results seem to be consistent with a strategy of survival that reflects a deep capacity for building relationships, not a strategy of pursuing targets at the expense of relationships.

Managers in Scania have often acted as if satisfactory results will occur in the long run if everyone seeks to master their special customer-focused practices. Such behavior implies a belief that the result is already there, that management's job is to cultivate the practices and nurture the relationships that bring forth the result. The late Marcus Wallenberg, as chairman of the board, encouraged Scania's postwar focus on modularization, on export-led expansion, and on avoiding growth by acquisition and merger. An astute financier, Wallenberg nevertheless did not view the company's operations through the lens of financial spreadsheets. Instead, he frequently visited Scania factories and workshops, telling people that he went there to "hear the music."[23] He said that what he saw and heard in the workshops told him if all was going well in the company or not. Obviously his leadership did not reflect "managing by results." One hopes that the "spirit in the walls" engendered by past leaders such as Marcus Wallenberg will enable Scania's present and future leaders to resist the market's pressure to "make targets" by engaging in the inevitable financial manipulations that can destroy a century of relationship building in a matter of months or years.[24]

5

....

Assess to Order

Progress is not doing better what should not be
done at all.

—Anonymous

As the two preceding chapters indicate, Toyota and Scania conduct
work in ways that obviate the need for management accounting information in their primary operations. Toyota has no reason to use
standard cost variances to drive work in the production area, and Scania does not use part-number cost information to drive work in the
design area. Neither company finds it necessary to use accounting targets to drive work because all the information they need to make a car
or design a truck is provided in the work itself. In every step of this
work, particular relationships unite company and customer. Primarily because managers and employees nurture these relationships between company and customer, satisfactory financial results emerge
year after year.

Both companies do, of course, rely on their accounting systems for
information about system-wide profitability and cost. Each uses such
information to assess their financial condition—the financial state of
the company. Such accounting information permits them to track the
overall financial results of their pursuits. However, neither company
uses accounting targets to direct or control the work of the people who
ultimately produce those results.

MOVING MANAGERS FROM TARGETS TO PATHWAYS

Unfortunately, today's business leaders almost without exception are not content to use accounting information exclusively to assess overall financial results. They also use it to control and assess the work that leads to those results. They fail to see the flaw in this position. There is nothing problematical about using accounting data to describe a business system's external state, condition, or results (such as its costs or profitabilities). A problem does arise, however, when these same accounting measures define targets which are then intended to direct and control operating activities. As noted earlier, while using quantitative targets to achieve desired results makes sense in mechanical systems, such a practice makes no sense in the long run for natural living systems, particularly business organizations.

For example, one can increase an engine's speed by a desired amount simply by increasing its fuel intake in a prescribed amount. This amount is determined by several variables, including the engine's horsepower. However, one cannot similarly increase an organization's profitability simply by boosting revenue or cutting costs by prescribed amounts. No neat linear connections link an organization's profitability, costs, and revenue to its work in the same way that an engine's speed is linked to its horsepower, fuel consumption, and other quantitative variables. Accounting information can measure and keep track of an organization's results at a system-wide level, but it offers no insight into the particular inner relationships that determine those results.

It is important to distinguish between system-wide accounting results and the information about the relationships that produce those results. It would be necessary to make the same distinction if accountants were assigned the job of tracking the flows of matter and energy in the universe. They could measure the number, size, temperature, and velocity of galaxies that emerge at any time. Such quantitative measures could tell nothing, however, about the underlying relationships that create galaxies from a cosmic sea of hydrogen and helium. The accountants' measures could not predict when or where a particular galaxy might appear, or if a galaxy might produce stars, or if those stars might become supernova that will implode and create new elements, new stars, planets, photosynthesis, and a cloud-covered blue sky. Similarly, the accountants' information in a business organization can describe the organization's features—its financial results, for example—but not explain the underlying forces that create those features.

Not accounting information, then, but information that comes from the work itself should guide, control, and assess the operations of living systems. An organization run like a living system does not rely for such information on "information systems" that are maintained separately from the work. Presumably, if workers "produce to order" or "design to order" according to principles such as those observed in natural living systems, then all workers at every moment can distinguish normal from abnormal conditions and can make adjustments to correct abnormalities when they occur. Everyone involved in the work can tell whether the company's production or design activities will be able to maintain and sustain its long-term financial well being.[1]

Such operational assessment focuses on the "means," not on the "results." Indeed, as the cases of Toyota and Scania show, the real-time information each uses to assess the ongoing flow of production or design is seldom financial data, and it never comes from accounting records. Instead, the real-time information, including "target prices" set before the work begins, consists of concrete evidence that work is being accomplished according to standards. These standards exist to make it possible to satisfy customer needs using as few resources as possible. They encompass adherence to design parameters, staffing, work layout, takt time, balance of work flows, customer delivery, and much more. Everything is done to standards. When proper standards are observed all the time at every stage of the work, then long-run financial results such as costs, margins, and profitability will be satisfactory. Those financial results can be tracked, of course, by an accounting system. But that is as far as accounting information goes.

It is difficult for today's managers to accept the premise illustrated by Toyota, that satisfactory long-run financial results do occur when work follows standards that emulate principles underlying nature. Because today's business leaders live in a milieu that is unconsciously influenced by Newtonian mechanistic thinking, they find this a difficult intellectual leap. True to a mechanistic outlook, they equate standards with targets that define end results, not with the path that leads to the results. They view the path as whatever combination of steps leads one to a particular result. Seen as ephemeral and incidental, those steps are regarded as inconsequential, insubstantial, compared to the end results.

Unlike mechanistic thinking, thinking that understands the way nature works recognizes that the right pathway, the means, is itself the true goal. Finding and nurturing the pathway should be as important in business organizations as it is in nature. Modern scientists have in the past few decades explained that throughout the universe rich diversity evolves from profoundly simple patterns. These patterns consist of recursive relationships that permeate the entire universe. In a sense, the "work" of the universe is to generate never-ending patterns of relationships that are cyclical, but not repetitive, and that yield unpredictable, ever-diversifying "results," from quasars to dolphins dancing in sunsets.

Business organizations that emulate the principles underlying the operation of this natural universal system reject conventional ideas of how one assesses progress toward a target, or goal. Defined simply, progress is "getting nearer to the place where you want to be."[2] Assessment concerns how we judge our efforts to reach that place. Virtually all companies typically define that place as a financial target or result that they reach through mechanistic work practices. Accordingly, they assess work using quantitative financial measures of growth and accumulation. That is what traditional modes of management accounting and financial analysis are all about.

The "place" a manage-by-means company wants to be is operating according to principles underlying nature. To assess this congruence with nature, it will use real-time indicators to assess how closely its work adheres to certain standards. These standards themselves embody the principles of natural systems. Both Toyota and Scania assess their ongoing operations—production and design—by attending to standards. In this sense, they manage the means, the pathway, and in so doing imitate nature.

Unfortunately, most companies' mechanistically inspired operations do not maintain the balanced continuous flows that permit them to assess work in terms of standards. They are trapped in a vicious circle. Using quantitative financial measures to assess operations, they organize their work in a way that inhibits the habits of thought and practices consistent with living systems. They therefore make it impossible to do anything except to drive work with quantitative targets. Using conventional measurement practices keeps managers from viewing progress primarily as adherence to proper standards, not just reaching quantitative financial targets.

As indicated earlier, merely modifying traditional management accounting information will not help managers discover the importance of developing standards. Management accounting simply takes accounting revenue, cost, and profitability information, which is appropriate for measuring the overall financial results of a business, and inappropriately attempts to trace it to the particular activities and products of the business that give rise to those results. Assigning such quantitative measures to parts of a mechanistic system makes sense. However, the parts of a natural living system cannot be so treated. Accounting measures are unable to penetrate the organic, multifaceted union between customer and company that ultimately is the source of a company's financial results. This union is the reason any company exists. It is the logical focal point for assessing how well the company complies with the principles underlying living systems. A company that uses accounting information to direct and control financial outcomes of that union risks destroying its ability to survive in the long run.[3]

Perhaps managers would be more likely to treat an organization as a living system were they able to assess its operations with information that *resembles* familiar management accounting, but is focused on the organic union between customer and company. It would be *financial* information, but it would not emerge from traditional accounting sources. Ideally, such "management accounting" information would emerge from the real-time information that flows naturally with the work that unites company and customer. In fact, managers will be able to "assess to order" with such nonaccounting financial information when they adopt a tool known as "order-line profitability analysis."

PROFITABILITY INFORMATION: ORDER LINE VERSUS ACCOUNTING

Profitability information compiled from the "order line," that is, from each line in every order that customers place with a company, comes from a completely different source than does the profitability information companies traditionally prepare from their accounting systems. An order line may refer to an entire product, such as an automobile or a truck, or it may refer to subcomponents of products, or to nontangible services that a company sells, such as maintenance contracts, insurance services, and so forth. To simplify, the following discussion will refer to order lines as though they refer to a complete product. Thus, if Scania were to sell 50,000 trucks in a year, those sales could be recorded in 50,000 order lines. In that case, order-line profitability analysis would enable Scania to calculate profit on each one of the 50,000 order lines.

The point of order-line profit information is to make the flow of profit visible with each item ordered, just as both Toyota's production system and Scania's design system make the flow of work visible with each item ordered. Order-line profitability data visibly connects the earning of profit with the conditions that exist where the customer's needs and the company's work come together in a natural union. Customer (revenue) and company (cost) are inextricably united at only that point of union. Order-line profitability information immediately draws one's attention to this union and to the human relationships responsible for it. In so doing, it enables managers to improve profitability by nurturing human relationships, unlike traditional management accounting information that encourages managers to improve profitability by using quantitative targets to haphazardly manipulate work. In other words, order-line profitability information supports management by means—management behavior and practices that are in accord with principles such as those which guide the operation of natural systems in the universe.

Compiling profit information at the order line departs radically, of course, from the practice of accountants. Accountants compile *aggregate* profit information in an income statement, not *detailed* profit information by order line. They collect revenue information from individual orders, but their cost information comes from myriad other sources such as invoices, purchase contracts, payroll records, and other records of spending. Accountants collect this revenue and cost information in separate sets of accounts which periodically they "close" into a profit and loss account. From this account they compile an income statement. The income statement determines profit by joining two separate streams of data that arise always from the accounting records, never from the order lines.

Compiling profitability by order line reaches the same total profit that accountants reach in the income statement. However, it yields a micro-level of detail unavailable in any accounting system. How it arrives at this level of detail matters profoundly. Compiling profit information by order line influences a company's thinking and behavior very differently than does the conventional means of compiling accounting profit information.

The person who probably deserves credit for originating the idea of order-line profitability information, Sten Drakenberg, had no formal training or experience in accounting or finance. Indeed, while Drakenberg was an engineering student at the Royal Institute of Technology (KTH) in Stockholm during the mid-1950s, he worked on a project for the director of a company who felt uneasy about basing decisions on overhead cost information from the accounting system. Working on this student project, Drakenberg devised a technique for tracing overhead costs to order lines. Not trained in accounting, he saw nothing unusual about using the order line as a "cost object." Moreover, he bypassed all the usual accounting cost allocation conventions and traced costs to order lines using information about work that he derived from interviews with employees in overhead functions, such as the pickers, packers, paperwork clerks, and other employees in the distribution function. Initially, Drakenberg gathered data and made calculations manually, foreshadowing techniques that some thirty years later would be known as "activity-based costing."

During the 1960s, while employed at Ericsson, the Swedish telecommunications equipment company, Drakenberg refined the order-line costing technique. In the mid-1960s, because computer programmers said the company's new IBM mainframe accounting system could not handle the order-line techniques, Ericsson's accounting department stopped using them.[4] About ten years later, with Ericsson's blessing, Drakenberg made these techniques the centerpiece of a consulting practice that he co-founded with Anders Bröms in Stockholm. Unlike the activity-based cost management practices that would eventually appear in the United States, the order-line practice developed by Drakenberg and Bröms was based neither on a management accounting nor on a cost accounting model.

Order-line profitability analysis recognizes that virtually all the use-

ful information about a company's profitability is contained in each
and every line item in every order the company has filled. Accountants
overlook the usefulness of this information by compiling revenue and
costs in separate accounts. Order-line profitability analysis circumvents
accounting practices by collecting and compiling detailed facts drawn
directly from a client's order lines. The information compiled from
each order line includes, at a minimum, customer identification, product or service identification, quantity sold, revenue earned, direct costs,
and indirect costs.

In general, profitability at each order line is calculated by deducting
direct and indirect costs from revenue. Compiling revenue and direct
cost information is almost always a straightforward matter requiring no
special attention. Revenue invariably is invoiced by order line, and direct costs are either identified by order line or can be drawn from bills
of material. The difficulty is to trace indirect costs to individual order
lines. Drakenberg's technique for tracing indirect costs to order lines is
deceptively similar to the technique of indirect cost tracing that came
to be known after the late 1980s as activity-based costing. Indeed, because Drakenberg and Bröms chose to describe their order-line technique as "activity-based costing" when that phrase became popular in
the late 1980s, most people today are not aware of the vast difference
between order-line profitability analysis and activity-based costing.

Like conventional activity-based costing, the order line procedure
departs from the traditional accounting practice of using only volume-
sensitive denominators such as direct labor hours or machine hours to
allocate indirect costs. Both order-line and activity-based procedures
also use nonvolume-sensitive denominators such as machine set-ups
and part-number counts to trace indirect costs. In all other respects, the
order-line way of tracing indirect costs is unique. In particular, order-
line practice differs from activity-based cost practice by not tracing indirect costs to products, customers, departments, regions, or other
independent "cost objects." Instead, it traces indirect costs in just one
step, only to order lines (Figure 5–1). Tracing indirect costs to order
lines reduces significantly the estimating errors that traditional costing
and activity-based costing techniques create by cascading costs through
multiple stages and departments into various final cost objects. Once
indirect costs are traced to order lines, the task of compiling costs for

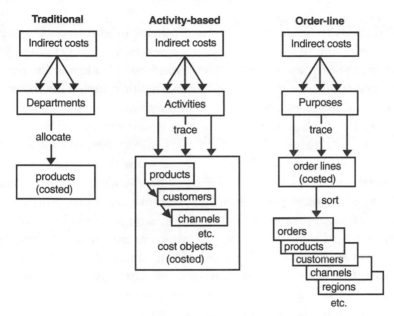

Figure 5–1: Costing Techniques

other cost objects such as products or customers simply requires sorting order lines according to the desired categories, using codes for each category that are identified each time an order line is created.

The procedure for tracing indirect costs to order lines begins by identifying all indirect costs with one of three basic purposes: supporting the *volume* of ongoing business—paid for out of current revenue; maintaining existing *structures* (systems) needed to conduct work in design, operations, administration, and logistics—also paid for out of today's revenue; and conducting extra work caused by *newness*—new products or processes—paid for out of savings in volume or structural costs.[5] These three purposes are analogous to those all natural living systems must fulfill if they are to survive, adapt, and evolve. A business must expend "volume" costs to generate the ongoing revenue needed to sustain its components over the business cycle. In the same way, a living organism must find the nutrients to sustain its basic metabolic functions. A business must also expend "structural" costs to refurbish the system that maintains its components. Similarly, a living organism must replace and replenish cells that die or become damaged. A business, furthermore, must expend "newness" costs to cope with changes in its structure, and reproduce itself. So must a living system adapt to its own development, maturation, and death. Viewing costs, revenue, and profitability in the context of these purposes recognizes that a business, like any life system, must maintain continuing and effective relationships with the world around it. Nurturing the relationships implicit in these purposes, not cutting costs, leads to improved levels of performance.

The order-line procedure divides costs among these purposes in relation to the work that people do in connection with each purpose. Once all indirect costs are divided among those three purposes, they are traced to each order line in proportion to common factors that influence the amount of work people must do to fulfill each purpose. Thus, indirect costs are traced to order lines in proportion to the intensity with which each order line requires each purpose. Order lines calling for more structural-related work, more volume-related work, and more newness-related work will receive proportionately more cost, and vice versa.

For example, the number of different part numbers in products creates complexity and causes work in design, ordering, sorting, stocking, making, and after-sale servicing. Therefore, the number of different part numbers contained in each product serves as a common denominator for apportioning structural costs among the order lines in a period. Other sources of complexity that cause structural costs include the number of product families, the number of product variants, the number of vendors, the number of dealers, and the number of customers, to name just a few. Sources of newness cost include numbers of new products, of new dealers, of new customers, and so forth. Finally, causes of volume costs include number of units produced, number of components actually used in production, number of labor hours, volume of space utilized, and more.

This technique for tracing indirect costs to the order line joins cost with revenue at the point where the company and a specific final customer actually come together. In contrast, activity-based costing and traditional costing simply average costs over all items of an object, such as all units sold of a particular product or all customers. Those average costs are then matched with average revenues earned by each class of product or each customer to determine profitabilities by product or by customer. Thus, with activity-based costing, the profitability of a particular product line is viewed as being the same for all units sold, no matter how many different customers in how many different circumstances bought those units. Similarly, activity-based costing information portrays the profitability of a particular customer's purchases of the same product with one average number, regardless of how many different times that customer purchased that product during the period.

Consequently, the likelihood that distortions and misinterpretations will corrupt the cost and profitability information is much, much greater with activity-based information than it is with order-line information. The order-line costing procedure is more reliable because it calculates cost and profitability only once—at the order line. All other determinations of cost and profitability—such as, for example, by product, by customer, or by region—emanate from nothing more than sorting the order-line data. The significance of this contrast between activity-based and order-line profitability information is explored in much greater depth below.

The order-line procedure for attributing indirect costs to "cost purposes" contrasts with the traditional activity-based costing approach of associating indirect costs with "cost drivers." The distinction between "purposes" and "drivers" is significant. Viewed in terms of drivers, costs are objects independent of revenue, to be "driven" mechanistically by external forces. To improve profitability, one cuts cost without having to be concerned for effects on revenue. Viewed in terms of purposes, however, costs fulfill purposes that generate revenue and revenue justifies costs. According to order-line practitioners, a cost is either "blessed by revenue" or it saves another cost that is blessed by revenue. In other words, costs arise *in relation to* the generation of revenue, and revenue, in turn, arises in relation to the generation of costs. Consequently, cutting costs to improve profitability is tantamount to "cutting purposes," the result of which is to diminish revenue. Without costs to fulfill purposes there is no revenue and, of course, no profit.

ORDER-LINE INFORMATION: THE FUTURE
OF PROFITABILITY ANALYSIS

There are many ways to compile and present order-line profitability information for purposes of analysis. The ultimate objective of such analysis is to understand how decisions about the organization of work affect conditions at the one and only place where revenue and cost naturally appear together—the order line. A company's order lines are a unique source of detailed and revealing information about profitability. They contain raw information typically lost in the averages that accountants compile for management purposes. Order-line profitability information gives a company insights into the effectiveness of operations, design, and administrative activities that are absolutely unattainable using management accounting information. As shown below, numbers, counts, and ratios visible at the order-line level make it possible to assess how well a company's design strategies and production procedures truly nurture profitable relationships with its customers. For this reason it is especially important to consider ways to compile order-line profitability information.

Perhaps the most fundamental issue is to determine the most effective way to present the profitability during the past year or so for each one of a company's order lines. One way to array individual order lines is in descending order of profitability, from positive to negative, as the bar-chart graph shows in Figure 5–2. In this chart, the envelope of the order lines' profits and losses traces an S-curve pattern that occurs in almost any array of order-line profits one might construct for any company.

Perhaps the next most logical way to portray the order-line profitability data from Figure 5–2 is to array the *cumulative* profit of the period by order line, as shown in Figure 5–3. In Figure 5–3, the horizontal line intersecting the vertical axis at 100 percent represents

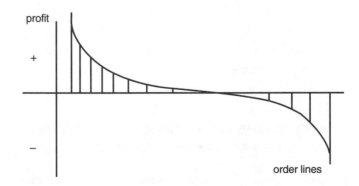

Figure 5–2: Profitability by Order Line

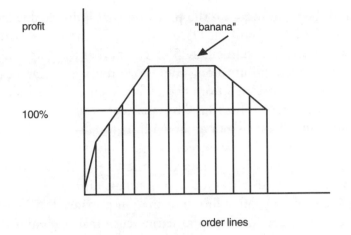

Figure 5–3: Cumulative Profit of the Period, by Order Line

the total profit actually earned in the period. The percentage added to total profit by each profitable order line is depicted by the rising order lines on the left-hand side of the array. The cumulative profit earned by profitable order lines often equals 150 to 250 percent of the period's actual profit. The amount by which each "loss" order line diminishes total profit is shown by the falling order lines on the right-hand side of the array. In the middle of the array are "break-even" order lines that neither add to nor detract from total profit. Order-line practitioners such as Sten Drakenberg and Anders Bröms who have been compiling such data since the late 1970s often refer to the envelope of the cumulative profit graph in Figure 5–3 as a "banana curve."

Order lines can also be sorted and grouped in order to show profitability information by categories, such as customers, products, geographic regions, or distribution channels. Usually each category member—for example, each customer, product, and region—will be represented by several order lines during a year. Total profit can be calculated for each member of a category by adding up the profits and losses of order lines for each individual customer, each product, or each region. Using such data, the members of a category can be arrayed in descending order of their total profitability as shown in the bar graph in Figure 5–4.

The graph in Figure 5–4 shows, in descending order, the profit by customer, calculated after sorting the order lines in Figure 5–2 by customer and then summing up the profit of each individual customer's order lines. The bar graph in Figure 5–4 traces the same pattern, of course, as the one shown in Figure 5–2, except that the graph in Figure 5–4 contains fewer points along the horizontal *x*-axis. One can also array the profit by customer from Figure 5–4 in cumulative fashion and generate a customer-profitability "banana" curve similar to the order-line-profitability "banana" curve shown in Figure 5–3.

Portraying profitability by categories, especially by customer, began to interest management accountants after the late 1980s when activity-based costing emerged. However, an important difference between the order-line customer profitability information portrayed in Figure 5–4 and the customer profitability information customarily compiled in activity-based costing systems is that order-line profitability information can penetrate below the level of category members, such as individual customers, and show each individual member's profitability order line by order line. This is possible because the order-line data is not compiled from accounting information that averages out the differences among order lines to allocate costs and revenue to each member of a category. Companies that rely on activity-based information know only average profitability by customer or product, not profitability by individual order line. In effect, activity-based information on customer or product profitability assumes that all of any one customer's or product's order lines have the same average revenue and cost, hence the same profitability.

This profound difference in the respective methods to determine the profitability of individual members of a category creates very different

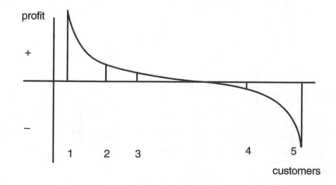

Figure 5–4: Profitability of Members in a Category (e.g., Customers)

information about "winners" and "losers" in each case. Because management accountants are unable to determine profitability at a level more detailed than that of the broad category, they would identify customers 4 and 5 in Figure 5–4 as unequivocal "losers" and customers 1, 2, and 3 as emphatic "winners." By contrast, the order-line method for determining the profitability of the individual customers in Figure 5–4 is to add up the different profits and losses of each distinct order line purchased by each customer in the year. This makes it possible to rank the particular, separate order lines of each customer—for example, the separate order lines of customer 5 in Figure 5–4—in terms of their relative profitability. The array of order lines for an individual customer inevitably looks like Figure 5–5.

The envelope of the graph in Figure 5–5 resembles the S-curves that we saw previously in Figures 5–2 and 5–4. This repeating "S" pattern is significant. It means that order-line profitability patterns seem to display the property of a fractal. The S-shape that exists when the individual order lines are examined (Figure 5–2) also exists among all the members of an entire category of order lines (Figure 5–4), and it exists, too, among the particular order lines belonging to any member of that category (Figure 5–5). The consulting firm founded by Drakenberg and Brölins has documented this fascinating relationship in innumerable studies it has done for its clients over the last two decades.[6] Notably, the order-line detail in Figure 5–5 reveals that customer 5, portrayed in Figure 5–4 as an unambiguous "loser," actually contributed to both profitable and unprofitable order lines during the year.

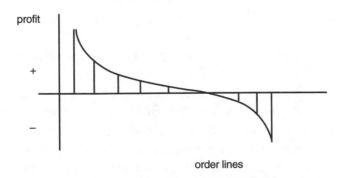

Figure 5–5: Profitability of Order Lines for Customer Number 5

Order-line profitability analysis reveals that the *total* profitability of a member of any customer, product, or other category almost always includes both profitable and unprofitable order lines. Activity-based management accounting, however, cannot reveal the different profitabilities of order lines for each member of a category. It shows only the total profitability of a member, as though that were all there is to it. Management accounting information, unlike order-line information, cannot rank the particular, separate order lines of each customer (e.g., customer 5 in Figure 5–4) in terms of their relative profitability (Figure 5–5).

Order-line profitability data put profitability analysis in a different light than would necessarily occur to management accountants. For instance, order-line information would cause one to think twice about proposals to improve overall financial results by pruning away unprofitable products, customers (such as customers 4 and 5 in Figure 5–4), or regions, or by eliminating the "losing" order lines that reduce cumulative profitability (see the right-hand side of the "banana" in Figure 5–3). Today, of course, management consultants around the world routinely advise clients to increase profits by pruning away unprofitable customers, products, or regions. Their advice assumes, however, that the profit or loss for a particular member of any category (e.g., a customer, a product, or a region) is the sum of identically profitable or unprofitable order lines. This flawed assumption treats the profitability of each individual customer, product, or region as if it emerged from homogeneous order lines.

A deficiency in management accounting profitability information gives rise to this flawed assumption. Management accounting information is not able to reveal what order-line data show, namely, that terminating one or more "losing" members of a category, such as customer 5 in Figure 5–4, can have an ambiguous impact on overall profitability. Customer 5's order lines are, on average, not profitable. But what if that customer is phased out in an effort to improve overall profitability?

The order-line statistics (shown in Figure 5–5) reveal what accounting information about customer profitability does not, namely, that several profitable order lines are contained within customer 5's overall "loss." Terminating that customer eliminates those profitable order lines along with the unprofitable ones. Order-line profitability statistics show, furthermore, that it may not be wise even for a company to prune away customer 5's *unprofitable* order lines, and leave the rest. To do so would fail to consider that the products found in those order lines will often show up as profitable in *other customers'* order lines. Rather than eliminate customer 5's "losing" purchases, a better proposal might be to learn how customer 5's purchases differ from those of other customers whose purchases of the same product are profitable. Companies cannot contemplate such knowledge, however, if they do not compile

Kanthal

To appreciate fully the distinctiveness of order-line profitability information, it is instructive to consider the following incident involving a 1990 Harvard Business School case about Kanthal, a Swedish company[7]. With help from the consulting firm that Drakenberg and Bröms founded in the late 1970s, Kanthal had compiled order-line profitability data in the mid-1980s and had used the data to construct product- and customer-level profitability statistics. Eager to spread the word about their distinctive analytical methods, Drakenberg and Bröms readily shared their work at Kanthal with a world-renowned American cost-management expert. They were surprised and disappointed, therefore, when the American expert's business school case about Kanthal focused on arrays of profitability data by product and by customer (resembling those shown above in Figure 5–4) and on cumulative profitability "bananas" (as in Figure 5–3), but failed to elaborate on the order-line data-gathering process that produced those arrays. Downplaying the importance of the information source—order-line profitability data—the author of the case presented Kanthal's profitability statistics in a form familiar to traditional management accounting academics and consultants in the United States.

Unfortunately, Kanthal, apparently following the American case writer's ideas, began using its order-line customer profitability information to cull "losers" from its product line in 1990. Kanthal's profits declined sharply in the early 1990s and half its work force in Sweden was laid off. The CEO who turned Kanthal around after 1992 blames the downturn on the effort to cull losers. Referring to the company's efforts to lay off "bad customers" located on the right-hand side of the "banana curve" in Figure 5–3, he said, "we need those customers too. Without them we would be worse off, running the business on the left-hand side of the curve. All business at any time consists of profitable and unprofitable customers. You cannot have only profitable customers. You need to maintain a healthy balance with not too many unprofitable ones."[8]

order-line data. Without this data, a firm cannot tell unambiguously *when* a product is a "loser" and *when* it is a "winner."

Sophisticated users of order-line profitability data use this information to explore relationships among customers and among individual customers' order lines. They do not encourage viewing a client's business as if it were a machine composed of separate parts that can be made to perform better by getting rid of product X or customer Y. They advocate, instead, using order-line profitability data to detect patterns and relationships among customers and among each customer's orders. They urge companies to consider, for example, whether an unprofitable order line is an aberration for the customer involved. Perhaps that customer, or another, has additional profitable orders with the same product or service, but under different conditions. In such a situation, one is well advised to study and replicate those conditions.

A useful tool for identifying and assessing the unique conditions affecting the profitability of each order line is the "order-line profit map" (Figure 5–6). This tool displays order line information in a format that shows patterns not disclosed by traditional management ac-

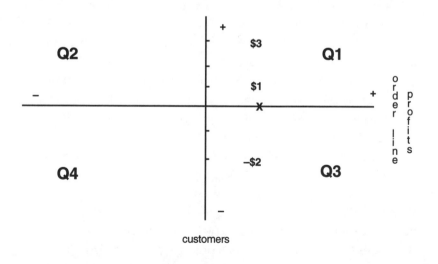

Customer X has $2 total profit from three
order lines with profits of $3, $1 and –$2

Figure 5–6: Order-Line Profit Map

counting information. To prepare data for a profit map, order lines are sorted by customer, and overall profit or loss is calculated for each customer. The point corresponding to that profit or loss is plotted for each customer on the x-axis of the map (Fig. 5–6). Then every order line of each customer is plotted at the appropriate profit or loss point along the y-axis. When all customers' order lines are plotted, the resulting points on the map fall into one of four quadrants that approximate the four zones on the cumulative order-line profitability "banana" curve (Figure 5–3). Quadrants 1 and 4 correspond, respectively, to the far left-hand ("winners") and far right-hand ("losers") zones of the banana, while quadrants 2 and 3 fall in the middle ("break-even") zones.

The order-line map helps one appreciate various complex relationships existing between customer and profitability. The determinants of profitability exist in each and every order line. One does not use aggregated averages or generalized quantitative models to analyze order-line profitability. To do so would be to miss the point. On the contrary, each order line is a self-contained universe of information sufficiently complete to explain why the history of orders for each customer, product, or service has, or has not, been profitable. Every order line tells its own peculiar story. In that sense, the order line resembles a holographic image of the whole. Each reflects a complete picture of conditions shaping the performance of the whole. The detailed knowledge available in order lines argues vigorously against the wholesale cut and slash strategies companies too often use to improve profitability. Instead of dropping unprofitable customers or products, a more effective way to improve profitability, as the map reveals, is to move order lines from quadrant 4 into either quadrant 2 or 3, and from there into quadrant 1.

If a company wants a quick boost to its overall profitability, the map suggests that customers falling into quadrant 4 might be candidates for disposal. After all, quadrant 4 contains only unprofitable sales to unprofitable customers. However, sales to those same customers that do bring a profit (quadrant 2) would be lost were the firm to drop all customers with order lines in quadrant 4. A better tactic than dropping customers is to explore the conditions that cause a product to be profitable in one customer's order line and unprofitable in another's; or to explore the conditions that cause one customer's purchases of a particular product to be profitable, while others' purchases of the same product are unprofitable.

Order-line information is invaluable for profitability management precisely because it reveals circumstances surrounding each and every purchase of a particular product or service. One learns from it about the situation of many customers ordering the identical product or service. From this information, a significant story unfolds that shapes business practices, always for company and customer working together. Management accounting information does nothing comparable.

An especially powerful way to discern the story implicit in any order line is to scrutinize the "neighbors to profit" that exist for profitable order lines. Insight into conditions affecting profitable order lines will provide clues as to how unprofitable order lines can earn profit. For example, aid workers recently hoping to ameliorate the plight of undernourished children in a region of Vietnam looked for conditions to explain the health of well-nourished children.[9] They found that parents of well-nourished children added locally available grasses and shellfish to the childrens' staple rice diet. By spreading the story of these families, aid workers improved the health of all children in the area. Furthermore, this improvement did not require additional technology or food. An experienced observer of order-line data can discern in studies of profitable order lines conditions that enable certain sales, to certain customers, to be profitable. Making as many customers as possible aware of these conditions may do more than any single thing to improve the profitability of "loss" order lines.

Four cases from the many in the files of Samarbetande Konsulter, the firm in which order-line profitability analysis originated in the late 1970s, demonstrate that when companies examine the context of any given situation with data from an order-line profit map, they learn to improve profitability without cutting out products, eliminating customers, or laying off workers:

1. Kanthal and the Furnace Builder

An anomaly in one very profitable customer's order lines disclosed an untapped opportunity that led to steps which moved several other customers' order lines from quadrant 2 to quadrant 1.

A salesperson in a division of Kanthal sold heating elements for industrial electric furnaces. From examining the order-line data of a furnace builder who was a very profitable customer for Kanthal, the salesperson observed that the profitability of a specific product Kanthal supplied to this customer was much lower than she had supposed. The reason was that the furnace builder had begun to use a new ceramic element which, while more expensive than Kanthal's, created much higher temperatures, used less power, lasted longer, and reduced furnace downtime. Therefore, the furnace builder had found it expedient to switch from Kanthal's product to this new ceramic element. Order-line profitability data enabled Kanthal's watchful salesperson to spot the switch much sooner and with more precision than would have been possible had she relied merely upon aggregated accounting-based product profitability data. This early warning enabled Kanthal to recoup its lost sales by introducing to the market sooner than it had intended its own version of the ceramic element.

2. Scania and the European Construction Industry

When Scania suffered losses in an entire group of customers' order lines, discovery of unusual conditions governing the customers' use of the product prompted changes that moved these order lines from quadrant 4 to quadrant 1.

An order-line profit map of one of Scania's European marketing regions located the heavy construction truck segment of its business squarely in quadrant 4. The map seemed to confirm what all makers of heavy trucks had long argued, namely, that any truck maker could improve its overall profitability by getting out of the construction truck business. An unusual feature of the map persuaded Scania's regional manager to investigate the situation carefully. He observed that all construction truck order lines in that region were not profitable for Scania. As a general rule unprofitable customers have at least a few profitable order lines. But that was not true for construction truck customers in this region.

Prompted by his study of the order-line profit map, the regional manager put the data in context by interviewing the executives of several construction companies in the region. These interviews revealed that construction companies purchase heavy trucks for very different reasons, and under very different financial conditions, than do long-distance haulers and urban distribution carriers. The latter prize Scania's heavy trucks for their low operating costs per kilometer, their service reliability, and their long economic life. Construction companies, on the other hand, work equipment around the clock for a fairly short contract period (usually two years or less). Therefore they care more about the truck's initial selling price than about either operating efficiency or longevity. Moreover, construction companies expect equipment to be ready to work the moment a contract is signed. They deplore downtime for any reason. Delays in the construction business can mean severe financial penalties, whereas finishing ahead of schedule may bring in large bonuses.

Given this knowledge, Scania's regional manager realized that major truck makers tended to sell trucks to construction users at prices and terms that generated losses for both customer and supplier. He concluded that it might make sense to lease trucks to the construction industry rather than sell them. Payments could be based on time, the single most important determinant of profitability to construction customers. Scania could meet tight contract deadlines by delivering, if necessary, from its stock of used equipment. All equipment could then be returned to Scania at the end of a contract. Should equipment fail for any reason, Scania would be ready to supply replacements immediately. The customer faced no downtime for repair work. Of course, Scania would build trucks as they always had—for long life, low operating costs, and high service reliability—because those factors improved Scania's bottom line, as owner of the vehicles, and they did nothing to diminish the construction customer's bottom line.

Within two years after implementing this win/win strategy, the Scania regional manager found that the profitability of his construction segment had moved from quadrant 4 to quadrant 1 of the order-line profit map. This change increased the region's overall net income by about 300 percent with no additional resources, no customers lost, no products dropped, and no layoffs.

3. Kanthal, Electrolux, and Parts Commonality

Teaching a profitable customer how to use common parts for widely different purposes moves that customer's unprofitable order lines from quadrant 3 to quadrant 1.

Kanthal sells Electrolux the wire that company uses to make heating elements on various consumer products such as electric ranges. A Kanthal order-line profit map revealed an alarming number of unprofitable order lines for sales of this product to Electrolux, a very large and profitable customer for Kanthal. At the same time, order-line maps revealed that similar products sold to much smaller customers were quite profitable. The context of profitable order lines revealed that while these firms bought the same product as Electrolux, they did so in a different way that paid more attention to the benefits of standardization.

At the time, Electrolux had several divisions making different varieties of similar consumer products, each with its own unique specifications for heating wire. Each Electrolux division ordered wire according to its own engineers' specifications. The engineers focused on designing the "ideal" wire for each end product. Hence, they saw themselves as saving "nonvalue material costs" by ordering #15 gauge wire where that was all the product needed and #10 gauge wire where the heavier wire was needed. The engineers did not know that the presumed savings in "volume" costs they made for Electrolux by fine-tuning the gauge of wire to suit each product design caused Kanthal to incur heavy "structural" assortment costs. Kanthal's engineers, apprised of the order-line profit map's story, suggested to Electrolux's engineers that because the gauge differences did not affect the performance of the consumer products involved, both companies could save a great deal of money if Electrolux simply ordered one gauge of wire—the heaviest needed—for all products. This solution called for occasional additional "volume" cost necessitated by sometimes using heavier gauge wire than was strictly necessary. However, this cost was much less than the assortment cost saved by supplying just one gauge of wire.

4. Avesta-Sheffield Steel Company and the Benefits of Variety

A study of customers' purchasing habits prompted changes in the purchasing practices of unprofitable customers that moved order lines from quadrant 4 to quadrants 3 and 2 and from quadrants 3 and 2 to quadrant 1.

Avesta-Sheffield gains competitive advantage and profitability by being known for supplying a full range of stainless products to customers. Customers who need a full range probably find it easier to buy in "one stop" from Avesta than to purchase different products from four or five specialized suppliers. Study of order-line profitability maps gives Avesta-Sheffield knowledge of the relative success it has selling its many products and selling to many different types of customers. Such information about products and customers has helped the company avoid unfortunate decisions to discontinue product lines or customers that on first glance seemed unprofitable.

Order-line profit data revealed to Avesta-Sheffield that unprofitable customers, contrary to popular wisdom, tended to concentrate their orders on one or a few of the eighteen different groups of stainless steel products the company sells. By sorting customers according to the number of different product groups each one purchased, Avesta discovered that those customers who purchased from the largest number of different groups, regardless of the customer's size, were the most profitable. Customers who purchased from only one product group, regardless of the group, were the least profitable, and small customers who purchased from only one product group were the least profitable of all. It seems, therefore, that the company's pathway to higher profitability lay not in dropping unprofitable customers so much as it lay in persuading single-product customers to increase the range of products that they purchase from Avesta-Sheffield. This insight, readily apparent from analysis of order-line profitability data, could never be gained by studying conventional management accounting information.

A further insight concerned the risks involved in dropping an apparently unprofitable product line, namely, stainless steel bars. Overall, the bar product group had a small volume and was unprofitable to Avesta-Sheffield. Order-line data revealed, however, that 45 percent of all its customers did purchase bars, and that these customers were profitable to Avesta. In other words, bars as a product group were unprofitable to Avesta, but at the customer level they were a neighbor to profitability. Dropping bars as an unprofitable line might disturb the 45 percent of Avesta-Sheffield's profitable customers who purchased bars. They might find that forcing customers to find a new supplier for that product may also prompt those customers to buy other products from the new supplier. The resulting customer defections could drive the company into a "death spiral."

. . . . .

These stories suggest that in any company possibilities to improve profitability abound that do not involve dropping products or customers, cutting resources, or laying off people. To identify such possibilities requires an order-line profit map and experienced personnel who can use it to analyze the context of sales of products and of a customer's situation. Astute analysis of an order-line profit map makes known the "neighbors" to profitability and it explains how relationships influence profitability. Working with this information, company personnel uncover the stories that underlie success, stories that hopefully focus on the specific customer—the customer with a face who can be located only at the order-line level.

Identifying cost with purposes encourages managers to improve profitability by *pulling* company resources into closer alignment with each customer's preferences, thereby enhancing the union between revenue and cost. Conversely, attempts to improve profitability that entail manipulating activity-based cost drivers (such as cutting drivers or batching work in order to use drivers more efficiently[10]) have the deleterious effect of *pushing* resources into alignment with targets that fit only the supplier's agenda, seldom the individual customer's agenda. Consequently, the manage-by-results thinkers who base decisions on conventional management accounting information fragment the union of revenue and cost, and thereby diminish long-term profitability.

Order-line profitability analysis illustrates that it is pointless, even self-defeating, to use accounting-based profit margin statistics by product, customer, or region in order to identify and discard "low runners" in pursuit of higher returns. Making decisions based only on the partial cost or revenue data from which those margin statistics are compiled is equally shortsighted. By contrast, using order-line information reveals the wisdom and expediency of mastering practices and nurturing patterns that create a profitable union of revenue and cost.

Order-line information presents the whole only as it is reflected in the particular details of each customer's purchases, never in terms of abstract averages. Therefore, it promotes thinking about profitability in terms of principles that guide the operation of systems in nature. Users of order-line information seek to understand key properties of the whole by painstakingly examining details in each and every part. They do this instead of using quantitative generalizations about the whole to draw inferences about how the parts should behave. Each and every order line invites consideration of the whole as a natural living system in which all work fulfills a customer-defined purpose necessary to the system's survival, all work follows a continuous flow which is balanced to the rate of customer demand, and every product anticipates the customer's potential needs before they are expressed.

ORDER-LINE PROFITABILITY ANALYSIS AND LIVING-SYSTEM PRINCIPLES

Analyzing profitability at the order line shifts the focus of management's attention away from quantitative abstractions to the actual work that unites the company with each of its customers. Order-line information does what conventional activity-based and other types of management accounting information cannot do. It connects profitability to the actual work that unites customer needs with company capabilities. In the late 1980s the lead author of this book (Johnson) created the terms "activity management" and "customer-focused activity management" to describe an approach for connecting work and profitability at the activity level.[11] Unfortunately, management accountants quickly transformed activity management into an accounting-oriented costing exercise that today is known as "activity-based management," or ABM. ABM, as practiced today, is little more than an extension of activity-based costing which, of course, is nothing more than an extension of conventional cost accounting. Order-line profitability analysis, by focusing attention on the connection between profitability and the work that joins the customer's needs with a company's competencies, can help restore the lost promise that activity management once offered.

Implicit in Johnson's activity management concept was the idea that disciplined attention to principles resembling those at work in natural systems enhances order-line profitability because it systematically *aligns* resources with customer needs. In so doing, it reduces the empty-handed use of resources, that is, the consumption of resources that serve neither present nor future customer needs. Empty-handed exertion distorts a balanced continuous flow and creates unwelcome complexity in design, production, and administration. It generates costs exceeding those necessary to maintain a healthy "metabolic" flow.

Traveling empty-handed, for example, might entail expending extra resources to produce more than current demand in order to achieve "economies of scale" or "economies of specialization." Avoiding such empty-handedness is implicit in the practices featured in this study: in Toyota's policy not to work ahead of current orders, nor to invest in capacity ahead of near-term market demand; in Scania's concern to design actual trucks only on demand; and in the practice of analyzing profitability only at the point where revenue and cost naturally occur together—the order line. Each of these practices reflects the view that profits *co-arise* with cost and revenue. Profit emerges from a symbiotic union of revenue and cost. It is not an outcome resulting from manipulating independent objects. Nor is it an outcome produced by a struggle between independent objects.

Moreover, viewing profitability in terms of relationships and of the need to incur costs to fulfill purposes, not to mindlessly cut costs, may restore lost respect for the tendency of all things in nature to recur in cycles. In nature, all needs are met in their appropriate time. There is a time to plant, a time to germinate and grow, a time to harvest, and a time to replenish. In nature, nothing grows infinitely.

Expecting companies and economies to grow endlessly has destructive consequences that could be averted if businesses were to think of costs as fulfilling purposes that recur in cycles, not caused by "drivers" that occur all the time. Companies that see costs in terms of purposes to be met at different times of the cycle will experience a boost in energy that comes from working in phase with, not at odds with, natural cycles. Leveraging opportunity by working in harmony with an otherwise antagonistic force is well known to practitioners of the Japanese martial art of Aikido. Viewing costs as an opportunity might mean, for example, that during peak expansion periods a company would shift resources away from handling new products or customers—"newness" costs in terms of the three-way classification of cost purposes—and into fulfilling current orders—"volume" costs. In other words, instead of

adding new (or additional) resources to capture growing sales in the expansion phase of a cycle, a company would shift existing resources from
sowing to harvesting. Neither would the company lay off resources during the contraction phase of the cycle. Instead, part of the work force
would shift from volume work to newness work—something Scania's
and Toyota's personnel have done for many years.

The payoff of such flexibility is enormous. A company can move
through the business cycle without suffering the costly effects of laying
off workers during downturns, losing their embodied experience.
Order-line thinking enables managers to see costs as purposes to be ful-
filled in their appropriate seasons, not as objects to slash and burn in a
constant quest for growth. The superior performance of hypothetical
Company B in Figure 2–4 suggests this.

The order-line approach to profitability analysis recognizes that
viewing a business as a life system entails improving its abilities to fulfill purposes. Anathema to this approach is cutting costs, reengineering,
or violating continuous flow with "empty-handed" efforts at pushing
work out in large batches to achieve scale economies. Such object-
oriented mechanistic thinking shapes traditional activity-based cost
management. In contrast, subject-oriented thinking shapes managing
by means, which was implicit in the concept of activity management
and now is implicit in order-line profitability analysis.

Notably, traditional mechanistic cost management focuses on quantities, whereas relational order-line analysis invites greater consideration of indexes and ratios—dimensionless numbers—not quantities.
Gregory Bateson once noted the importance of the distinction between
number and quantity.[12] As Bateson said, "number is of the world of pattern, gestalt, and digital communication; quantity [the product of measurement, i.e., comparison to a scale] is of the world of analogic and
probabilistic computation." The upshot of this distinction is that
"quantity and pattern are of different logical type and do not readily fit
together in the same thinking." Therefore, number (or ratio), because
it can be used to denote differences in patterns, can aid our understanding of a multivalent world where all is explained by relationships.
Quantity, however, only enables us to understand continuous, mono-
tonic variation in a one-dimensional world where all difference is explained by size. The quantity-focused management accounting tools

dominating contemporary organizations—in business, government, education, and elsewhere—substitute measurement for discipline. In the United States and increasingly throughout the world, measurement alone dominates management thinking.

The term "quantity" implies *something that has no relation to anything but itself.* Quantitative management accounting tools do not identify cost and profit as emergent properties of a multivalent web of relationships. Instead, management accounting reduces cost and profit to objects, to mere particles that are moved only by external force. This shows that quantity and measurement are not germane to a world of interdependent relationships and mutual causality, the world that is implicit in natural living systems. Quantification and measurement separate any system into isolated parts, eliminating all relationships except those concerning an increase or decrease in the magnitude of something. The costs, revenues, and other financial and nonfinancial quantities that management accountants and controllers customarily supply to decision makers speak only to the single dimension of size. Those quantities cannot reflect the patterns of interdependence and mutual causality—the qualitative relationships—implicit in natural living systems and the essence of operations in Toyota and Scania.

CONCLUSION

Managers brought up in the Western world seem instinctively to seek answers from quantitative measures. To quantify requires seeing things as independent objects. Westerners, especially in the United States, almost automatically assume that by nature all things are independent of one another. Independence and the related notion of lineal causality are not, however, self-evident truths. Rather, they are a fairly recent product of the human mind, rooted in the same intellectual ground from which quantitative thinking emerged in the seventeenth century. As modern biologist Lynn Margulis has said, "independence is a political, not a scientific, term."[13]

Order-line profitability analysis causes managers to see a company as a complex set of relationships. It emphasizes that a company is a whole requiring that each part should contribute disciplined work. It implicitly asks managers to master practices that treat costs as purposes, rather than as objects. It implicitly rejects quick and easy management that aims mindlessly at quantitative targets and asks, instead, for an awareness that was lost when we reduced the features of natural systems to quantity. Order-line information brings forth stories of interrelationships and neighbors. It portrays cost and profitability as emerging from relationships among parts of a living system. A business cultivates these relationships through disciplined attention to mastery of practices that emulate principles present in nature's systems.

Techniques of order-line profitability analysis help managers focus a company's work on interdependent relationships and the patterns of mutual causality implicit in them. When organizations concentrate on nurturing relationships rather than on achieving quantitative targets, they will spontaneously generate financial results consonant with healthy long-term survival. This is evident in the strong financial results that natural-system management practices have generated for years at Toyota and Scania. Adopting order-line techniques will encourage other companies also to replicate such practices and to achieve the same long-term results.

When run from a natural-system perspective, a company's systems will replicate "dependent co-arising." Both ancient religious and philosophical thought and modern science affirm universal interdependence. Modern science and ancient intellectual traditions alike declare that interdependence and mutual causality are among nature's deepest patterns. Everything in the universe is inseparably connected to everything else, and has always been so. Modern science draws this conclusion from recent theories of cosmogenesis and evolution. According to these theories, everything in the universe since the beginning of time has evolved, and continues to evolve, from one constantly changing bundle of matter and energy. The scientific hypothesis that all natural processes are absolutely interdependent also is consistent with ancient mythical and religious teachings. For example, Joanna Macy finds a particularly elegant way "for perceiving the dynamics of interdependent power in our own lives" in Buddha's central teaching of "dependent co-arising."[14] Adopting the thinking implicit in order-line profitability analysis offers managers this magnificent perspective.

6

....

Results Are in the Details

To see a World in a Grain of Sand
And a Heaven in a Wild Flowere,
Hold Infinity in the palm of your hand
And Eternity in an hour.

—William Blake[1]

A good traveler has no fixed plans
and is not intent upon arriving.

—Lao Tzu[2]

Toyota's way of organizing production, Scania's design engineering practices, and order-line profitability analyses differ enormously from mainstream business practices. These practices exemplify the approach to management that this book refers to as "managing by means," or MBM. In that approach, a business fulfills each customer's needs and simultaneously nurtures its own human capabilities by attending carefully to each minute particular—each action, each design decision, and each order. By nurturing the details, MBM balances the opposing interests of company and customer in a self-sustaining cycle that generates profit naturally, without seeking endless quantitative growth in outputs and inputs.

Managing by means is the antithesis of "managing by results," MBR, which wrenches the particulars until they fit into the Procrustean mold of a preconceived quantitative model. MBR views company and customer as separate, opposing objects whose respective needs to consume and accumulate must grow independently forever. Managing by results is the fundamental habit of thought that dominates business today. MBR practices do not emulate the basic principles governing the operation of all natural living systems. The MBM approach to management embraces principles that permeate the way nature works. Companies hoping to gain the long-term benefits of MBM must align their practices with these principles. Only in this manner, and not merely by introducing a few isolated new practices, will managers create organizations in which the means generate the desired results.

The purpose of this chapter is to show companies how to adopt MBM thinking and build new practices on a foundation of principles resembling those that govern the operation of natural living systems. The pathway companies are urged to follow is a cycle in which principles feed the discovery of practices and practices are judged in the light of principles—a cycle of "doing is knowing and knowing is doing." This cycle resembles the recurring metabolic cycle that sustains activities in all living systems. When replicating that cycle, an organization continually assesses peoples' actions not by how well they reach quantitative targets, but by how well they emulate the principles that guide the activities of a natural living system.

Companies that follow this cycle improve their long-term performance. Adhering to practices that nurture every detail in the web of relationships that is the company eventually connects the company's employees and suppliers (including suppliers of capital) with the company's customers, its community, and the natural systems that support all life on Earth.

PRINCIPLES IN LIVING SYSTEMS: NEW THINKING TO SHAPE NEW WAYS OF ORGANIZING WORK

The first chapter described the modern scientific view of the universe as a system that produces continuously evolving diversity from perpetually changing fields of relationships. As that chapter indicates, a business is a natural living system that arises from, and is explained by, the same three principles that seem to explain the operation of all natural living systems in the universe. Each of these principles is described below:

1. SELF-ORGANIZATION: *Creative energy continually and spontaneously materializes in self-organizing forms that strive to maintain their unique self-identity.* Every natural living system has a unique identity which it strives to preserve with feedback among its parts. Information fed back among its parts preserves the system's self-identity in the face of influences from the external environment. Living systems reflect the self-actualization, or unique embodiment, of creative potential in material form.

2. INTERDEPENDENCE: *Interdependent natural systems interact with each other through a web of relationships that connects everything in the universe.* The word "relationships" expresses the essential nature of reality. Nothing exists in isolation from the rest of the universe. Fields of "gravitational curvature," an image derived from Einstein's theory of general relativity, may be the most pervasive and one of the most fundamental expressions of the radical interconnectedness of all things in the universe. In the presence of such interconnectedness, everything exists "in the context of" something else.

3. DIVERSITY: *Diversity results from the continual interaction of unique identities always relating to one another.* Diverse forms result from constant interactions within a fixed budget of matter and energy in the universe. From those interactions there has evolved a rich variety of forms including, for example, quarks, galaxies, planets, starfish, and business organizations.

Increasingly these three principles must provide the basis for management practices in modern business organizations. They already shape key practices found at Toyota and, in the design area, at Scania. Nature's principles are a model for procedures such as continuous flow of work to order, work balanced to customer needs, design to order using common parts wherever possible, and making information an integral part of the work at all times. It is time to explain now how the principles that guide the operation of natural living systems can shape the development of new business practices consistent with the way nature works.

PRACTICES BASED ON LIVING-SYSTEM PRINCIPLES

The practices mentioned below have all been described at length in earlier chapters. They succeed because of their connection with the basic principles underlying nature's systems. This connection produces the new thinking that informs company practices. As the following pages show, each particular practice is related to some extent with each of the three principles underlying natural systems.

Principle 1: Creative energy continually and spontaneously materializes in self-organizing forms that strive to maintain their unique self-identity.

One of the most pervasive patterns in the universe is the unique identity of every material form. No two members of a species—from atoms to human beings to galaxies—are identical. Remarkably, at every level of the universe, self-referencing feedback mechanisms in every entity seem to enable all natural systems to maintain a sense of identity and order. Presumably each carbon atom maintains a unique identity whether it is found in interplanetary clouds, a lump of coal, or a protein molecule in the cell of a lion's heart. Similarly, each galaxy maintains a distinct identity in the midst of thousands of millions of other galaxies.[3]

This principle of self-organization that governs natural living systems has numerous implications for the practices that should guide the operations of a business. Undoubtedly the most important implication for a company seeking to operate according to the principles of natural living systems is the need to replace traditional MBR control systems—especially financial targets—with various practices that promote the standardization of each unique part of the work. Standardization is an indispensable element of internal feedback essential to preserve and sustain an organization's sense of identity. It is not surprising that Toyota's training portrays standardization as the foundation of a production system depicted as a building with supporting columns and a roof.

Moreover, one of the first lessons of the Toyota Production System is to show how standardized work practices give each individual worker the ability to distinguish normal from abnormal conditions in every detail, at all times. Standardized work practices profoundly emulate the self-referencing powers inherent in the feedback process of any natural living system. Having such practices in place greatly increases a system's flexibility.

Among the many practices included in standardized work, an especially important procedure is having workers define, describe, graphically depict, and document the steps they perform in any work they do. Documenting present procedures creates the first standard in any work setting. When workers document the expected pattern in their work, they make normal expectations visible. This information makes it possible for workers to assess their own ongoing work and to easily accommodate change in designs and processes. Standardized work also makes it possible to pace work to the rate at which customer orders are filled. Such pacing leads to establishing, as much as possible, uniform takt times throughout the work system. Uniform takt times greatly strengthen the relationships that connect employees to each other and to the final customer.

Standardized work and other practices which mirror the principle of self-organization, the first principle of living systems, will be implemented and sustained primarily from the ground up, not enforced from above. For people in business today it is natural to think otherwise. Typically managers advocate and exercise strong-willed assertion. While direction and prescribed behavior are sometimes necessary to influence and coordinate people's actions, they should be the exception. Companies whose practices emulate what is observed in living systems will not divide knowing and doing into separate tasks performed by different classes of employees, such as bosses and workers.

Every person in a company must participate in both knowing and doing. "Knowing" implies firsthand detailed awareness of both customer needs and company processes. "Doing" implies detailed knowledge of how to conduct design, production, and logistical procedures. Linking knowing and doing means that bosses will frequently visit and participate in shopfloor activities, and workers will frequently offer ideas for changing designs and processes. Moreover, all employees, regardless of position, will visit as often as possible with customers to learn about and share their experiences with the company's products and services.

Principle 2: Interdependent natural systems interact with each other through a web of relationships that connects everything in the universe.

The imperative to relate prevents the imperative to self-organize from becoming so voracious and destructive that one self-organizing species destroys all others. Thus, absent the imperative to relate, "the desires of a single pair of aphids, if satisfied, would destroy the Earth. After only a single year such aphids would generate over half a trillion offspring. . . . To energize those aphids means to remove energy from other regions, from other beings, and for these others to perish."[4] However, the imperative to relate introduces a balancing mechanism that insures that once evolution has given rise to aphids, the aphids' presence will be contained and will not bring further evolution to a halt.

In business, a system of continuous flow is a vivid example of a balancing mechanism that embodies the imperative to relate. Linking all work in a continuous flow is perhaps the most potent practice a company can introduce to abide by the principle of interdependence that characterizes all natural living systems. A continuous flow makes visible the connection between each employee's activities and the satisfaction of customer wants. It also facilitates the feedback necessary to insure the integrity of the system's unique identity. And having a continuous flow indicates more readily the level of resources being consumed to fill each customer order. In effect, a continuous flow helps to insure that the work itself, at no additional cost, provides all the information that is required to meet each customer's needs. It thereby reduces the need for much of the information that companies today process at great cost and delay outside of the work stream, in what we have referred to as "the information factory."

Besides continuous flow, order-line profitability analysis is another practice that derives from nature's principle of interdependence. When companies strive assiduously to nurture relationships among designers, producers, and customers in every step of the work, they will naturally and inevitably come to view profitability and costs at the order-line level. This in turn will cause managers to assess performance in terms of how well each worker's practices adhere to natural life-system principles, not how close they come to reaching financial targets.

Principle 3: Diversity results from the continual interaction of unique identities always relating to one another.

In natural systems, diverse results emerge spontaneously from relationships among interrelated unique parts, not from moving homogeneous parts about according to external designs. Rich diversity, a hallmark of nature's system in the universe, derives, ironically, from nature's exquisitely parsimonious use of matter and energy. In nature, nothing is added or wasted as changing fields of relationships continually transform old into new. Energy continually turns into matter, and matter turns into energy, and yet, remarkably, the total budget of matter and energy in the universe has not changed since the big bang. All the diverse phenomena we see manifest around us arise from the perpetual churning of that fixed budget of matter and energy.

The creation of diversity from limited resources by means of practices consistent with nature typifies companies that manage by means. Evidence from Toyota and Scania demonstrates that when companies focus on the way nature works, they can produce great varieties of high quality products and services at very low costs. Their accomplishment runs contrary to the results achieved by companies that manage by results. MBR companies drive people to reach planned financial results by aiming for a target, without regard for the wasteful means used to hit the target. They are able to reach targets for short periods—even several years during expansion phases of the business cycle. Invariably, however, their performance lags behind MBM companies, and they survive for significantly shorter periods.

The pursuit in MBR companies of targets for financial growth and accumulation necessarily subordinates relationships to abstract financial goals. Such pursuit disrupts nature's inherently balancing processes and generates, instead, unnatural pressures that force organizations in the long run to underperform and eventually to collapse. In other words, MBR, mass production, and other practices feature growth but ignore relationships. They ignore, in other words, the fundamental principle in nature—interdependence—that exists expressly to check growth and thus to avoid destruction of the entire system. Unlike MBR companies, MBM companies behave according to nature's principles, thus insuring longer life and superior long-term performance. MBM practices sustain satisfactory performance consistently, year in and year out, without layoffs, cutbacks, mergers, sell-offs, and the like. They are devoid of pressures that impair profitability over the long haul and that lead eventually to unwanted cutbacks and even to bankruptcy.

Practices that address the principle of diversity can be said to fulfill the imperative "do no harm." Such practices insure that growth will not be allowed to overpower relationships. One crucial practice that enables MBM companies to generate diversity at low cost is that of reflective patience, or in other words the discipline to leave well enough alone and let results unfold. It takes discipline, as well as a modicum of courage, to focus attention on nurturing relationships among steps in the work and among employees doing the work. However, it is a mistake to yield to the temptation to define financial expectations, especially financial targets, and to intervene and "manage" whenever results fall short of those expectations. An MBM company avoids that temptation and the harm it causes precisely because of disciplined mastery that values the system from which results emanate.

The practice of patiently letting results unfold while concentrating on nurturing the relationships that connect each part of an organization was foreshadowed centuries ago in a Japanese fable about three rulers from different parts of Japan. The fable concerns a bird that would not sing. When asked what to do about the bird, one ruler said "kill the bird if it will not sing." The second ruler said "make it sing." But the third ruler simply said "wait." Perhaps it is not coincidental that the third ruler lived in the area surrounding present-day Nagoya, the area the Toyoda family comes from. The spirit of "waiting for the bird to sing" that must be present in all MBM companies has permeated Toyoda family enterprises from the late nineteenth century to the present time.

That same spirit is also expressed in W. Edwards Deming's admonition to managers: "Don't just *do* something; *sit* there!"[5] Both the Japanese fable and Deming's admonition reflect a belief that the best results come to those who value and nurture proper relationships and who refrain from trying to force results by arbitrarily manipulating the system. Modern managers must learn to reflect on the dynamics of the system they inhabit, honor processes that mirror the workings of life systems, and then wait for results.

Another practice that will help companies fulfill the principle of diversity, in addition to waiting patiently for results, is the use of common patterns again and again in the design of products and services. Nature achieves immense diversity from surprisingly few patterns. For example: a small number of different particles recombine in many ways to produce only one hundred or so chemical elements that make up all material substances in the universe; the same branching pattern shapes the veins in your hand, the veins in the leaf on a tree, and the tributaries and rivers that form a regional watershed; a common pattern shapes the bones, shell, and joints in the limbs of a human, a horse, and a crab; five chemical elements (P, O, N, H, and C) combine to form four structures (A, T, C, and G) that unite in almost infinite combinations to form the genetic code (DNA) of organic life forms; over 70 percent of the DNA in humans and in pumpkins is shared in common. The search for ways to achieve greater diversity with more commonality, as we saw in Scania's modular design system, is a largely unexplored practice that, by emulating a profound feature of natural living systems, will greatly improve business performance.

Finally, a practice that follows from all the other practices we have enumerated is to consciously and intentionally design work so that the information needed to link company and customer flows with the work, and the work itself becomes that information. When information and work flow together as one, there is no need for computer information systems to manage the flow of work that connects company with customer. This integration of work and information not only eliminates an enormous layer of overhead costs, it also enables any worker at any moment to make the small changes that create variety to order at low cost. Thus, careful design of the continuous flow of work transforms the relationships among workers, at no additional cost, into a vehicle for creating variety to order.

APPLYING PRACTICES: MAKING THE WORKPLACE
A LIVING SYSTEM

Learning about the practices enumerated here is not simply a matter of observing them from a detached and "objective" perspective in existing workplaces. Very few businesses in the world today offer examples of such practices at work. The only way for most companies to discover and learn how to apply these practices is to create projects designed to emulate the principles of natural living systems within their own workplaces. In effect, this is tantamount to proposing that organizations incorporate the scientific study of work into their regular routines. But that means viewing science as something other than just the "objective" study of "measurable" aspects of phenomena. It suggests viewing the organization's members as both participants and observers of the phenomenon being studied. This learning will be accomplished only by doing.[6]

Science for over three hundred years has viewed the human observer as separate from the phenomenon being studied. This emphasis on separateness, and on studying only what can be measured, is meant to insure "objectivity." Unfortunately, this quest for objectivity forces one to ignore what cannot be measured. It denies the influence of unseen fields of relationships. By admitting only what can be sensed and measured, it considers as causative influences only forces that are external to the phenomena being studied. While this viewpoint has provided a foundation for mechanistic understanding of the material world, it has excluded the living human situation as a subject for contemplation and analysis. Ironically, traditional science has enabled humans to gain a marvelous understanding of the world around them from a vantage point that denies a place for the living human as a proper object of study, except to the degree that the human can be seen in purely measurable, mechanical terms. In other words, the understanding of the world that our objective science has given us does not admit the presence of life itself, especially human life.[7]

Moving the study of work into the workplace is comparable to shifting the study of dolphins from examining dissected creatures on an embalming table to swimming with dolphins. This move does not mean that one stops studying parts in order to focus exclusively on examining a whole. On the contrary. It means focusing more intently than ever on *how parts reflect the unity of the whole.* It means examining how each part contributes to the whole not as a separate thing in itself, but through its relationships with all the other parts. In the end, this shift of emphasis alters what we consider to be scientific work. Instead of focusing on how parts connect quantitatively, the work now centers on understanding and nurturing nonquantitative relationships among parts.

An obvious place to introduce the study of work into the workplace is with problems that exist because work has been organized, probably in the interest of achieving some financial target, so that people elude rather than embrace relationships. An example of such a problem is the defects found in a product or service after it is ready for delivery or is in the customer's hands. Such deficiencies too often cause rework, complaints, and returns in all businesses, resulting in avoidable costs and lost revenue. Seldom is the problem traced to the practice of using quantitative targets to drive work. However, the drive to produce more, faster is usually the main cause of defects, rework, complaints, and returns.

To address this problem, managers must spend time at work stations and bring with them knowledge of the principles that guide living systems. Then they will see how to organize work from a fresh perspective. Perhaps they will realize that separation among parts— separation instigated by the quest to reach quantitative targets—is the central issue to be addressed. Their commitment to nature's principles should prompt them to search for ways to overcome this separation, not search for ways to "improve" results within the separated system. MBM managers will realize that, to end the separation causing dysfunction, they must establish relationships among people doing the work in every step of the process. Relationships, aided by feedback, must enable work to flow continuously from company to customer. Building such relationships will stimulate employees to search for ways to standardize work steps, so that every person at every moment can identify abnormal events. Once work is flowing continuously in standardized steps, everyone can recognize that it is possible (and simpler) to find defects when they occur, not after all the work has been done.

Organizing work into a continuous flow insures finding defects as they occur because it demands that each person see his or her work in terms of a relationship to the next (internal) customer, not in terms of independent effort to reach a remote target. Nurturing relationships in a continuous flow of work coincides with the principle of interdependence basic to living systems. When a company emulates living systems by organizing work into relationships that flow from step to step, it reduces defects, reduces costs, and improves quality. Costs and lead times inevitably fall and revenue improves. Nurture the means. The results will take care of themselves.

Having self-conscious efforts to emulate nature's principles become part of the regular workplace routine makes leaders of everyone. Everyone at all times will pay attention to practice and assessment—doing and knowing. Everyone will be engaged in the task of assessing how well their practices coincide with principles informing nature. Workers and bosses will make this judgment by constantly attending to details. Bosses, for example, will regularly visit worksites. Instead of relying upon secondhand reports that filter information after the fact, they will "go and see" the work and any problems that arise. Workers will focus attention not only on their immediate task, but also on how it might be improved and on how it might best serve the needs of the internal customer who will soon receive it. Ultimately, everyone's work thereby satisfies a final paying customer.

Unquestionably one of the most profound benefits of organizing work according to the principles that govern living systems is the joy humans feel when participating in community. While politicians may preach the virtues of independence, the scientific reality is that we emerge from, and cannot live apart from, relationships. We are *naturally* *inter*dependent creatures. Relationships fulfill our deepest needs. Businesses that organize work as a system of relationships do more than any institution in society, perhaps, to heal the destructive fragmentation caused in large part by a mechanistic worldview that sees human beings as inanimate blocks to be manipulated arbitrarily and cast off cavalierly. Companies that evaluate and assess their problems and practices in the context of living-system principles help restore community to our lives.

LESSONS ABOUT MBM PRACTICES

MBM practices such as those in place at Toyota, and to a lesser degree at Scania, embody several specific lessons. A company is wise to have these lessons in mind as it attempts to implement similar practices itself.[8] Such lessons can provide signposts for assessing how well specific practices conform to principles in nature. These lessons are presented below in the form of questions that managers must ask themselves:

LESSON ONE: *Are resources used parsimoniously?* When work links customer with company in a balanced, continuous flow every step of the way, it satisfies every new customer demand with minimum resources. Toyota's "produce to order" system, for example, balances resources at every stage to the amount needed to advance one customer's order one more step along the way to completion. Similarly, Scania's "design to order" modular design system meets a customer's needs for something new and different by changing as few parts of the truck as possible and using common parts for the rest. And using order-line information to "assess to order" obviates the need for many of the wasteful, disembodied information systems companies feel they need to assess financial performance.

LESSON TWO: *Does work attend at all times to the relationship between company and customer?* All production, design, and logistical work in an MBM system will attend at *all* times to both sides of the company-customer relationship. Such work is never "empty-handed," meaning that it never attends to one side of that relationship while ignoring the other. Work that is organized according to MBM principles never reflects an empty-handed pursuit of cost or revenue targets, as when output is pushed indiscriminately to achieve so-called scale economies.

LESSON THREE: *Is money regarded primarily as energy to fuel the union between company and customer, never merely as a commodity to be accumulated for its own sake?* Revenue provides energy to do what is needed to serve customers, and costs use energy to fulfill customer-oriented purposes. "Energy" that is diverted from fueling the union between company and customer can be effectively saved and stored only to accommodate variation produced by natural cycles of expansion and contraction. Efforts to accumulate energy without limit are inevitably wasteful and destructive.

LESSON FOUR: *Do managers focus profitability measurement on the point where profit actually occurs, that is, the point where customer and company meet—the order line?* Only at the order line is profit visible and open to measurement. All the conditions that determine profit exist at that point, and the only possible way to alter profitability in the long run is to alter those conditions. It is especially important at that point to assess how well those conditions reflect the principles governing living systems. Nurturing minute particulars at each and every point where company and customer meet underlies the success of managing by means. Profitability is managed in the long run not by wrenching those particulars to fit the terms of a quantitative financial model, but by helping each person connect in a relationship with others that emulates principles found in natural systems.

LESSON FIVE: *Is work assessed real-time ("to order") with index numbers, ratios, and words instead of after the fact with quantitative management accounting artifacts?* Indexes and ratios enable one to compare and contrast the principles underlying systems of relationships. The density index, for example, enables product designers to compare different products in terms of commonality of parts. The density index discloses how well designers conform to principles congruent with nature and encourages nurturing them. Since deviating from nature's principles will invariably increase resource consumption and costs, therefore, ratios and indexes gauging these deviations are crucial. They are to MBM managers analogous to, but vastly superior to, the product cost information and gross margin information used by MBR managers.[9] Assessing work with words is discussed in the next section.

LESSON SIX: *Do stories from the order line replace traditional management accounting information?*[10] Order-line profitability analysis requires examining information about the unique story each order line conveys. Order lines reveal stories that focus on the real and the concrete. By understanding and sharing order-line stories, one can interpret and analyze profit. In the world of MBM, improving long-run profitability hinges not on manipulating financial variables, but on knowing "how to make sad stories better."

These lessons are meant to help managers assess how closely their company's practices reflect the principles that govern behavior in natural living systems. They provide a nonquantitative template that can assist people's efforts to evaluate whether or not a company's practices are likely to generate results such as those that emerge spontaneously from the operations of natural systems. Another such nonquantitative template for assessing practices in the workplace is found in word patterns, that is, in the words and phrases we coin or use repeatedly to describe the work we do.

NONQUANTITATIVE ASSESSMENT OF MBM PRACTICES
WITH REFLECTION AND WORDS

How can those who manage by means tell when their practices adhere to principles responsible for order and harmony in nature? How are they to assess not only the success of their daily practices, but also their adherence to principles? Certainly quantitative signals used by MBR managers are not germane. Instead of quantitative data, MBM managers will rely on meditative reflection and words. Reflection may show us hidden qualities, or patterns, that "stir the heart of nature," as the architect Christopher Alexander says, and that create harmony and contentment when present in human surroundings.[11] One such pattern, Alexander observes, is that when people see each other's faces, they understand each other better. An architect reflecting further on Alexander's observation will notice that light entering a room from two sides enables people to better see one another's faces and so achieve more understanding than would be possible in a room with light coming from only one side, where shadows and dark corners create glare. This discovery about a natural pattern—a "quality without a name"—can become widely incorporated into architectural practice, Alexander suggests, if it is expressed in a "a pattern language," or, simply stated, in a phrase such as "light on two sides of every room."[12]

Similarly, in business reflection yields insights about natural patterns, and these insights can be expressed in words. Mindful reflection occurs when a manager participates closely in the daily life of an organization. Only from immediate and direct experience within a company does the manager gain a clear understanding of the relationships connecting parts of the organization. Living within the system means being immersed in the day-to-day operations—to "go and see." Most managers today, of course, are unaccustomed to immersing themselves in the daily operations of a company. They see no need to master concrete details. Confident that "objective" quantitative data allow them to make sound decisions, they are content to maintain a detached position. Unaware of a "nameless quality which stirs the heart of nature" and oblivious to a pattern implicit in nature, traditional managers see no reason to reflect. Unhesitatingly they settle for the barren revelations of abstract quantitative analysis.

MBM managers, prompted to reflect, search for an appropriate language, for a phrase, for "pattern language," as Christopher Alexander terms it. Using words demands precise thinking about how work is done. Managers who reflect choose words with exactitude to explain precisely how the behavior of "minute particulars" in the company corresponds to the principles governing living systems in nature. They tell stories that enrich understanding, rather than depend upon bloodless quantities and equations.

Those who manage by means must develop certain phrases that express their understanding of how an organization's work reflects nature's patterns. These phrases will help convey two essential differences between MBR and MBM. One is the difference in worldview (Box 6–1). The other is a difference in action (Box 6–2).

W. Edwards Deming, in one of the first items on his fourteen-point list of management principles, urged managers to "adopt . . . [a] new phi-

Box 6-1	
PHRASES EXPRESSING THE OLD AND THE NEW WORLDVIEWS	
MECHANICAL: MBR	NATURAL: MBM
The "I" stands alone Eliminate competitors Overpower the other Control the result Win with scale Escape	Relationships are reality Increase each customer's options Empty the self Nurture relationships Win with diversity Embrace

losophy." They need to adopt, in Gregory Bateson's terminology, a new epistemology. Phrases that articulate the thinking of MBM are compared in Box 6–1 to phrases that convey the mechanistic thinking of those who manage by results (MBR). The contrast underscores the profoundly different worldviews of those who see companies as mechanistic entities and those who see them as living systems. The language that values living systems includes such phrases as "relationships are reality," "increase each customer's options," "empty the self," "nurture the pattern," and "win with diversity." Conversely, the language of the mechanistic, MBR outlook includes, for example, "the 'I' stands alone," "eliminate competitors," "overpower the other," "control the result," and "win with scale."

From these very different worldviews inevitably spring radically different actions. The connection between worldview and action is captured by Maturana and Varela in their phrase "all doing is knowing and all knowing is doing." Executives who use such word patterns as "relationships are reality" and encourage us to "nurture relationships" promote actions that embody life-system principles. Executives who believe that "the 'I' stands alone" and seek to "eliminate competitors" by "overpowering the other" of course promote actions contrary to principles implicit in living systems. Actions that spring from these different habits of thought are described by the phrases in Box 6–2.

Box 6-2	
PHRASES DEFINING CHARACTERISTIC ACTIONS OF THE OLD AND NEW WORLDVIEWS	
MECHANISTIC ACTIONS (MBR)	NATURAL ACTIONS (MBM)
Remove constraints to growth	Embrace constraints creatively
Follow finance-driven rules	Master life-oriented practices
Manipulate output to control costs	Provide output as needed, on time
Persuade and sell	Build customer loyalty
Build for scale and size	Build for flexibility
Increase speed of work	Change how work is done
Specialize and decouple processes	Enhance continuous flow
Utilize resources fully	Keep idle resources ready
An individual is the cause: blame	Complex, mutual interaction is the cause: reflect

The phrases describing actions make it possible to assess work in an MBM organization. In fact, they provide a nonquantitative means of evaluating the entire organization. Those who wish to manage by means should examine the words they use to describe their work. Do they describe their own work with words that resemble life-system phrases or mechanistic phrases?

Without words one cannot fully capture complex qualitative insights. Quantitative measures express only one dimension of reality, that of size. Size matters, of course, where size is relevant, as in systems where the whole is reducible to the sum of its parts and the size of the part is, therefore, significant. In a business, for example, it is often appropriate to measure the pounds of material consumed, the hours of labor employed, or the distance something is shipped. It is impossible, however, to quantify and measure relationships, and it is the web of relationships connecting the parts of a company from which financial results such as cost and profit ultimately emerge. Because cost and profit are not objects, but are properties that emerge from relationships, quantitative measures can only describe them, they cannot explain them. Quantitative measures, unlike art, music, or the stories and myths that humans fashion with words, cannot convey understanding of the multidimensional patterns that shape the relationships from which results, such as cost and profit, emerge in a living system.

Chapter 1's comparison of Toyota and its American counterparts after World War II highlights a particularly unfortunate aspect of directing action with quantitative measurement. The experience of the American Big Three auto makers in that story reveals how such action cannot generate the infinite diversity of outcomes that is the hallmark of nature's robust process of creation. Diversity—a condition of robust survival in natural systems—is not created by following abstract designs or blueprints derived from quantifying and measuring. Instead, using quantitative measurements to shape outcomes leads to recurring iterations that monotonously repeat the same, unvarying output. The result, of course, is the homogeneous output that we associate in the business world with mass production, but in nature with instability and, ultimately, extinction. Oblivious of these considerations, MBR managers adhere to thinking that produces repetition and homogeneity. Because repetition is contrary to nature's pattern, eventually its use has destructive consequences both for humans and for the ecosystem that sustains them.

TAKING MBM PRACTICES TO THE NEXT STEP

Managers who understand clearly the different principles underlying mechanistic and life-system thinking are able to distinguish the management practices that these two modes of thought inspire. Even without realizing it, managers demonstrate life-system principles when they concentrate on practices that continuously link company and customer in every step of an organization's work. When virtually every action in every one of a company's parts links a customer's need and the company's ability to serve that need, the ends and means are seamlessly connected. And where adherence to MBM principles seamlessly connects means and ends, one sees more than gratified customers. Equally pleased are employees themselves.

Once people in business believe that better long-term results inevitably emerge if one concentrates attention on nurturing proper relationships rather than on striving to reach quantitative targets, it would not be surprising to see that message spread quickly to people in government and in education. Indeed, the public's perception that mechanistic practices brought efficiency to businesses had much to do with the spread of those practices to government and education in the last forty or fifty years. Surely it is not unreasonable to expect a similar transfer of MBM management thinking and practice to occur in the next generation.

Beyond that, those who learn to live by cultivating relationships in organizations will grow to appreciate a connectedness with nature that people in the last two generations have lost by trying to run organizations with quantitative targets. An example of this new appreciation is found today among those who are trying to restore traditional farming practices in agriculture. Unlike modern techno-farmers who myopically focus on quantity, traditional farmers always knew that preserving soil, essential to support and renew life, takes precedence over meeting arbitrary financial targets, particularly targets that require damaging the soil. However, today's techno-farmers, driving to achieve quantitative results, disregard practices that join farming to a healthy ecosystem. Instead, they use chemicals, pesticides, and capital-intensive processes to drive output. They seek only to achieve computer-driven, commercial targets. A traditional farmer recognizes the natural patterns in the soil, that great repository of "decay and repose." He preserves the rich humus of natural soil that spontaneously generates, according to some biologists, energy equivalent to one horsepower per acre every day.[13]

Surely, if MBM were to become the habitual way of conducting work in business, in government, and in education, it would inevitably shape the way humans interact with the ecosystem that supports life on Earth itself. MBM is predicated, of course, on the belief that the best long-term results await organizations whose practices emulate those principles that govern the behavior of natural living systems. MBM reunites that which human mechanistic thinking has separated. In effect, MBM organizations *by definition* move closer to working in harmony with nature's living system. This does nothing to change that living system itself. However, it will markedly improve the human condition. The next and final chapter will explore this ultimate consequence of MBM in more detail.

CONCLUSION

Management practices must harmonize with the principles that govern the operation of natural systems. Enlightened managers will use words and stories to identify and describe how practices in every part of the organization may become consistent with nature's principles. By adhering to practices characteristic of nature's system, companies will experience success. Each part of the organization, each individual and each system, must embody the principles adhered to in life systems. In so doing, the organization becomes a web of relationships that produces results which exceed the sum of its parts. The pattern embodied in that web of relationships is the "spirit in the walls," as Scania's people say. Nurture this spirit, and the organization will flourish.

Further, by nurturing the spirit that prevails in nature's system, organizations will contribute immeasurably toward lessening the dissonance between human thinking and "the way nature works" that is the root of most problems in modern society. For this way of thinking gave rise to the highly mechanical view of business that led, after the 1950s, to the practices we refer to as "managing by results." These MBR practices focus attention on achieving unlimited homogeneous growth of quantitative targets, not on *the creative and sustainable pursuit of unlimited qualitative enrichment with limited means.* Accordingly, today's managers ignore all properties and relationships in their organizations that cannot be quantified. Values and nonquantifiable patterns are passed over in favor of simply accumulating more and more of quantifiable "bottom-line" targets.

Quantification requires "separating into parts" a world that *naturally belongs together.* Nature equips human beings to do what is needed to harmonize with its system. Our problem is to let go of the need to achieve financial targets and to concentrate instead on doing what is right. Modern science reinforces again and again the point that a hidden wholeness underlies the manifold variety of visible things around us. Physicist David Bohm, reflecting ideas similar to thinkers as various as Pythagoras, Aristotle, William Blake, Johann Wolfgang von Goethe, and Gregory Bateson, referred to this wholeness as an "implicate order." Modern organizational thought obscures for us this implicit wholeness. To find this wholeness involves what is aptly called "organizational healing."[14] Recovery, healing, a return to health are possible if managers focus on the means, not results. They will be capable of focusing on the means—on processes and details, on every worker and each step—only when they understand that organizations are adaptive living systems and as such must adhere to nature's principles. Upon their adherence depend the health and well-being of businesses and all other human organizations.

7

....

What's Natural Comes Hard

The major problems of the world are the result of
the difference between the way nature works and
the way man thinks.

—Gregory Bateson[1]

Most businesses have difficulty achieving satisfactory long-term financial performance because their mechanistic management practices ignore nature's principle of interdependence and give virtually no consideration to relationships. Instead, they focus almost exclusively on the quantitative dimensions of size and scale. Virtually every business in the world today strives to grow perpetually. Each business currently sees itself entitled to expand as much as its ability to earn money will allow it to grow.

For all practical purposes, today's businesses acknowledge no limit to size. However, for centuries most businesses did recognize limits. Limits were imposed by family, community, and regional relationships. Businesses served local needs as defined by a well-understood nexus of relationships. The extent of one's money-making was circumscribed by the limits of family capital, community resources, and regional markets.[2] Although the boundaries of family, community, and region were breached in the late nineteenth century by a few very large companies, those large companies still remained exceptions until the 1950s. But since the 1950s businesses have pursued unending growth as if it were a normal way of life.

In view of the business world's obsession with growth, it is notable that no system in the universe seems ever to grow in size without limit. The only exception may be the universe itself, which appears always to be expanding in every direction, albeit perhaps at a decelerating rate. Apart from that one exception, nothing in the universe grows endlessly in size. Rather than quantitative growth, the universe displays endless growth in quality, manifest by the continual diversification of its parts.

The desire of businesses to grow endlessly in size presupposes a system in which the principle of self-organization in natural living systems operates, but not the principles of interdependence and diversity. In other words, relentless economic growth assumes that the human species can with impunity articulate its own purposes unchecked by imperatives to relate to, or to honor, the diverse purposes of other species. The inevitable consequence is "one of the most terrible things of our time—the destruction of species and their habitats, the elimination of some living beings forever."[3]

Managing by means may to some extent curtail this destruction. MBM will increase the level and reduce the volatility of a company's long-term profitability (B in Figure 2–4). That may be reason enough for most companies to take it seriously. However, there is a far more important reason to promote MBM practices. These practices force humans in their daily lives to honor nature's principles of interdependence and diversity as well as the principle of self-articulation. Possessing their own unique and ineffable creative power, human beings attend less than do other species to the imperatives to relate and to honor diversity. The fact is, human creativity is both a grave danger and a great blessing. Balancing that twin potential for danger and fulfillment in every moment, in every act, is the essence of the human condition. Today's global economic activity, because it equates fulfillment too much with quantitative growth rather than qualitative enrichment, prompts humans to encroach too far, too fast on the habitats of other species. MBM practices may do more than any single thing in the next generation to reverse the deteriorating human and environmental conditions that accompany unchecked human expansion. Limiting and reducing that damage, while working relentlessly to raise living standards of the poorest third of humanity, is arguably the most pressing problem of our time. MBM calls for new thinking that may enable business organizations to lead the way toward resolving that problem in the next century.

For hundreds of centuries, humans have used their unique creative powers to escape what they perceive to be the terror, violence, and insecurity of living in nature's system. In so doing, they have in effect created a separate support system to serve their desires. Although this separate system—the human economic system—has generated some very remarkable features in its brief ten thousand or so years, it has done so by drawing down Earth's restorative capacity to a dangerous degree. Working with tools and language, humans have steadily created a situation separate from the conditions existing in nature's system. For example, by domesticating other life forms—plants and animals—humans created a food supply that they intended would always be more predictable and more abundant than the supply of food that nature provides for the taking. Moreover, humans fabricated shelter and clothing that enabled families, clans, and tribes to remain settled in the same place over long periods of time rather than having to migrate with nature's seasons and with the patterns of other animals they relied on for food. They have created technologies associated with agriculture, settlement, and modern industrial activity. Their mechanistic thinking has enabled human population to grow until humans now occupy space in virtually every corner of Earth, and even beyond Earth. They have planted footprints on the Moon and machine tracks on Mars. However, these very triumphs have increasingly divorced humankind from the natural ecosystem that does sustain all life on Earth. Among human inventions that particularly threaten the health of nature's ecosystem is the modern global business enterprise. Their extreme emphasis on quantitative growth causes global businesses to operate according to very different principles than those which govern the cyclical and restorative practices of the natural ecosystem.

The human economic system can persist, ironically, only as long as nature's ecosystem has the capacity to absorb and restore the destructive consequences that occur when human striving is at variance with nature. Nature does have an enormous capacity to regenerate the resources destroyed each year by human activity. It has absorbed the costs of human activities for eons. But recent signs such as global warming and high rates of species extinction cause many concerned observers to believe that the exponentially rising power of human technology is approaching the limits of nature's capacity to replenish the resources that human expansion destroys.[4] These concerns echo the prescient warnings of Gregory Bateson, Rachel Carson, Barry Commoner, Paul Ehrlich, Aldo Leopold, and others over forty years ago who predicted these consequences if human beings did not begin to cooperate more and clash less with the ecosystem. Widespread adoption of MBM practices in large businesses should do much to alleviate these consequences.

MBM does not deny the value of human creative self-articulation. It does not ask of humans that they sacrifice their inborn technological prowess and revert to the life style of hunter-gatherers. Far from it. Instead, it continually stimulates awareness of relationships and of the power of diversity so that creativity will occur "in the context of," not "to the exclusion of." The cost of increasing exclusion includes poisoned rivers and lakes, depleted aquifers, eroded plains, forests of farmed trees devoid of wildlife and as monotonous to walk through as a cornfield, oceans where the hum of high-speed ships replaces the sounds of cetaceans, starless light-polluted night skies, endless miles of unbroken densely packed urban development, and much, much worse.

Attempts to explain how the unparalleled gift of human creativity has led to what many consider the brink of human desolation have produced one particularly compelling answer in recent years. Modern science tells us, really for the first time ever, that the human being is a self-correcting system immersed in a virtually infinite web of self-correcting systems encompassing the entire Earth and all the universe beyond. The lesson of this discovery is that a self-correcting system imbedded in a sea of self-correcting systems *must act very, very carefully.* The key property of such a system of systems is that it makes continual small changes to check and balance against the excesses of any one component in the system becoming a threat to the system's survival. Hence, any component of the system that somehow acquires the power to promote its own particular agenda, like the human species on Earth, faces difficult conditions and ultimate extinction if it pursues its own self-interest for a long enough period.

The nineteenth-century naturalist and evolutionary biologist Alfred Russel Wallace saw the concept of natural selection as an example of

this check-and-balancing power of natural living systems. He anticipated the modern cybernetic explanation of natural selection when he
compared it metaphorically to the governor that stabilizes the speed of
a steam engine. He said "[the governor] checks and corrects any irreg-
ularities almost before they become evident; and in like manner [nat-
ural selection insures that] no unbalanced deficiency in the animal
kingdom can ever reach any conspicuous magnitude, because it would
make itself felt at the very first step, by rendering existence difficult and
extinction almost sure to follow."[5] The human being implicitly defies
natural selection, and all other self-balancing mechanisms in nature, by
using its unique creative power to extend its own domain without
regard for the welfare of other species or the total life-support system
itself.

Writing a century after Wallace, the pioneering systems thinker
Gregory Bateson attributed this human tendency to our unique ability
to pursue conscious purpose. Bateson asserted that the human mind
has a unique power to override its innate awareness, or wisdom, of nature's interactive self-corrective system and to self-consciously pursue
what it wants—its own purposes. As a consequence, human techno-
economic activity, like a spear ripping through delicate fabric, cuts a
linear path through a world of intricately interrelated systems, leaving
disorder and ugliness in its wake. While humans have exercised this
power for eons, the effect today is particularly devastating because of
the unusually destructive potential of modern high technology. Describing this process, Bateson said:

> On the one hand, we have the systemic nature of the individual human
> being, the systemic nature of the culture in which he lives, and the sys-
> temic nature of the biological, ecological system around him; and, on
> the other hand, the curious twist in the systemic nature of the individ-
> ual man whereby consciousness is, almost of necessity, blinded to the
> systemic nature of the man himself. Purposive consciousness pulls out,
> from the total mind, sequences which do not have the loop structure
> which is characteristic of the whole systemic structure. If you follow the
> "common-sense" dictates of consciousness you become, effectively,
> greedy and unwise—again I use "wisdom" as a word for recognition of
> and guidance by a knowledge of the total systemic creature.

Lack of systemic wisdom is always punished. We may say that the biological systems—the individual, the culture, and the ecology—are partly living sustainers of their component cells or organisms. But the systems are nonetheless punishing of any species unwise enough to quarrel with its ecology.[6]

Bateson went on to point out that we fail to see the systemic forces underlying the problems—the desolation—created by the human pursuit of goals and purposes. We blame the problems either on our own shortcomings or on the system's vengeance. Either way, the solutions we pursue all share one thing in common—a belief that we can overcome the problems simply by gaining more knowledge, by trying harder, by doing more of the same, only smarter.

In a sense, what Bateson describes as the pursuit of conscious purpose resembles what we have described as MBR—managing by results. With blatant disregard of the means, of how a system of self-correcting systems works, the MBR culture pursues its own particular purposes relentlessly. This pursuit generates growth and accumulation—what are considered its necessary results—for a time at least. The progress toward goals is not without periodic setbacks, of course. Yet, exponential "progress" can occur for periods that on a human time scale are quite long, say centuries. But, as Bateson says, "lack of systemic wisdom is always punished."

The punishment may come with a bang, or it may elicit no more than a whimper. No one knows, yet. However, we might escape punishment, or at least delay it indefinitely, if we pay heed to the message of Bateson, and many others, that there is hope if we become more attentive to wisdom—"the way nature works"—and be less intent on using technological knowledge to evade constraints—"the way man thinks." This approach to life resembles what this book refers to as MBM—managing by means. It advocates recognizing and submitting to the dictates of the system that sustains all life. MBM thereby can sustain more satisfying results for longer than can any MBR process that humans design to meet their own particular purposes.

Adopting MBM thought and practices—following the "natural" way—is not easy. There is no simple way, no royal road to substituting "the way nature works" for "the way man thinks." One reason for the difficulty is that the human mind, the source of our perceptions that define conscious purpose, is itself a system that self-corrects against disturbance. It has the capacity to learn what disturbs its own status quo and what, therefore, should be checked against in order to protect and conserve that status quo. Moreover, we create cultural, social, and educational institutions designed to reinforce that learning and to conserve the status quo. Indeed, our minds and our institutions make it much simpler to stay with "the way man thinks" than to pursue "the way nature works."

This dilemma is expressed succinctly in two lines from a song by Stephen Sondheim: "What's hard is simple, What's natural comes hard."[7] The lines are sung by a young woman who finds it simple to do things most people find hard, namely, read Greek, do higher mathematics, and dance ballet. She is troubled, however, that she finds it hard to whistle, *something that should be natural.* What's natural—to whistle (or to reflect on and master how nature works)—is hard. Pleading for help, the young woman in Sondheim's song acknowledges that learning to whistle may require her to learn "how to let go, lower my guard, learn to be free." *Learn to be free.* The promise that MBM holds out to those who only manage by results is freedom—the freedom that comes from realizing *the result is already there,* and is ours to have as a gift, if only we will surrender to the "spirit in the walls" and master practices that nurture life-system principles. The writer Henry Miller expressed this idea beautifully when he said that "the world is not to be put in order, the world is order incarnate. It is for us to put ourselves in unison with this order."[8]

According to Bateson, we can do this if we acquire humility, lose the scientific arrogance that tells us we have limitless power to control nature, and engage our minds in realms that encompass more than just the consciously purposeful part. In other words, nurture the *entire* creative process as humans have expressed it in art, poetry, music, mythology, and religion. Understand that evolution is not the story of species learning more tricks for controlling their environment, with the human being having the best tricks of all. Come to see that we humans ultimately have no control over nature. Nevertheless, humans do have a special power that enables them to reflect on the working of the system itself. With that power, humans are, in Thomas Berry's words, "the universe reflecting upon itself." MBM has the potential to restore, in business organizations at least, the power to reflect on and act in partnership with that natural system, as opposed to creating processes designed to reach unnatural targets that fly in the face of that system.

This same message has been expressed eloquently by the poet Gary Snyder who says that "the longing for growth is not wrong. The nub of the problem now is how to flip over, as in jujitsu, the magnificent growth energy of modern civilization into a nonacquisitive search for deeper knowledge of self and nature. Self-nature. Mother Nature. If people come to realize that there are many nonmaterial, nondestructive paths of growth—of the highest and most fascinating order—it would help dampen the common fear that a steady state economy would mean deadly stagnation."[9]

What Snyder says about growth gets to the heart of what the shift from MBR to MBM will entail. The desire of living systems to grow is natural, not wrong. Indeed, the first principle of living systems is about growth. The issue we face in the business world is to transform our obsession with quantitative growth in size into a delight with qualitative growth in diversity, until that delight becomes the energizing force in our lives. This transformation can completely change our use of the term energy. Instead of seeing energy as something we take from natural sources to alter and mold matter to our purposes, MBM can cause us to see it as a life force that we acquire from nurturing and delighting in an inherent property of nature that already exists in all the matter around us. More to the point, by delighting in natural qualitative growth we are less inclined to use natural sources of energy to destroy order in nature for our increasingly homogeneous mass-production purposes. Instead, we will discover energy in the delight that comes from participating in the order that already exists in nature's continually diversifying system.[10]

HOW MBM MIGHT HEAL THE RIFT BETWEEN BUSINESS AND NATURE

Managers who accept the above propositions and who choose to manage the means will implicitly engage their companies in healing the rift between nature's ecosystem and humankind's economic system. An MBM company will certainly pursue various healing activities once it extends the scope of its interests from focusing only on the organization's quantitative growth to enhancing the diversity of nature's life system. The following five subsections contain examples of such activities that companies might pursue to bring human economic affairs into closer harmony with nature's support system.

Transportation

Makers of automobiles are already showing increased awareness of human and environmental concerns by searching for economically viable ways to dramatically reduce fossil fuel consumption, to promote more recycling of materials used to make cars, and to design cars that are safer, longer lasting, and maintenance free. We can hope that their concern for the impact automobiles have on the human community and on nature's ecosystem will cause auto makers also to explore how they might profitably help society alter its use of urban and recreational space to reduce, ultimately, the demand for automobiles. No greater concentration of talent exists in the world to deal with this issue than that found in the engineering and marketing talent currently employed in the automotive industry. Undoubtedly their efforts to ameliorate the impact of the past half-century's unchecked automotive consumption could generate as much, or more, employment and income as that currently generated to produce the world's entire auto output.

In this spirit, auto makers might profitably address their energies to helping communities achieve the following possibilities: Make shopping and work accessible on foot or on bicycle by reducing the scale, and decentralizing the location, of commercial sites in urban areas. Criss-cross urban areas with truly safe bicycle and pedestrian pathways separate from automobile highways and streets. Downsize and decentralize public transportation systems to make door-to-door public transport services a reality. Decrease commuting by enhancing access to interactive video communication systems in homes and in neighborhood sites. Create large and significantly varied open spaces for human recreation in urban areas, thus reducing the demand to travel to find "nature." Create truly useful and dependable regional and interregional railroad systems devoted primarily to transporting people between large urban areas. Sharply curtail automotive access in the few genuinely wild areas left in the world and work to expand the size of those areas.

Initially, these possibilities probably will strike most business executives as irresponsible, even foolish. Implementing such projects will lead, they will say, to economic depression and social disaster. Any proposal for change that, for example, systematically reduces automobile production over the long haul, automobile manufacturers will reject outright. But more is at stake here than economic consequences. If efforts to increase the quantitative output of the human economic system threaten our place in nature's ecosystem, we need to rethink how we do business in the long term. Since efforts to protect and restore the human niche in the ecosystem will protect and sustain the human economic system in the long term, it behooves us to plan strategies that reduce the human threat to other life forms. Widespread adoption of MBM thought and practice, hopefully, will help business leaders understand that business is inextricably linked with and affects all of nature.

Other, nonautomotive, modes of transportation have also become implicated in serious environmental problems in recent years because of the rapid expansion of global business activity. One such problem is the increased demand for local and regional shipping that is fueled both by the worldwide adoption of "just-in-time" (JIT) practices that began in manufacturing in the 1980s and by the boom in outsourcing that occurred in the 1990s. The results of JIT and outsourcing, on the whole, have been beneficial to manufacturers' bottom lines and to their customers' prices. Companies discovered that by rethinking how they organized work inside the factory, they could produce more output at less cost, use less space, move material shorter distances, and shorten production lead times. The savings, for the most part, have been passed on to customers.

Often overlooked, however, is the cost of JIT and outsourcing beyond the individual company's factory. Using JIT has generally caused companies to ship far more frequently and outsourcing has prompted more shipping over longer distances. The costs of this more frequent and more distant shipping are not reflected, of course, on the books of the organizations implementing JIT and outsourcing. Instead, they are recorded externally on the books of shippers and others who are charging for services that did not exist before JIT and outsourcing were adopted. The net impact on society at large and on the ecosystem of increasingly congested highways, seaways, and airways seems so far to have gone largely unremarked. On the other hand, a potential long-term benefit of outsourcing may be the spread of strong local manufacturing activities and greater self-reliance in all parts of the world.

Energy

The adoption of manage-by-means thought and practice in fuel or mineral extraction companies opens the door to resolving what is one of the most pressing environmental problems of our time—the release into Earth's atmosphere at unsustainable rates of substances that nature extracted from the atmosphere and stored inside Earth millions of years ago. Lynn Margulis speculates that the Earth's deposits of oil and coal are the carbon "fixed" by photosynthesis in vast forests of vegetation that grew everywhere on Earth at a time before there were microbes capable of decomposing plant cells.[11] Buried deep beneath the surface by massive tectonic shifts and covered by countless layers of volcanic material, these plant deposits, under extreme pressure and heat, simply reverted directly back into the carbon state from which they originated. With the carbon that is fixed in those deposits removed from the Earth's atmosphere millions of years ago by natural photosynthesis, the resulting atmosphere allowed animal life as we know it, including all mammalian life, to emerge and flourish. We should recall this story as we release each year into the atmosphere the amount of carbon that nature took tens of thousands of years to remove from the atmosphere. This present rate of consumption seriously damages the atmosphere, as "global warming" suggests.

Were oil and coal companies to adopt manage-by-means thinking and practices, they would wish to build and nurture relationships that encompass the ecosystem that supports all life. Such a focus would put high on the list of an oil or coal company's projects, the study of activities and processes, such as solar energy projects, that make fossil-fuel consumption unnecessary. To develop efficient non-fossil-fuel-using processes and activities might be as profitable as is the extraction and sale of oil and coal today.

Environmental Management Practices and MBM

Many environmental management concepts, including life-cycle thinking, design for environment, industrial ecology, and total quality environmental management, will conceivably stimulate manage-by-means thinking by encouraging companies to follow practices that address social and ecological concerns. Those concepts encourage practices such as environmental impact assessment, environmental performance evaluation, and integrated substance chain management.[12] Certainly those practices are compatible with the principles that guide living systems. However, companies seeking to be identified as environmentally caring and "green" often pursue such practices within a growth-oriented, target-driven, mechanistic MBR context that scarcely conforms to the principles of a living system. Environmental watchdogs refer to such pursuits as "green washing."

The new *thinking* identified with living system principles and MBM practices is the key transformation that must occur in companies today. Companies cannot make that transformation simply by adopting environmental programs that do not change traditional management thinking. Reducing toxic effluents and replanting cut-over forest are commendable actions. However, if they are part of an overall strategy of unrestricted growth in production and consumption to maximize shareholder wealth, their long-term significance must be considered ambiguous at best. If an environmental program is supposed to cause a company's thinking and behavior to harmonize more with living system principles, then surely it will alter traditional attitudes about growth. If a company's leaders still view endless growth in size and output as a critical determinant of business success, then it is not certain that the environmental program has helped them understand nature's principles and MBM practices.

The conflict between ecology and growth is seen in programs of "The Natural Step," an environmental management movement that recently has gained enormous popularity around the world. Conceived in the late 1980s by Karl-Henrik Róbert, a Swedish biologist and physician whose career was devoted to the study and cure of cancer, The Natural Step is an organization that promotes a framework of concepts for evaluating the environmental impact of an organization's activities.[13]

Essentially, TNS proposes that businesses see their activities through the lens of life systems, especially those systems observed in the plant and animal cells that are ubiquitous building blocks of life on Earth. Basic "system conditions" that TNS urges businesses to follow reflect two fundamental rules: engage only in practices that benefit cellular processes, or at least do no harm; and desist from actions that reduce natural habitat and impair its ability to nurture diversity of life forms.

It is encouraging that many companies around the world are evaluating their affairs in the light of TNS principles. Unfortunately, companies often adopt TNS principles without first evaluating and challenging their existing MBR thinking and practices. The upshot of pursuing TNS under MBR conditions may be the same as adopting any one of the recently popular programs for performance improvement such as reengineering, TQM, time-compression management, or lean manufacturing while still being driven by financial targets and results. Such improvement programs have too often failed in the past decade or so because they were seen merely as another way to improve profitability by cutting costs or raising revenue, not by mastering disciplined practices that emulate the pattern in natural life systems.

The same fate might befall TNS if companies that adopt its principles fail to understand the difference between the quantitative focus of MBR and the qualitative focus of MBM. A company committed to practices that are based on MBR principles cannot achieve the original goals of TNS.[14] Consuming less and recycling are innate features of the natural world that companies and individuals strive to emulate by following TNS principles. But businesses that recycle more do little to restore health to the natural world if what is recycled arises from a continuing stream of growing output. Likewise, individuals who simplify their life styles do little to help the natural world if consuming less consists of no more than "downscaling" their purchases from expensive department stores to discount houses.

Expanding Order-Line Stories to Encompass Bateson's Wider View

Organizations that adopt MBM thought and practices will discover the advantage of extending order-line stories to encompass the consequences of nurturing all life forms. Ideally, efforts to accommodate ecosystemic imperatives will become an automatic part of the continuous flow of work that accompanies each order in a business. Such efforts should be included in all studies of the order line, the place where customer and company unite.

Order-line profitability analysis provides companies with an answer to those who argue that "environmental" initiatives must pass cost-benefit tests before being adopted. In an MBM world, a company will evaluate such initiatives in terms of their impact on the company's ability to fulfill the principles governing the operation of natural life systems. Living by such principles means emulating the most efficient and effective systems yet contemplated by the human mind. Doing so implicitly meets long-term cost-benefit tests. That implies talking in words, not in quantities, about how an initiative affects the company's ability to embrace constraints that will sustain the union between company, customer, community, and the ecosystem for generations to come.

The Internet

The Internet is a technological breakthrough of such import that it virtually defies description at this time. On the one hand it is a global system of electronic interconnections that some people believe rivals the human brain in complexity and power. On the other hand, it has the potential to turn virtually every human act into an economic transaction and thereby commercialize all human affairs. As a global system of interconnections it has the power to reverse much of the encroachment on Earth's habitat caused by the last century or two of economic development. For example, it can sharply reduce the demand for interregional travel by allowing people in the near future to communicate at virtually no cost with anyone, anytime, anywhere by audio and visual means. At the same time, as an instrument for conducting commercial transactions instantaneously from anywhere on Earth it has the power to accelerate human encroachment on habitat to a degree never thought possible even five to ten years ago. The prospect of a world overrun by interregional and local transport carrying every single product consumed from its producer anywhere to final consumers everywhere is an unimaginable horror.

How humans choose to use the Internet is a decision that warrants global conversations on a scale never before contemplated. Whether or not such dialogue unfolds, it is important not to lose sight of the fact that economic activity will still entail as much, or more, consumption and waste of resources whether or not it is mediated by the Internet. Don't be beguiled by notions that the electronic age has moved humans out of an industrial economy. Today there is more manufacturing of material products than ever before in history, and the amount is growing exponentially at this moment. A physical product ordered over the Internet still must be made by someone, somewhere, and it must be shipped somehow to the buyer. The activities that people engage in to make and ship those things still consume materials from the Earth and still generate waste that must be disposed of for better or worse.

Thus, the message in this book applies more than ever in an age of Internet commerce. Humans conducting economic activity need to think about relationships between supplier and customer, relationships among the people who make up the supply chain—whether that chain be a virtual electronic network of free-market agents or a company of employees working under one roof—and relationships between humans and the ecosystem that supports all life on Earth. Whether those relationships will honor the imperative of diversity or generate stultifying mass homogeneity is still an open issue even when commerce is conducted via electronic means. Whether they communicate electronically or by signal fire, people in businesses always will face the question: does my behavior reflect thinking that honors principles guiding the operation of natural living systems, or does it reflect thinking that emulates the principles of mechanistic systems?

CONCLUSION

The decade of the 1990s was a remarkable time for businesses around the world. Business conditions everywhere produced bullish economic news and glowing company reports. Businesses everywhere experienced steady growth and constantly improving financial performance. It is widely recognized, however, that the world's booming economy, with its successful global enterprises, is threatening Earth's life-sustaining ecosystem. The best of times for businesses proves also to be the most dangerous of times. A booming economy built on the financial success of global enterprises seems inexorably linked to environmental destruction so great that it threatens humanity's long-term survival. This economy also seems linked to human disaffection. At the same time that companies of every kind are reporting record-breaking financial performance, numerous publications and seminars dwell on the need to restore spirit and soul to business. These circumstances suggest that the very companies breaking financial performance records are among those contributing both to ecological devastation and to alienation, fragmentation, fear, and burnout in the workplace.

Although business organizations are an example of a life system, humans choose repeatedly to treat them as machines. Thinking mechanistically, oblivious to the principles underlying the evolution of all matter in the universe, today's business and economic leaders have devised systems that threaten mass extinction. These leaders not only do not grasp and nurture the pattern underlying life, but they thwart it. Therefore, our now widely acclaimed global economic system promises, in the words of poet Gary Snyder, "the death of birth." This system inordinately pursues growth at the cost of the individual worker's dignity, distress in the company and the community, and the health of the ecosystem.

Humankind disturbs and disrupts the delicately poised universe. Why? Because conscious purpose enables human beings to remove constraints that interfere with their ambitions and impede their progress. In short, humankind disposes of whatever it perceives to be an obstacle. Erroneously, humankind regards as obstacles all impediments to endless human expansion, infinite growth, and limitless ambition. Indulging infinite longing for security, wealth, and power, human beings use their technological prowess to obliterate impediments. This technological expertise diminishes or otherwise destroys the habitats of all living creatures, disrupts evolution, and threatens the extinction, if not of all life, certainly of human and most animal life.

To put in perspective the devastating impact of the voracious human appetite to realize its every single aspiration, consider that no prehuman life forms ever attempted to remove obstacles to serve their own purposes. Rather, earlier life forms *embraced* obstacles. For example, efforts to "embrace . . . gravity's hindrances to motion" gave rise in time to "the wings of the birds . . . the musculature of the elephants . . . and the anatomy of the cheetah."[15] Humans, on the other hand, to avoid pain, sacrifice, and suffering, "took control" of nature's processes in order to "enjoy" relentless expansion of human space. These efforts to control by *removing* perceived obstacles have brought unarguable benefits, but have also prompted unimaginable disruption, loss, misery, and violence.

Currently managers responsible for bulldozing everything on the pathway to achieve shareholder wealth are the strongest proponents of MBR. Their results-oriented style of management prompts them to "take control" for the sake of growth, expansion, and accumulation. Those who manage by results, oblivious to nature's patterns, impose human objectives on nature's system. In so doing, they violate nature's fundamental principles of self-organization, interdependence, and diversity. In place of those principles they impose their own artificial construct: a measurable, quantifiable arrow aimed at a measurable target.

A massive disjunction exists between the mechanistic practices most business managers embrace and the way nature works. The remarkable differences between nature's processes and the practices of those who manage by results explains why so many corporations are sources of increasing personal, social, and ecological misery. Until managers abandon the growth-oriented practices called for by mechanistic, MBR thinking, this misery will only increase and intensify. It is therefore imperative that leaders of businesses, indeed of all organizations, adopt a new way of thinking and behaving. They need to promote all life on Earth. They need to discover that true order is not imposed by human agents. It is immanent in nature.

Surely business leaders must eventually realize that they do have a choice. They can choose to either nurture or destroy humankind's place in the ecosystem. Business leaders can choose to either fashion organizations that trespass against nature's pattern or create organizations that blend harmoniously and constructively with the rest of nature, thus enhancing all life. Business organizations are sufficiently flexible to adopt a new worldview that reflects nature's principles. Businesses are positioned to lead the way. Ultimately, every human organization—in business, government, or education—must incorporate the new worldview if the Earth is to prove a viable home for future generations.

Business and national leaders would do well to conduct economic affairs according to the three principles that guide the operation of natural living systems. Pursuit of nature's principle of self-organization, coupled with adherence to nature's principle of interdependence, will lead to businesses that nurture relationships. When the human creative impulse focuses on relationships, humankind will reinforce nature's principle of diversity. The flowering of diversity sustains all life in the universe. Businesses leaders who cultivate diversity maintain nature's delicate balance between creation and absorption.

This book urges leaders in business to accept the findings of recent science. It urges them to pay attention to scientific evidence that a universal pattern of connectedness embraces all matter in the universe. It calls upon leaders of *all* organizations to see that a universal pattern permeates each individual and every human organization. It calls upon them to honor this pattern and in so doing to lead the world into a new century of harmony to be enjoyed by businesses, workers, society, and the ecosystem which sustains all life.

....

by Leif Östling

During almost thirty years in the automotive industry, I have had the privilege to work for a company named Scania, which is a Swedish manufacturer of heavy commercial vehicles. For the last ten years, I have acted as the CEO of the company.

The commercial vehicle industry has gone through a radical consolidation in Europe since the beginning of the 1970s, dwindling from almost thirty manufacturers to six today. During these years, Scania has always been looked upon as being too small in scale. However, Scania has always been by far the most profitable company in the commercial vehicle industry. The wave of consolidation finally hit Scania in August 1999, when another, more well-known Swedish manufacturer, Volvo, acquired Scania. This acquisition marks the beginning of a new era for Scania. I approach this new era with keen interest in part because of what I have learned from working with Anders Bröms and, more recently, with Tom Johnson.

In late 1992, Anders Bröms sent me Tom Johnson's book *Relevance Regained.* In *Relevance Regained,* Bröms and I found confirmation of studies we had initiated fifteen years ago. Carried out in the Netherlands and Germany, these analyses demonstrated that known accounting methods were by far not enough to understand a complex business organization. With the order-line profitability analysis, I realized for the first time how important the interconnections of different work or activities in an organization are for its overall efficiency. This is something accounting never measures. Early in 1993, Anders Bröms and I invited Tom Johnson to talk about his work and to discuss using Scania as a site for his ongoing field research. He readily agreed, and a long collaboration started, as a result of which I have moved from seeing a business through the lens of a cost-focused macro model—bottom-line thinking—to a micro model based on how the different parts are linked together. Focusing on the connections among parts, on how the work is done, is a fundamental principle of "managing by means," the phrase in *Profit Beyond Measure* that describes new management thinking. "Managing by means" involves examining how work is done rather than driving work with financial targets.

It is interesting to consider Scania's efficient product design system from the perspective of "managing by means" principles. That system, which we call a "modular design system," cannot be understood with a pure financial model. A financial model merely indicates that the system is superior to that used in other companies. It does reveal that for generations, Scania has developed and nurtured a specific, distinctive design practice. This design practice is deeply imbedded in the culture of the company and drives design work in a certain direction. Scania's close attention to the design system is similar to Toyota's attention to its production system. Toyota's production system (TPS) is built on deeply rooted practices which have been developed during many years and which are always the subject of continuous improvement. With Tom Johnson's help and Anders Bröms's support, Scania established contacts with Toyota Motor Manufacturing in Georgetown, Kentucky. Both Toyota and Scania have developed similar strategies to achieve an immense variation in specifications of vehicles, Scania with a unique modular design system and Toyota with a unique production system. These "management by means" cultures have contributed at both Toyota and Scania to an enviable record of long-term financial success. No other companies in their respective industries can match these long-term records.

The acquisition of Scania by Volvo will certainly be an interesting case to follow. Scania, on the one hand, emphasizes through its design system the "management by means" described in *Profit Beyond Measure*. Moreover, since the 1920s Scania has been guided by a strong owner, the Wallenberg family. Volvo, on the other hand, is a traditional "management by results" company driven by financial targets. The two different cultures of Volvo and Scania will from now on be co-managed. But the Wallenbergs will also step in as dominating share-holder, which could lead to a radical change for an "ownerless" com-pany such as Volvo. An "ownerless" company, a company owned entirely by mutual funds, hedge funds, and so forth, often fares differ-ently than one that has an owner.

During my many years working in Scania with its approximately 25,000 employees, I have met and worked with a number of small and medium-sized companies often owned by an entrepreneur. My experi-ence has been that those entrepreneurs understand and apply the prin-ciples of "management by means." They know that the success of their business depends on the people working with them. It depends on how these people carry out their work. These entrepreneurs live the message in *Profit Beyond Measure*. The bottom line is useful for the banks that loan companies money and for the fiscal authorities. It is not useful for running the company. Some of these companies owned by entrepre-neurs have grown into worldwide organizations. As long as the entre-preneur stays with his company, the focus continues to be rather on the "means" than on the "results."

Invariably when the entrepreneur leaves and professional man-agers—"hired gunmen"—take over, the "result" orientation starts to dominate management's thinking. In an "ownerless" company, the "management by means" is in many cases forgotten. In the eyes of many of the fund managers running "ownerless" companies, a com-pany represents a black box which can be plugged into a PC model. The task for the company's CEO, who frequently meets with these fund managers, is, together with his executive team, to take the box and subdivide it into new boxes, pushing these to steadily lower levels in the hierarchy. Few in the top seem to understand that the sub-boxes con-tinuously interact with each other in an immense web of information and activities. Instead, top managers focus on measurements. To para-phrase Dr. W. Edwards Deming, although we can only quantify 3 per-cent of all that is going on in an organization, management seems to devote 97 percent of its time to that measurement effort.

The traditional bottom-line focus taught today in universities around the world inhibits the student's ability to understand the 97 percent of a business organization that Deming said it is impossible to quantify. More could indeed be quantified with nonlinear models, but we have found it is typically hard to conceptualize those and even more difficult to apply them. But we can take a much easier way: we can study how nature takes care of its business, in a manner of speaking, by developing simple, robust, and efficient learning structures with a minimum of waste and with immense variation to satisfy every individual customer's demands. The book *Profit Beyond Measure* will help every reader better understand the 97 percent which is not quantifiable. It will explain what really determines a business organization's profit performance. Personally, I believe that the old-timers in business like myself born in the mid 1940s will have problems taking this message to their hearts, but I am definitely convinced that the coming generation of top managers born in the 1970s will find the message is quite "natural."

The connection between the way nature works and how companies operate made in *Profit Beyond Measure* raises interesting ways to look at the Scania-Volvo merger. For example, in nature, mergers are commonplace. Different entities come together, each retains its own identity, and together they cooperate to create yet another entity. As Tom Johnson explains it—and I will not go deeply at this point into the scientific details—the evolution of the plant cell involved such a merger.[1] Some bacteria at one point swallowed, but did not digest, types of cells known as chloroplasts and mitochondria, with beneficial consequences for the bacteria, the chloroplasts, and the mitochondria. Each of these unique life forms retained its own identity while at the same time developing a mutually beneficial cooperative system that became the plant cell. Inside the plant cell to this day reside bacteria, chloroplasts and mitochondria, maintaining their separate identities as, working together, they make it possible for the plant cell to exist. Since business organizations are themselves natural systems, the story of the plant cell raises possibilities for the Scania-Volvo merger. Perhaps each company will be able to keep its separate identity and at the same time collaborate to create a third unique entity. Scania's modular design expertise could make a distinctive contribution to the Scania-Volvo merger. Undoubtedly Volvo's system contains unique strategies that could make a distinctive contribution to the merger. Serious dialogue between Volvo and Scania should aim

at discovering their distinctive qualities and cultures. Mutual understanding grounded in knowledge of the principles of *Profit Beyond
Measure* might help each company retain its separate identity while
achieving one of the most exciting organizational transformations of
the twenty-first century.

. . . .

CHAPTER I

Market Capitalizations Compared

Studies of the automotive industry have documented the superiority of Toyota's performance in terms such as employee productivity, customer satisfaction ratings, production costs, and new model concept-to-market lead times.[1] Presumably because it is more difficult to compare accounting data among different companies, long-term profitability seldom is shown as an index of Toyota's superior performance. Certainly it is undeniably impressive that Toyota, without ever resorting to layoffs, has not reported an accounting loss in any year since 1960, a record not equaled by any other company in the industry. Still, the level of Toyota's accounting earnings, and the size of those earnings in relation to sales and assets, have elicited only a lukewarm response from auto industry observers.

Market capitalization comparisons, however, tell a different story. The American magazine *Business Week* since 1988 has published an annual ranking of the market capitalization of the world's 1,000 largest public corporations. Less well known than the famous *Fortune* 500 list, which ranks corporations according to revenue and profitability numbers found in annual accounting reports, the *Business Week* "Global 1000" list ranks companies according to one statistic—total market value. The five curves in Figure I–1 compare the trends in total market value from 1988 through 1998 for Toyota, for each of the American Big Three auto makers (Chrysler, Ford, and General Motors), and for the Big Three combined. Remarkably, Toyota's market value is close to the *combined* market value of the Big Three in almost every year but 1998. Indeed, Toyota's market value in 1989 equaled, and in 1997 *exceeded,* the combined market value of the Big Three. The divergence between the market capitalization of Toyota and the Big Three in 1998 reflects, among other things, the spectacular climb of U.S. stocks, the simultaneous collapse of Japanese financial markets, and the fall of the Japanese yen against the U.S. dollar in early 1998. Despite those

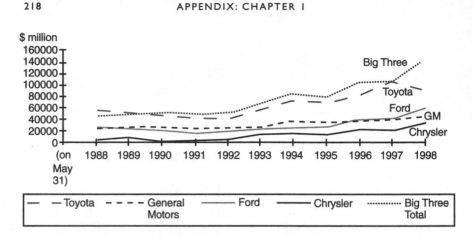

Figure I–1: Market Capitalizations

strongly adverse trends in the Japanese economic situation, Toyota's market capitalization still remained far above that of Ford, the highest ranked U.S. auto maker in mid-1998.

Market value statistics avoid many of the problems inherent in comparisons of financial accounting numbers such as revenue, operating income, and return on equity. By most financial accounting measures the U.S. Big Three occasionally come out sharply ahead of Toyota. However, despite Toyota's smaller size in terms of sales and total accounting profits, and despite adverse trends in exchange rates and in Japanese domestic economic conditions in recent years, Toyota's continuing high valuation indicates that the market perceives its operations as somehow different, and much more robust, than the operations of its largest global competitors.

The market's assessment may seem ironic since Toyota, unlike Ford, General Motors, and Chrysler, has never driven operating managers with financial targets. Actually, the connection between Toyota's well-known aversion to "management by results" and its higher market valuation should not be considered ironic at all. No doubt a primary reason for Toyota's superior long-term performance, reflected in its high market value, is its mindful attention to how work is done, as opposed to a mere manipulation of work in the pursuit of financial and nonfinancial targets. As indicated at the start of chapter 1, the factor that makes all the difference between Toyota and its major competitors is its systemic thinking. And the main difference between Toyota's thinking and that of other competitors lies in how they approach bottom-line results.

···

CHAPTER 2

Two Perspectives on Profit Information

The problem caused by using accounting profit and loss information to direct and control a natural living system is evident if one examines the behavior implied by the conventional accounting equation for profit. An algebraic expression for this equation is $P = R - C$: P is profit, R is revenue, and C is cost. This seemingly innocuous arithmetic equality expresses lineal and mechanistic thinking—thinking that produces specific behavior.[2] Profit occurs because one *removes* cost or *adds* revenue. To *increase* profit, one *increases* revenue, or *reduces* cost, or does both.

When this thinking causes managers to decide to improve profit by cutting cost, it prompts behavior like that portrayed by the diagram in Figure II–1. In the figure, a "chunk" is cut away from cost and added to profit. This satisfies the algebraic rule that a change in one part of an equation must be offset by an equal and opposite change in another part of the equation, in order to preserve the equation's balance. Cost is affected, of course, by having the chunk removed. But revenue is unchanged. Looked at this way, an attempt to increase profit by cutting

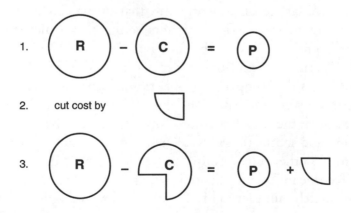

Figure II–1: Cut Cost to Increase Profit

cost might seem slightly ridiculous. Surely the attempt disregards the complexities created by the interdependencies, interconnections, and cybernetic feedback loops that exist in human organizations.

Ironically, this equation—with its severely limited application—is a cornerstone of present-day management practice. It is reflected, for example, in the downsizing praised almost universally by business writers and journalists. It is taught as gospel in many of the world's most highly regarded executive education programs. It depicts profit in mechanistic terms. Profit is the sum of neatly divided parts; the parts are independent and noninteracting; and all change occurs as a result of external force applied to the parts, according to the equation that links the parts with the whole. In other words, a change in either revenue or cost simply changes profit by the same magnitude, in the direction indicated by the equation. When this equation frames the way managers think about an organization's affairs, almost inevitably they think about performance improvement in terms of increasing profit either by raising revenue or cutting cost.[3]

How to raise revenue and *how* to cut cost are, of course, not addressed by the equation. The choice of means is up to individual managers. They may increase revenue by reducing selling prices, running promotional campaigns, or courting individual customers. They may cut costs by postponing training and maintenance, cutting research outlays, laying off workers, or outsourcing work to lower-cost outsiders. Since in a purely mechanistic world, changes in costs are not seen as interacting with revenue and vice versa, any action is deemed acceptable. Managers need worry only that changes are in the right direction, and involve the right amounts, so that they achieve the desired change in profit defined by the equation.

Managerial thinking that accepts this conventional accounting equation sees the company as consisting of separate parts, and treats each part only as an independent object. Each object is regarded, however, through the one-dimensional lens of quantitative measurement. Addition and subtraction signs alone are used to connect parts of this system. No other relationships are acknowledged. Profit itself is regarded as one independent part among many.

Fortunately, another kind of managerial thinking is possible, and another way of assessing work and profit. When managers view a company's system as comparable to that found in natural life systems, they regard profit, revenue, and cost as occurring in a world of mutual causality and interdependence. They observe that not independent parts, but rather relationships and patterns, influence success. They view profit as a consequence of organizational health, not as an isolated object to be increased or decreased by moving other objects.

Managers who perceive companies as actual living systems deem it impossible to enhance the overall profit of an organization simply by removing or adding amounts of revenue or cost. Their knowledge of interrelatedness among parts of the whole prevents such an assumption. An ancient Hindu metaphor for the interrelatedness of everything in the universe is that of the Net of Indra. This mythical net is made from an intricate web, each node of which contains a multifaceted jewel. Each jewel in the web constituting this net perfectly reflects every other jewel in the net, and is itself perfectly reflected in the face of every other jewel. It is not possible to add or remove one jewel in the Net of Indra without diminishing the lustre of the net as a whole. In other words, moving its parts does not make it possible to control the beauty of the net, but only to disturb it. In the same way, manipulating revenue or cost in a company does not improve its long-term profitability, but only gives the illusion of doing so.

The belief that long-term profitability can be shaped by manipulating cost and revenue—reflected in Figure II–1—rests on an error in logic. It is illogical to equate the quantitative measures of profit, cost, and revenue—which are, after all, abstract fabrications of the intellect—with the concrete reality from which these abstractions have been derived. Quantitative measures might *describe* abstract features of a complex system of interdependent parts, but they cannot explain or enhance one's *understanding of how change occurs* in such a system. In other words, quantitative measures can describe end results, but they cannot penetrate the means—the relationships and patterns—from which results emerge in a life system characterized by interrelatedness and mutual causality.

Management accountants need to make existing practices reinforce the life-systemic patterns and relationships implicit in all organizations. To do so, they might consider portraying profit from the perspective of a natural system of interdependent parts. Figure II–2 shows that profit

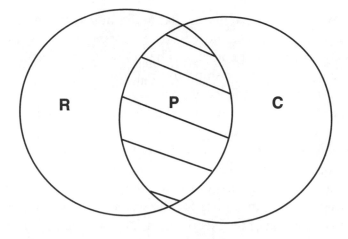

Figure II–2: A Natural-System View of Profit

(P) occurs in the space marked by the *intersection* of revenue (R) and cost (C). This contrasts with the mechanistic view of cost, revenue, and profit shown in Figure II–1, where profit is defined as what is left over when cost is subtracted from revenue. The life-system view defines profit as emerging from *relationships* between revenue and cost.

The diagram in Figure II–2 should *not* be interpreted to mean that profit is a *magnitude* equal in *size* to the area where revenue and cost intersect. Were that mechanistic interpretation valid, then profit—the area of intersection shown in Figure II–2— is maximized when revenue and cost are equal in size and occupy exactly the same space. However, the same equality of revenue and cost also guarantees profit to be *zero* from the mechanistic perspective of Figure II–1. Ironically, equality between revenue and cost appears to create both *zero* profit, from the mechanistic perspective of Figure II–1, and *maximum* profit, from the natural-system perspective of Figure II–2. This paradox is intriguing, but it arises simply because equating profit with the *size of the area* of intersection in Figure II–2 erroneously applies mechanistic thinking to the natural-system view of profit that is meant to be portrayed there. Instead, identifying profit with the space where revenue and cost intersect is only meant to imply that profit is a state or condition arising out of relationships. The diagram in Figure II–2 implies that *profit emerges from relationships that unite revenue and cost.* In other words, the important features that determine profit reside in systemic relationships within the organization. Such relationships are necessarily multifaceted, a fact that is ignored by traditional management thinkers who believe that using one-dimensional, quantitative measures to drive work can improve an organization's long-term financial performance.

The flaw in such traditional management thinking is illustrated by the story of Flatland. In the imaginary world of Flatland, the human inhabitants, their thoughts, and all things have only two dimensions.[4] If a three-dimensional hollow sphere were to pass through the two-dimensional plane of their world, Flatlanders would see a single point when the surface of the sphere first touched the plane of their world. As the sphere passed through Flatland, the point would grow into a circle that increased in circumference until it reached the size of the equator of the sphere. Then the circle would shrink in size as the sphere continued its journey, eventually diminishing to a point and disappearing at the moment the sphere finally passed completely through Flatland. At no time would Flatlanders perceive the concept "sphere." They would see only the two-dimensional intersection of the sphere with their plane of existence.

Flatland is analogous to the world of modern management accounting. In that world, people try to use one-dimensional quantitative measures to penetrate the causes of a multidimensional organization's financial performance. Referring only to those measures, top managers urge employees to take actions which they believe will move results in the direction of desired targets. However, such belief reflects a view of reality as distorted as that of the Flatlanders who, lacking knowledge of a sphere, see only an expanding and shrinking circle. Companies run from such a distorted perspective can manage, of course, as the causal-loop analysis portrayed in Figures 2–1, 2–2, and 2–3 suggests, to meet bottom-line results for a limited time. However, such success entails using a financial management strategy that actually distorts and disturbs relationships inherent in any human organization. This disruption of the relationships implicit in a natural system invariably causes unanticipated imbalances that increase the cost of attaining desired results.

As noted earlier, consequences of that higher cost include greater instability of long-term performance (as shown for company A in Figure

2–4), increased cost of operations, and generally lower organizational morale. However, typical MBR executives can see no better than do the residents of Flatland. They fail to understand that what causes these unwanted consequences is the one-dimensional focus of their results-driven actions, which disrupts and destabilizes the system's natural multidimensional relationships. They do not understand that these relationships, if left undisturbed, generate far better results, with less cost, than does MBR inspired by management accounting. A company guided by MBM principles—one that recognizes, honors, and nurtures principles that govern the operation of natural systems, as Toyota seems to do—consistently achieves far more robust and satisfying long-term financial results than do any of its "Flatland" competitors.

A comparison of these two views of profit (Figures II–1 and II–2) indicates the change executives experience when a company moves from a mechanistic to a natural-system view of business. Managers in the mechanistic, manage-by-results world (Figure II–1) attempt to improve profit by cutting cost, by raising revenue, or by substituting high-margin for low-margin products and customers. Crucial to good decision making in that world are data about cost, revenue, and margins, such as the data provided, for example, by today's activity-based cost management system and ERP systems. Managers versed in MBM principles (Figure II–2), however, improve profit by nurturing specific relationships that exist in the union of customer (revenue) and company (cost). Managers who regard organizations as natural living systems address two issues that do not occur to managers when they regard organizations from a mechanistic perspective. First, they know where to find and study the union between customer and company. Second, they understand how to identify and nurture the particular conditions that strengthen and sustain this union. Both issues are highlighted in the discussion of order-line profitability analysis in chapter 5.

APPENDIX

· ·

CHAPTER 6

MBR versus MBM Thinking and Behavior

Box VI–1 heightens awareness of how the differences between MBR and MBM practices reflect differences between the principles that govern natural living systems and those that govern mechanistic systems:

Box VI–1	
PRINCIPLES OF MECHANICAL SYSTEMS THOUGHT (MBR)	PRINCIPLES OF NATURAL LIFE-SYSTEMS THOUGHT (MBM)
1. Observers and the objects they observe are separate from and independent of each other. In other words, nothing inherent in an observer affects an object that is being observed, or vice versa. Your smile does not affect a tree or a mountain, nor are you affected if a tree falls or a hillside blossoms.	1. Observers and objects being observed are inextricably interconnected and interdependent. Relationships are the basis of reality and shaping all relationships are what Gregory Bateson referred to as the pattern which connects." Therefore, the ultimate object of your attention is not a "thing" that you observe; instead, it is a pattern underlying the relationships that connect all things.
2 Change occurs only as a result of external force or impact, according to top-down external laws that govern the behavior of all matter in the universe.	2. Change occurs as a result of a difference, not simply because of external force or impact. Differences arise from relationships, and the appearance of a difference is all that is needed to trigger change. The universe is replete with examples of differences (two) combining to create a difference (a third) that fulfills without diminishing: e.g., sexual reproduction, sounds combining to make harmonies, two eyes or two ears combined to create visual depth and aural richness, "bid and ask" creating an exchange that enriches both.

3. All systems in the universe naturally tend toward a state of entropy (random disorder, uniformity, sameness) in the absence of an external source of energy or control.	3. Life systems are self-generating, self-defining and self-sustaining. They autonomously generate order; they naturally dissipate entropy.
4. Quantity is sufficient to describe all differences. What you cannot measure—love or hate, for example—does not affect matter or your understanding of it.	4. Patterns that connect relationships, not quantity and measure, describe all differences that make a difference in life systems. Patterns can be described with number or ratio, but never with quantity.
5. Cause and effect sequences are sequential and lineal; that is, effects do not feed back to influence prior causes.	5. Cause and effect sequences are recursive and cyclical, not lineal; effects can feed back and subsequently influence prior causes, often in self-regulating ways.

   Adhering to principles of mechanistic thought yields behavior radically unlike the behavior that results from adhering to principles of natural life systems. This radical difference becomes evident if one considers how differently mechanical and life systems treat three phenomena—change, order, and the relation of parts to whole. First, in a mechanical system quantity alone is sufficient to bring about change from one state, or one period, to another. In that nonliving world, size alone—measured in dimensions such as mass, volume, velocity, acceleration, force, distance, and time—affects events or outcomes. Varying quantities causes different outcomes. Leaving quantities unchanged causes outcomes to remain the same. In a mechanical system, direct impact from an outside force provokes change. In a life system, however, change occurs simply as the result of a difference. Any difference can precipitate the emergence of something new. For example, if the light changes, a plant responds. If a parent's facial expression shifts, the child's behavior alters.[5]

   Just as change occurs differently in mechanical and living systems, so order arises differently in each system. Order in the mechanical realm can be imposed temporarily by external flows of energy and control. When external influences are withdrawn, however, the order in a mechanical system inevitably dissipates and entropy follows. Such dissipation does not occur in living systems. Quite the opposite. In these life systems, order emerges spontaneously. Indeed, scientists now characterize living systems as open systems that generate order and dissipate entropy as they continually process matter and energy "at the edge of equilibrium."[6] A marked difference exists in the nature of change and in the source of order for mechanical and living systems.

A great difference also exists between the relationships of parts in the mechanical realm and those in nature's life systems. In the mechanical realm, managers manipulate independent parts to make a whole. When they combine parts to make the whole, furthermore, the whole never exceeds the sum of its parts. If one alters the quantitative measure of a part, this variation instantly changes the whole by an equal amount. Any action that affects a part also affects the whole identically and simultaneously. However, this is not the case in living systems where parts and wholes are not linked so neatly. An object or event in the living world exists in the context of intricate feedback relationships among all parts of the system. Thus, a small change in one place may have enormous consequences in another place, and a large change may be diminished and become imperceptible in the final analysis. The outcome is shaped by the infinitely recursive and multiplicative patterns in living systems. Patterns in life systems repeat, reinforce, and dampen themselves in intricate ways.

These distinctions in how managers handle change, order, and the relationship of parts to the whole reveal the impact of the competing worldviews being discussed here. Change, order, and the relationship of parts to the whole are handled differently by those who manage by results than by those who manage by means. Still, in one respect, those who manage by results and those who manage by means behave in the same way. Both rely upon the mechanical principles of quantitative science to design a company's products or services. These same quantitative principles should not be applied, however, to running the organization. In so doing, those who manage by results make a great mistake.

ACKNOWLEDGMENTS

....

Profit Beyond Measure expands on management themes first addressed by Tom Johnson in his 1992 book *Relevance Regained: From Top-Down Control to Bottom-Up Empowerment* (The Free Press). The catalyst that triggered the writing of this new book, and that ultimately provided its core message, is the field research Johnson conducted at Toyota in Georgetown, Kentucky, in 1992 and 1993. Enriching that message after 1993 was a program of field research in Europe and America that Anders Bröms supported. Several people deserve special thanks for their contributions to this book.

Elaine B. Johnson tirelessly edited two preliminary versions of the book. Readers who find pages that sing with clarity and force have her to thank. Tom Johnson is responsible, however, for passages that even her talented pen might not have untangled.

Beginning in the early 1990s, W. Edwards Deming and Peter Senge greatly influenced Johnson's interest in quality management, systems thinking, organizational learning, and modern physics. Since Dr. Deming's death in 1993, the Deming Institute has continued to encourage and support this interest. Peter Senge also continues to stimulate and support this interest by reviewing manuscripts, by listening and sharing ideas, and by providing frequent opportunities to speak to and meet with his colleagues in the Society for Organizational Learning.

Kazuhiro Mishina introduced Johnson to TMM-K, Toyota's organization in Georgetown, Kentucky, and he shared with him his deep knowledge and understanding of Toyota's system. Chapters 1 and 3 draw on Johnson's many meetings with Mishina in 1992 and 1993 in Georgetown and in Boston, where Mishina taught at the Harvard Business School. Those two chapters, and much more in the book, also benefited enormously from countless conversations with Ken Kreafle and Glenn Uminger, two patient mentors and the warmest of friends, and with many of their associates at TMM-K, especially Michael DaPrile and past president Fujio Cho.

Anders Bröms facilitated Johnson's research on the material in chapters 4 and 5 by sponsoring him on several trips to Stockholm, to Kentucky, and elsewhere between 1993 and 1999. Bröms introduced Johnson to Leif Östling who opened doors at Scania. Bröms also introduced Johnson to his colleagues at Samarbetande Konsulter in Stockholm and to the order-line mode of profitability analysis they use in their consulting practice.

Many others who have made special contributions that it is a great pleasure to acknowledge include (in alphabetical order): Edward Baker, Shige Baker, William J. Bellows, Jeffrey Blumberg, Juanita Brown, David S. Cochran, Jan-Erik Dantoft, Robert W. Hall, Ken Hanioka, Anders Isaksson, Robert R. Locke, Norman B. Macintosh, Bartley J. Madden, Paul McNeill, Tyrone Norrman, John Oh, Carl-Erik Ridderstråle, Roger Saillant, Michiharu Sakurai, Håkan Samuelsson, Richard Sapp, Richard Schonberger, Johann Siberg, Michael E. Smith, and Ben Solis.

Finally, Johnson and Bröms express their deepest gratitude to their families—Elaine and Thom Johnson and Christina, Ulrika, and Katarina Bröms.

NOTES

....

Introduction
1. William Shakespeare, *Hamlet*, II, ii, 257.
2. A. E. Housman, *A Shropshire Lad* (1896), "The Welsh Marches," 49.
3. W. Edwards Deming, *Out of the Crisis* (Cambridge, MA: MIT Center for Advanced Engineering Study, 1986), p. 76.
4. Arie de Geus, *The Living Company* (Boston: Harvard Business School Press, 1997), pp. 3–9.

Chapter 1: Lessons From the Rouge
1. Thomas Berry, *The Dream of the Earth* (San Francisco: Sierra Club Books, 1988), p. 134.
2. *Jerusalem*, plate 55, lines 60 and 61. Quoted in Gregory Bateson, *Steps to an Ecology of Mind*, (New York: Ballantine Books, 1972), p. 469.
3. Daily production schedules for Model Ts matched consumer demand closely enough to not incur stockouts nor build costly inventories, except in severe recessions and near the end of the model's life.
4. Henry Ford (in collaboration with Samuel Crowther), *Today and Tomorrow* (Cambridge, MA: Productivity Press, 1988 reprint edition. Original edition by Doubleday, Page, 1926), p. 118. A seldom-noted person whose work was essential to the smooth operation of Ford's system was the "shortage chaser." See David S. Cochran, *The Design and Control of Manufacturing Systems* (Auburn University PhD dissertation, 1994), pp. 105-111.
5. On auto makers' prewar efforts to mass-produce variety in cars, see Daniel M. G. Raff, "Making Cars and Making Money in the Interwar Automobile Industry: The Manufacturing that Stood Behind the Marketing" (unpublished Harvard Business School working paper), and David A. Hounshell, *From the American System to Mass Production, 1800–1932: The Development of Manufacturing Technology in the United States* (Baltimore: Johns Hopkins University Press, 1984), ch. 7.
6. Quoted in David Halberstam, *The Reckoning* (New York: William Morrow, 1986), p. 81. Emphasis added.
7. The different modes of thinking described here are evident in late-1990s news stories

about Ford's and Toyota's respective strategies for expanding market share around the world. See, e.g., "The World that Changed the Machine," *Economist* (March 30, 1996), pp. 63–64. Ford's strategy, as outlined by chairman Alex Trotman, focuses on achieving scale economies by mass producing the "world car," i.e., a common design for one type of vehicle that will sell globally. Toyota's strategy focuses on intensive customization by proliferating designs to appeal to local differences in any part of the world. Thus, reflecting the same thinking that has been in place since the 1950s, Ford attempts to shape the local to the global, while Toyota attends to the local as it builds globally.

8. Peter R. Scholtes, *The Leader's Handbook* (New York: McGraw-Hill, 1998), ch. 9.

9. What is said here about decoupling is not to be construed as a diatribe against specialization. All efforts to partition work do not automatically create imbalance and waste. Efficient specialization does occur when each specialized task is accomplished at the same rate, as in Henry Ford's original system at the Rouge (Figure 1–1). Adam Smith's eighteenth-century pin-making "factory" illustrates the efficient cooperation possible among workers doing separate tasks. In that system, workers who specialized in each step of the pin-making process—wire drawing, cutting, grinding, stamping, and so forth—presumably produced output at the same rate as the finished output rate. Working together these people generated more finished products than could be made by any one member performing all tasks independently. Smith's factory, however, featured continuous flow. Batches delivered to, and distributed from, warehouses were not part of Smith's thinking.

10. Excellent critiques of this changed perspective in the 1970s are found in Robert H. Hayes and William A. Abernathy, "Managing Our Way to Economic Decline," *Harvard Business Review* (July–August 1980), pp. 67–77, and Jeffrey G. Miller and Thomas E. Vollmann, "The Hidden Factory," *Harvard Business Review* (September–October 1985), pp. 141–150.

11. Michael Porter, *Competitive Advantage: Creating and Sustaining Superior Performance* (New York: Free Press, 1985), p. 3. Porter is the leading advocate of this strategic viewpoint. Based on neoclassical economic theory, this either/or strategic viewpoint reflects a mechanistic Newtonian worldview. By contrast, the both/and viewpoint of low-cost variety in large markets, achieved by Toyota, reflects the quantum-evolutionary worldview of modern physics.

12. The Toyota story as told by Taiichi Ohno is found in his *Toyota Production System: Beyond Large-Scale Production* (1978); *Workplace Management* (1982); and *Just-In-Time for Today and Tomorrow* (1986). All three books are translated and reprinted by Productivity Press, Inc.

13. Toyota's concern to produce many varieties efficiently grew in large part out of the fact that the postwar Japanese auto market was not only small in numbers; it also manifested the Japanese customers' ancient preference for differentiation. Thus, manufacturers could sell only very small volumes of any particular model. Given the resource scarcity at that time, this meant that plants had to be able to produce many different varieties *on virtually the same equipment.* No one could afford specialized model-

specific equipment, nor could anyone afford to stockpile inventories for multimodel assembly. Systems had to be flexible. Moreover, this necessitated trust between managers and workers. At Toyota managers became the worker's protector, so that the worker was not discouraged from continually finding new ways to improve work methods.

14. On the inability of imitators to catch up with Toyota, see Alex Taylor III, "How Toyota Defies Gravity," *Fortune* (December 8, 1997), pp. 100–108.

15. Bernard Lovell, *In the Center of Immensities* (New York: Harper & Row, 1978); Stephen Hawking, *A Brief History of Time* (New York: Bantam Books, 1988 and 1998); David Layzer, *Cosmogenesis: The Growth of Order in the Universe* (New York: Oxford University Press, 1990); Brian Swimme and Thomas Berry, *The Universe Story* (San Francisco: HarperSanFrancisco, 1992); Christian de Duve, *Vital Dust: Life as a Cosmic Imperative* (New York: Basic Books, 1995); Brian Swimme, *The Hidden Heart of the Cosmos* (Maryknoll, NY: Orbis Books, 1996); Lee Smolin, *The Life of the Cosmos* (New York: Oxford University Press, 1997); Sidney Liebes, Elisabet Sahtouris, and Brian Swimme, *A Walk Through Time* (New York: John Wiley & Sons, 1998); Brian Greene, *The Elegant Universe: Superstrings, Hidden Dimensions, and the Quest for the Ultimate Theory* (New York: W. W. Norton, 1999).

16. This conclusion, based on ideas from the biologists Lynn Margulis, Humberto Maturana, and Francisco Varela, is developed in H. Thomas Johnson, "Using Performance Measurement to Improve Results: A Life-System Perspective," *The International Journal of Strategic Cost Management*, Vol. 1, No. 1 (1998), pp. 1–6. The essential point is that human organizations emerge from roots deeply embedded in the genetic patterns that link humans with the rest of life on Earth and, implicitly, with the universal system from which Earth and its living systems emerged. Social organizing among humans emerged from the internal dynamic implicit in all living systems, not from a design of the human intellect. Thus, business organizations evolved naturally from the same ecosystemic pattern that creates life on Earth and continues to influence its evolution.

17. Swimme and Berry, *The Universe Story*, pp. 66–79.

18. Nature is recursive, not repetitive. A *recursive* process is a sequence of steps that acts on the output of its own operation without repeating itself. The opposite of recursive is *lineal*. A lineal process is a sequence of cause-effect relations where the output never comes back to the origin point. A special case of lineal is *linear*, a series of relations which plot a straight line on a two-dimensional Cartesian grid. The opposite of linear is nonlinear. See Gregory Bateson, *Mind and Nature: A Necessary Unity* (New York: Bantam, 1980), pp. 250–251. Recursive and lineal process offer two different ways to explain the appearance of order: order self-emerges from a pattern embodied in the recursive process; order is imposed from outside the process, by design, in the lineal process.

19. An ancient mythic symbol reminiscent of this process is a snake swallowing its own tail.

20. Gregory Bateson alluded to this idea many times in his writings, for example, in the story of how the tightrope walker "survives" (maintains balance) by constantly changing position.

21. Naess expressed this concept variously in many writings. For example, see David

Rothenberg, *Is It Painful to Think? Conversations with Arne Naess* (Minneapolis: University of Minnesota Press, 1993), p. 65.

22. A living system is "dependent upon, but not determined by" conditions in the environment that surrounds it. In other words, life systems respond to outside influences, but such influences do not instruct them how to change. This idea is discussed in Humberto R. Maturana and Francisco J. Varela, *The Tree of Knowledge: The Biological Roots of Human Understanding* (Boston: Shambhala Publications, 1987), pp. 95–96. This idea implies that information should not be viewed as an object that imposes change from outside a life system. Rather, a life system internally forms (i.e., it "in" forms) and embodies outside influences so as to affirm its own identity. This is what biologists such as Maturana and Varela mean when they say that a living system "brings forth the world" that it inhabits.

23. This is a central theme in H. Thomas Johnson's *Relevance Regained: From Top-Down Control to Bottom-Up Empowerment* (New York: Free Press, 1992) and is reiterated in two more recent studies, Arie de Geus, *The Living Company* (Boston: Harvard Business School Press, 1997), and James C. Collins and Jerry I. Porras, *Built to Last* (New York: Harper-Collins Publishers, 1994).

24. A framework that promotes the thinking referred to here and that derives both mass-production and Toyota-style behavior from axiomatic principles is the production system design model being developed by Professor David S. Cochran at MIT. See the MIT Production System Design Laboratory website at http://psd.mit.edu.

Chapter 2: Relationships (MBM) versus Quantity (MBR)

1. James DePreist, *The Distant Siren* (Salem, OR: Willamette University Press, 1989), p. 43.

2. Albert Einstein, source unknown.

3. Johnson thanks Lynne Halpin for sharing her "puppy IQ test" with him.

4. Bartley J. Madden, "A Transactional Approach to Economic Research," *The Journal of Socio-Economics,* Vol. 20, No. 1 (1991), pp. 57–71, presents an excellent discussion of The Ames Distorted Room, a striking demonstration of the limitations of abstract, mechanistic thinking.

5. Henri Bortoft, *The Wholeness of Nature: Goethe's Way toward a Science of Conscious Participation in Nature* (Hudson, NY: Lindisfarne Press, 1996), pp. 173–174.

6. Bortoft points out that Aristotle, unlike modern social scientists, did not perceive quantity to be "a specific content of the world which is given materially, but to a way of seeing which constitutes the world in the *form* of 'parts external to one another.'" Ibid., p. 173.

7. Ibid., p. 174.

8. Clinical pathologists make this point when they tell physicians, "Never treat a test result; treat a patient."

9. Gregory Bateson, "Paradigmatic Conservatism," in *Rigor & Imagination: Essays from the Legacy of Gregory Bateson,* edited by C. Wilder-Mott and John H. Weakland (New York: Praeger Publishers, 1981), pp. 347–355.

10. *The Best of Deming,* collected by Ron McCoy (Knoxville, TN: SPC Press, 1994).

11. Eric Lampard, "Figures in the Landscape: Some Historiographical Implications of Environmental Psychology," *Comparative Urban Research*, Vol. 5 (1977), p. 27. Emphasis added.

12. Maturana and Varela, *The Tree of Knowledge*, pp. 209–212.

13. Ibid., p. 212.

14. A timeless parable of mankind's relationship with "tree" is Shel Silverstein, *The Giving Tree* (New York: Harper & Row, 1964).

15. Joanna Macy, *Mutual Causality in Buddhism and General Systems Theory: The Dharma of Natural Systems* (Albany: State University of New York Press, 1991), p. 208.

16. The following historical material on management accounting draws on H. Thomas Johnson, "Accounting and the Rise of Remote-Control Management: Holding Firm by Losing Touch," in *Cities and Markets: Studies in the Organization of Human Space Presented to Eric E. Lampard*, edited by Rondo Cameron and Leo F. Schnore (Lanham, New York: University Press of America, 1997), pp. 191–221. Also see H. Thomas Johnson, "Moving Upstream from Measurement: A Former Management Accountant's Perspective on the Great Dilemma of Assessing Results," in Peter Senge et al., *The Dance of Change: The Challenges to Sustaining Momentum in Learning Organizations* (New York: Doubleday/Currency, 1999), pp. 291–298.

17. Johnson's co-authored 1987 book *Relevance Lost* offered, among other things, a tentative solution to management accounting's post-1950s malaise. This solution came to be known as activity-based cost accounting. See H. Thomas Johnson and Robert S. Kaplan, *Relevance Lost: The Rise and Fall of Management Accounting* (Boston: Harvard Business School Press, 1987).

18. Promoting the spread of multidivisional organizations and further abetting the rise of MBR was the first postwar wave of mergers and acquisitions (referred to then as "conglomeration") in the 1950s. This wave all but erased the influence of manufacturers and engineers in the corporate suite. Manufacturing authority Richard Schonberger recalls that overcapacity in U.S. companies immediately after the war triggered fierce zero-sum marketing wars in which marketing executives shoved engineers out of high places. When the dust settled, winning companies with hordes of cash gobbled up losers that were attractive acquisition targets. At that time the finance and legal people replaced the marketing people at the top. Subsequent waves of mergers and acquisitions, down to the late 1990s, have only reinforced the finance executives' role at the top.

19. Ironically, many techno-oriented government and business leaders since the 1950s associate their work with "systems" theory, thereby implying that the work reflects a new non-Newtonian worldview. However, they often use the word "systems" in a mechanistic engineering sense that connotes design and control with feedback from quantitative targets, not self-organization with self-referencing feedback.

20. David A. Hounshell, "Ford Automates: Technology and Organization in Theory and Practice," *Business and Economic History: The Journal of the Business History Conference*, Vol. 24, No. 1 (Fall 1995), pp. 59–71.

21. George B. Leonard, *The Transformation: A Guide to the Inevitable Changes in Humankind* (New York: Delacorte Press, 1972), pp. 43–44.

22. David Milobsky and Louis Galambos, "The McNamara Bank and Its Legacy, 1968–1987," *Business and Economic History: The Journal of the Business History Conference,* Vol. 24, No. 2 (Winter 1995), p. 173.

23. Ibid., p. 175.

24. Jerry Mander and Edward Goldsmith, eds., *The Case Against the Global Economy / and For a Turn Toward the Local* (San Francisco: Sierra Club Books, 1996), p. 14.

25. The diagrams and related discussion are based on H. Thomas Johnson, "Management Accounting: Catalyst for Inquiry or Weapon for Control?," *The Systems Thinker* (November 1995), pp. 1–5. Basic discussion of causal-loop mapping techniques is found in Peter Senge, *The Fifth Discipline: The Art & Practice of The Learning Organization* (New York: Doubleday/Currency, 1990), ch. 5 and appendix 2, and in Karl Weick, *The Social Psychology of Organizing,* second edition (Reading, MA: Addison-Wesley, 1979), ch. 3.

26. On the short life expectancy of most corporations, see Arie de Geus, *The Living Company* (Boston: The Harvard Business School Press, 1997), pp. 1–3.

27. Two excellent examples of the unexpected consequences of applying force to natural systems are found in Bateson, *Steps to an Ecology of Mind,* pp. 30–31 [Alice's croquet game] and pp. 481–482 [kicking a dog].

28. W. Edwards Deming, *The New Economics for Industry, Government, Education,* second edition (Cambridge, MA: MIT CAES, 1994), ch. 2 (esp. p. 37). Also see Edward M. Baker, "Springing Ourselves from the Measurement Trap: The Quality Effort at the Ford Motor Company," in Peter Senge et al., *The Fifth Discipline Fieldbook: Strategies and Tools for Building a Learning Organization* (New York: Currency/Doubleday, 1994), pp. 454–457.

29. Macy, *Mutual Causality in Buddhism and General Systems Theory,* p. 209. Emphasis added.

30. Maturana and Varela, *The Tree of Knowledge,* p. 26.

31. David Bohm, *Wholeness and the Implicate Order* (London: Routledge/Ark, 1983), pp. 145–146.

32. When asked to define the purpose of their company, MBR managers often reply, "to make money." One way to answer this is to say, "technically it is illegal for any organization but the national government to 'make' money. More likely, what your company does is to *earn* money by providing useful service to customers." It is then useful to ask if a company "earns" money by any of the usual steps that MBR managers pursue to "make" money, such as cutting cost, stimulating sales, increasing market share, etc.

Chapter 3: Produce to Order

1. Quoted in James Gleick, *Genius: The Life and Science of Richard Feynman* (New York: Pantheon, 1992), p. 13.

2. In particular see James P. Womack, Daniel T. Jones, and Daniel Roos, *The Machine That Changed the World* (New York: Rawson Associates, 1990).

3. The Toyota story as told by Taiichi Ohno is found in his *Toyota Production System: Beyond Large-Scale Production* (1978); *Workplace Management* (1982); and *Just-In-Time for Today and Tomorrow* (1986). All three books are translated and reprinted by Productivity Press. Also see Yukiyasu Toga and William Wartman, *Against All Odds: The*

Story of the Toyota Motor Corporation and the Family That Created It (New York: St. Martin's Press, 1993), and Michael A. Cusumano, *The Japanese Automobile Industry* (Cambridge, MA: Harvard University Press, 1985), ch. 5.

4. Information for this section comes in part from "Toyota Information Seminar," a frequently updated brochure available to visitors to TMM-K, and in part from over 30 private study missions to TMM-K, beginning with Johnson's visits accompanied by Kazuhiro Mishina in 1992 and 1993.

5. On the inability of imitators to catch up with Toyota, see Alex Taylor III, "How Toyota Defies Gravity," *Fortune* (December 8, 1997), pp. 100–108.

6. An electronic metering system monitors andon pulls in every segment of the plant, thereby allowing supervisors to detect unusual activity signifying an unsolved local problem, a new team member requiring extra assistance, or a work station in which cycle time may require attention.

7. There is probably more component making co-located with final assembly at TMM-K than in any auto making facility in the world, including Toyota's plants in Japan. Toyota's Japanese assembly plants tend to make fewer major components under the same roof and therefore receive more from outside suppliers than is the case at TMM-K. However, this difference does not indicate that the Japanese plants "outsource" more component making, as that term is used by American and European auto makers. Indeed, Toyota does not outsource work in the frequently disjointed transaction-oriented manner that is currently so popular among European and American companies that often spin off component making into separate companies merely to reduce accounting costs. Toyota always strives, as much as possible, to integrate all work into a balanced continuous flow, whether the work is done in Toyota's own plant or in another company's plant. For reasons of history and geography Toyota relied on nearby companies to supply the major components to its main assembly facilities in Japan and then chose to make most of the same components alongside assembly at TMM-K.

8. In addition to sources already cited previously, specific sources of information for this section include: Toyota Motor Corporation, Operations Management Consulting Division, *The Toyota Production System* (October 1995); and William Mass and Andrew Robertson, "From Textiles to Automobiles: Mechanical and Organizational Innovation in the Toyoda Enterprises, 1895–1933," *Business and Economic History*, Vol. 25, No. 3 (Winter 1996), pp. 1–37.

9. So that work can follow a balanced and continuous flow, TMM-K batches orders three days ahead of delivery and then releases them in stable takt-time intervals in proportionately balanced sequences known as heijunka (see below)—a practical way to schedule customer orders for a production system that is designed to efficiently handle a different build sequence and different parts requirements for each order.

10. Where replenishment lead times are a few hours, like the seat maker in Figure 3–1, or ten hours, like a heat treatment facility, the increased likelihood of a slip between the planned sequence of work and actual demand requires a buffer.

11. Kazuhiro Mishina, "Johnson Controls, Automotive Systems Group: The Georgetown, Kentucky Plant," Harvard Business School Case # 9-693-086 (1993).

12. Mass customization attempts to achieve variety at low cost in a mass-production setting by locating out-of-sequence work, needed to achieve variety, as far downstream in the production process as possible.

13. Aiding Toyota's efforts to co-locate material transformation, machining, and assembly is their long-standing and exclusive use of unit-body construction. Others who use body-on-frame construction find it easier to ship stamped and welded parts to final assembly. With unit bodies, however, Toyota more easily integrates stamping and welding into assembly. Moreover, unit-body construction—especially with palletized conveyance systems—makes it easier to vary models and platforms on the same assembly line.

14. Efforts to cope with these indirect costs in the past decade have led companies inspired by mass-production thinking to pursue "improvement" programs labeled by various names such as "activity-based management," "reengineering," and "lean manufacturing." Commonly these programs refer to the source of those indirect costs as "non value activity."

15. Overall, Toyota operates with larger plants that produce greater varieties of vehicles than other auto makers. This tends to reduce variation of *total* vehicle volume over time in each plant. Other makers, with more and smaller *dedicated* final assembly plants, experience less stable output volume over time in each plant.

16. In addition to sources already cited, the following Harvard Business School cases by Kazuhiro Mishina are excellent guides to TPS as it is practiced at TMM-K: "Toyota Motor Manufacturing, U.S.A., Inc.," case # 9-693-019 (1992) and "Project Ghost Busters (A-E)," case #s 9-694-066 through -071 (1994).

17. Toyota's training depicts TPS as resting on a foundation of standardization which supports two pillars, JIT and jidoka, and a rooftop pinnacle, kaizen. The discussion of TPS in this chapter deviates from that format only to emphasize the natural life-system attributes of TPS, not to change the spirit of Toyota's format.

18. Richard Schonberger offered the points about Taylor in the last two sentences.

19. Akira Kawahara, a distinguished senior executive of Toyota when he retired in 1996 after forty years with the company, praises the 1990 MIT study *The Machine That Changed The World* for revealing to the world the effectiveness of Toyota's production system. However, he faults the book for not mentioning production leveling. He contends that no one fully comprehends TPS who does not mention production leveling, as he believes that it provides one of the key reasons for the low costs that Toyota achieves with its production system. In a 1991 interview, one of the MIT study's authors told Kawahara that sharp market fluctuations in America make production leveling impossible. Kawahara concluded from this that the author did not fully understand TPS, because in his view production leveling for Toyota is an indispensable tool for coping efficiently with market fluctuations. Akira Kawahara, *The Origin of Competitive Strength: Fifty Years of the Auto Industry in Japan and the U.S.* (published by the author, 1995 in Japanese and 1997 in English), ch. VII, especially pp. 205–210.

20. Batch lots are produced in a few cases, especially in stamping and plastic injection molding. However, the lot sizes and setup times are assiduously kept as low as possi-

ble. The drive to flow all work continuously in lot sizes of one is relentless. This key feature of TPS is not understood by many exponents of "mass customization," a manufacturing paradigm for achieving variety at low cost by assembling to order in lot sizes of one from parts that are mass-produced in large batches. See the comparison of this concept to TPS found in B. Joseph Pine II, Bart Victor, and Andrew C. Boynton, "Making Mass Customization Work, " *Harvard Business Review* (September–October 1993), pp. 108–119.

21. Taiichi Ohno, *Toyota Production System: Beyond Large-Scale Production* (Cambridge, MA: Productivity Press, 1988 translation of 1978 Japanese text), pp. 97, 100, 107, and 109. Emphasis added.

22. Technically, the goal is to scale resource needs to the smallest period of time needed to meet an order, not to the needs of making one unit as such. To simplify the explanation, however, the discussion here is couched in terms of units.

23. The ideas in this paragraph draw on a conversation between Johnson and Humberto Maturana on June 24, 1998.

24. The analogy between TPS and the nervous system is based on the discussion of nervous systems in Maturana and Varela, *The Tree of Knowledge,* ch. 7.

25. An interesting anecdote about pulling andon cords comes from a visit to TMM-K by plant managers from one of the American Big Three auto makers that had implemented andon cords in one of its plants. The manager of that plant told a TMM-K manager that his people pulled the cord about fifteen times in an average shift. When the TMM-K manager said that his people pull the cord on average more than a thousand times in a shift, the Big Three manager replied, "You have that many problems?" To which the TMM-K manager replied, "You don't?"

26. Nothing said here is meant to imply that Toyota does not compile master plans that project upper and lower limits of capacity and supplier requirements. Indeed, the company projects such plans a year out, with monthly and quarterly updates. However, their skill at keeping short model cycles and short production cycles enables them to readily adapt production capability to market changes at very low cost.

27. Interview with Ohno quoted in Isao Shinohara, *NPS: New Production System,* English translation edition (Cambridge, MA: Productivity Press, 1988), p. 147.

28. Proponents of "lean" manufacturing, by "eliminating" waste without also changing embedded manage-by-results thinking, often create stress and make inevitable the need to restore at least some of the "nonvalue" work eliminated. This resembles "yo-yo dieting" that eliminates calories without changing how one thinks about food. Ohno's "limited" thinking emphasizes continually balancing work to demand. ("Eliminating waste" is like trying to cut product design costs by "removing parts." See chapter 4.)

29. Seldom is it acknowledged that computers often save time by enabling work to be done at a faster pace, not by enabling it to be done in less time at the same rhythm. Perhaps because the computer's work is invisible to them, employees do not ascribe to the computer the increased speed of tasks and the diminished contact with processes that its coming often brings to their work. It should not be surprising to learn that

Toyota, historically, has eschewed the use of computers to direct work on the shopfloor, preferring instead that all information needed to guide work be visible and subject to control of employees who do the actual work. However, Richard Schonberger indicates that where the scale of production activity is microscopically small—as in making electronic circuits—computer-aided bar code tracking may provide the only way to make abnormality visible.

30. In Toyota's Japanese plants in the mid-1990s, with an unusually weak domestic auto market, a prominent tool for absorbing workers was the company's patience to wait for normal attrition.

31. Gregory Bateson and Mary Catherine Bateson, *Angels Fear: Towards an Epistemology of the Sacred* (New York: Bantam Books, 1988), p. 181.

32. Although computer-based information announces the arrival of a customer order that starts work on the line, the overwhelming practice at Toyota is to have visible physical movement, not invisible electronic signals, trigger work.

33. It is noteworthy in this regard that Toyota has nearly dispensed with the statistical information gathering required to maintain statistical process control (SPC) systems. Toyota was one of the first companies in the world to pioneer the use of SPC nearly fifty years ago. Today it maintains virtually all its processes in control without explicit use of SPC. But Toyota achieved this level of process sophistication only through decades of disciplined attention to mastering standards and creating fail-safe processes.

34. Comments based on numerous interviews and tours of TMM-K with Uminger, and on examining his "Manufacturing Cost Management: A Practical Life-Cycle Cost Perspective" in *New Management Accounting: How Leading-Edge Companies Use Management Accounting to Improve Performance* (Menlo Park, CA: Crisp Publications, 1998), chapter 3.

35. Toyota does maintain cost systems for pricing and project purposes, but never to drive operations. In any event, the cost systems maintained reflect actual, not standard, costs, and they compile costs only as needed, not on a regular basis. The general practice is to compile in most detail the costs of the high volume models, and to add and subtract incrementally from those numbers to estimate costs of lower volume models. The principle in cost estimating is to adjust incrementally from carefully prepared base estimates, not to compile new cost figures every time a number is needed.

36. Work is designed in Toyota plants to avoid, as much as humanly possible, "unused takt time." That is, no slack exists between the time available to do a task (takt time) and the time required (cycle time). This absence of slack time is another reason for the andon system. Team members pull the andon cord to signal when they are short of time to finish a task.

37. These cost data are devised by estimating the cost of *changes* to existing processes or products, not by compiling new cost information from the ground up.

38. One indication of Toyota's success at avoiding the fixed (or indirect) costs incurred by traditional mass producers is their ability to reduce the minimum "break-even" scale of an auto-making facility, from about 250,000 units per year for most makers in the 1980s to about 100,000 units per year for Toyota by the late 1980s.

Chapter 4: Design to Order

1. *Dialogues Concerning the Two Great Systems of the World,* Salisbury translation, London, 1661, p. 99. Quoted in E.A. Burtt, *The Metaphysical Foundations of Modern Science* (Garden City, NY: Doubleday, 1932), p. 75.
2. *Scania—100 Years* (Södertälje, Sweden: Saab—Scania AB, 1990), pp. 111 and 128 ff.
3. Ibid., p. 128. Emphasis added.
4. "Organic Growth at Scania: A Case Study of Quantum Management," white paper prepared for Scania top management by H. Thomas Johnson and SAM Samarbetande Konsulter AB (May 1994). An article based on that white paper is H. Thomas Johnson and Anders Bröms, "'The Spirit in the Walls': A Pattern for High Performance at Scania," *Target,* Vol. 11, No. 3 (May/June, 1995), pp. 9–17.
5. The material in this section draws extensively on Sverker Sjöström, "The Modular System in Truck Manufacturing," *The Saab-Scania Griffin* (1990/91), pp. 2–12, and on interviews with several Scania executives, including especially Lars Gardell, Kaj Holmelius, Lars Orehall, Håkan Samuelsson, and Sverker Sjöström.
6. General observations about product design architecture are based on Karl T. Ulrich and Steven D. Eppinger, *Product Design and Development* (New York: McGraw-Hill, 1995), ch. 7, and Karl T. Ulrich and Karen Tung, "Fundamentals of Product Modularity," MIT Working Paper #3335–91-MSA (September 1991).
7. One exception is the largest V-8 engine, which does not fit under the small P-type cab.
8. Scania's modular design matrix has the potential to provide much better information about the impact that design changes have on costs and profitability than the information supplied in traditional sources such as cost-driver data from activity-based cost systems or part-number data from balanced scorecards.
9. By extending the focus of design from serving customers' needs at the moment of sale to serving those needs over the life of a truck, modularization has the potential to put Scania's activities into a more harmonious balance with nature. For one thing, it should direct more attention to programs for recyclability and remanufacturability. It also should shift attention from extensive growth by churning customers to growing intensively by providing more services to existing customers over time.
10. Examples of companies using part-number cost drivers to motivate ambiguous design and marketing decisions are found in early Harvard Business School activity-based product costing cases concerning Hewlett-Packard, John Deere, and Tektronix.
11. These different modes of thinking are evident in Ford's and Toyota's recent strategies for expanding market share around the world. See chapter 1, note 7.
12. The 1994 white paper mentioned above in note 4 refers to this metric as a "technical commonality coefficient," or TCC.
13. The density index is a proxy for the indirect costs that arise from work caused by complexity—i.e., by departures from commonality. That includes most, if not all, indirect costs in today's average manufacturing establishment.
14. Some executives in Scania view it as desirable to link mass production of standardized components with assemble-to-order in final assembly, a practice sometimes referred to as "mass customization." Few advocate taking the step beyond that, achieved only par-

tially and by a handful of relatively small manufacturers to date, which is to assemble-to-order from unique parts that are fabricated to order with nearly zero setup time, including design time. Indeed, Scania's 1997 annual report speaks favorably of the company's long-standing policy of specializing component production in separate plants. That policy reflects, in large part, a quest for lower costs through economies of scale. However, by locating key component-making plants far from assembly plants, this policy makes it virtually impossible to maintain stable takt times and balanced continuous flows in both component-making and final assembly sites.

15. *Scania—100 Years,* p. 191.

16. The U.S. strategy produces earnings pattern A in Figure 2–4, just as Scania's strategy produces B.

17. The large fleet buyers' focus on purchase price may change if hiring good drivers requires having more comfortable cabs and state-of-the-art safety features.

18. Conny Hetting, "Mexico Looks to Europe," *Scania World Bulletin: International Edition,* No. 2 (1998), p. 18.

19. This difference was described recently by a veteran Scania driver who moved to the United States in the early 1980s and, after a brief stint driving American rigs, imported a Scania to the States. At first he was impressed by the "flashy, powerful American rigs." But he soon discovered "that there wasn't really all that much glamour in driving heavy monoliths with dead steering, non-synchromesh crash gearboxes and noisy engines." Although he found the American trucks' drivelines "immensely robust and powerful, . . . the entire truck as a whole is raw, unpolished, unsophisticated. My Scania is the very height of smooth sophistication—it drives like a car." Bo Östlund, "Kikka From Finland . . . ," *Scania World Bulletin International,* No. 2 (1995), p. 36.

20. Martin Haag, "Leif Östling behöver ett mirakel [Leif Östling needs a miracle]," *Veckans Affärer* (April 14, 1998), pp. 60–62.

21. To gain expertise in making aluminum bodies, Scania in 1994 acquired a small (about two hundred employees) bus-making company in Denmark.

22. Scania around 1990 eliminated about two hundred jobs in connection with a non-financial decision to outsource canteen, health care, cleaning, and security services. A few years later a reduction in force of about six hundred was prompted by a one-time systemic change in Swedish social insurance benefits that sharply reduced turnover and absentee rates for employers throughout the country. In both cases, those terminated received substantial compensation.

23. Sensing the presence of music in the shopfloor connections between each work step and a customer's needs is reminiscent of the comparison that string theorists draw between a universe of uniquely vibrating strings and a "cosmic symphony." See Brian Greene, *The Elegant Universe,* pp. 145–146 and 206.

24. Based on his study of forty of the world's longest-lived public corporations, former Royal Dutch Shell executive Arie de Geus concluded that it is possible to destroy a centuries-old company in less than twelve months by following three easy steps: declare that the company's goal, henceforth, is to achieve a specific rate of return; develop

a plan to trim assets and so forth to meet this goal; follow the plan. See de Geus, *The Living Company*, p. 126.

Chapter 5: Assess to Order

1. Indicators used to assess work at Toyota, for example, include andon pull statistics, operating ratio and overtime data, presence of scrap, quality statistics such as direct run ratios to assess off-line work and final-test ratios, and much more.
2. C. S. Lewis, *Mere Christianity* (New York: Touchstone Books, 1996), p. 36.
3. This is one of the central points of the evidence marshaled by Arie de Geus in *The Living Company*.
4. To speed the transfer of telephone network manufacturing overseas, Drakenberg designed a standardized training format that used what we now would refer to as activity and process maps. The accounting group at Ericsson used those maps until the mid-1960s.
5. Costs incurred to create future business are paid out of tomorrow's revenues. R&D departments have volume, structural, and newness costs—not just newness costs.
6. The S-shaped pattern revealed by order-line analyses is astonishingly similar to the fractal patterns that repeat at successive orders of magnitude in natural systems, from the subatomic level to the level of galaxies. Those repeating patterns reflect the fundamental interrelatedness of everything in the universe that is observed in modern physics and ancient mythology. The same interrelatedness is implicit in the union of revenue and cost that defines the reason for any company's existence. Because order-line-based measures of profit inherently reflect conditions at that union, they therefore reinforce management practices designed to nurture those conditions.
7. Kanthal (A) and Kanthal (B) (Harvard Business School Cases 9-190-002 and -003; 1989), prepared by Robert S. Kaplan.
8. Interview with Ola Rollén in February 1998.
9. Richard Pascale, "Adapting Complex Systems Theory to a Social Problem," *Timeline*, No. 37 (January/February 1998), p. 10.
10. Examples of companies such as Tektronix, Hewlett-Packard, and John Deere attempting to improve profitability by manipulating activity-based cost "drivers" are found in several of the early Harvard Business School cases on activity-based costing (ca. 1987–1992). For more on this see H. Thomas Johnson, *Relevance Regained*, ch. 8.
11. H. Thomas Johnson first enunciated this concept in 1987 in "Let's Return the Controller to Relevance," keynote address to the NAA Second Conference on Cost Accounting for the 1990s, Chicago (September 1987). He elaborated further on the idea in his "Activity-based Information: A Blueprint for World-Class Management Accounting," *Management Accounting* (June 1988), pp. 23–30, and his "Activity-Based Information: Accounting for Competitive Excellence," *Target* (Spring 1989), pp. 4–9.
12. Gregory Bateson, *Mind and Nature: A Necessary Unity* (New York: Bantam Books, 1980), pp. 50–56.

13. Lynn Margulis and Dorion Sagan, *What Is Life?* (New York: Simon & Schuster, 1995), p. 26.
14. Joanna Macy, *World As Lover, World As Self* (Berkeley, CA: Parallax Press, 1991), p. xi.

Chapter 6: Results Are in the Details
 1. "Auguries of Innocence" (c. 1804).
 2. Stephen Mitchell, *Tao Te Ching: A New English Version* (New York: Harper & Row, 1988), chapter 27, verse 1.
 3. Physicists who espouse "string theory" hypothesize the existence of undifferentiated primal "strings," each infinitely smaller than an electron, as the foundation of all matter and all forces in the universe. Despite their monotonous similarity, each string is presumed to "vibrate" uniquely. This diversity in vibrations supposedly creates patterns that give rise to every material form and every force in the universe. See Brian Greene, *The Elegant Universe: Superstrings, Hidden Dimensions, and the Quest for the Ultimate Theory* (New York: W. W. Norton, 1999), pp. 142–146.
 4. Brian Swimme and Thomas Berry, *The Universe Story* (San Francisco: HarperSanFrancisco, 1992), p. 54. Consider in this light what it would mean to view money as energy, not as a commodity to accumulate. One company or individual accumulating unneeded energy (money) denies life to another, thereby reducing diversity and threatening the long-term sustainability of the system as a whole.
 5. Statement by Dr. Deming at his June 1992 four-day seminar attended by one of the authors (Johnson) in Seattle, Washington.
 6. For more on this view of science see Stephen Edelglass, Georg Maier, Hans Gebert, and John Davy, *The Marriage of Sense & Thought: Imaginative Participation in Science* (Hudson, NY: Lindisfarne Books, 1997), ch. 5.
 7. Ironically, much of the work by modern biologists admits no place for life. "The current focus on genetic-molecular entities . . . treats life as an epiphenomenon of ultimate realities that are body-spatial, reduced, and mechanistic." This work explains biological functions in terms of mechanisms and it focuses thinking on how to manipulate and control biological processes. "In the process, however, the wholeness of the organism is lost." Edelglass et al., *The Marriage of Sense & Thought,* p. 125.
 8. These lessons do not provide a blueprint showing how to install particular MBM practices. That is not feasible, because such practices are necessarily unique to the context of every organization.
 9. Words, index numbers, and ratios are also important components of the sixteen principles that Richard Schonberger enunciates under the heading "principles-based management" in *World Class Manufacturing: The Next Decade* (New York: Free Press, 1996), ch. 2 and appendix.
10. This change reflects the inability of management accounting to deal with the minute particulars that occur where revenue meets cost. Management accounting information exists only by separating revenue, cost, and profit and thereafter treating each as independent objects. Management accounting is, in fact, the *sine qua non* of MBR. By deduction, therefore, substituting means for results at the focal point of management

attention insures the irrelevance and obsolescence of management accounting.

11. Christopher Alexander, *The Timeless Way of Building* (New York: Oxford University Press, 1979), ch. 27.

12. Christopher Alexander, *A Pattern Language* (New York: Oxford University Press, 1977), pp. 746–751.

13. William Bryant Logan, *Dirt: The Ecstatic Skin of the Earth* (New York: Berkley Publishing Group, 1995), p. 2.

14. For an example of thoughts in this spirit, see Fetzer Institute, *The Institute Report* (Kalamazoo, MI: 1995), esp. pp. 3–5.

Chapter 7: What's Natural Comes Hard

1. Quoted in Bill Devall and George Sessions, *Deep Ecology: Living As If Nature Mattered* (Salt Lake City: Gibbs Smith, Publisher, 1985), p. 1.

2. Art Kleiner, *The Age of Heretics: Heroes, Outlaws, and the Forerunners of Corporate Change* (New York: Currency Doubleday, 1996), pp. 6–9.

3. Gary Snyder, "Unnatural Writing," in *The Gary Snyder Reader: Prose, Poetry, and Translations, 1952–1998* (Washington, DC: Counterpoint, 1999), p. 261.

4. Lester Brown, Paul Ehrlich, Paul Hawken, and William McDonough are a few of the many people from varied scientific and professional backgrounds who express this concern.

5. Gregory Bateson, *Steps to an Ecology of Mind: A Revolutionary Approach to Man's Understanding of Himself* (New York: Ballantine Books, 1972), p. 428.

6. Ibid., p. 434.

7. Lyric from the song entitled "Anyone Can Whistle" (1965).

8. Henry Miller, source unknown.

9. Snyder, "Energy Is Eternal Delight," op. cit., p. 255.

10. Ibid., p. 256.

11. Comment made during a November 1998 presentation to the Institute for Science, Engineering, and Public Policy in Portland, Oregon.

12. Charlotte Bjuggren brought these concepts and tools to our attention.

13. The discussion of TNS is based on discussions with Róbert and his colleagues since 1995, including participation by Johnson in a 1996 international TNS training seminar in Idebörg, Sweden, and recent participation in seminars conducted by TNS of Oregon.

14. Indeed, if space and time are equivalent, as Einstein's theory of special relativity suggests they are, then the "time compression" that all MBR strategies seek today is not compatible with efforts to economize resource consumption. Technically, nothing can be made to go the speed of light because to do so implies consuming an infinite amount of matter (space). Efforts to make time "go faster" are necessarily accompanied by increased consumption of material space. Hence, programs aimed at conserving resource consumption (e.g., TNS) are doomed to fail if they are carried out by organizations committed to MBR time-compression strategies.

15. Swimme and Berry, *The Universe Story*, p. 55.

Afterword

1. This idea, based on the work of biologist Lynn Margulis, is described at greater length in H. Thomas Johnson, "Using Performance Measurement to Improve Results: A Life-System Perspective," *The International Journal of Strategic Cost Management,* Vol. 1, No. 1 (1998), pp. 1–6.

Appendix

1. In particular see James P. Womack, Daniel T. Jones, and Daniel Roos, *The Machine That Changed The World* (New York: Rawson Associates, 1990).

2. Management accounting textbooks often express the monetary totals in this equation by multiplying average per unit monetary coefficients by total volume. The equation then might be PV–CV = MV, where V is total volume of output, P is average price per unit, C is average cost per unit, and M is average margin per unit. Further refinements of the equation might divide CV into fixed cost and a variable cost component, in which case M might be referred to as the contribution margin per unit. These refinements permit one to use differential calculus to articulate instantaneous marginal values for revenue, cost, and margin. However, none of this changes the fact that the equation portrays results as a continuous and lineal function of output. At no time does the equation allow for the nonlinear feedback that characterizes nature's inherently interdependent systems.

3. The Newtonian thinking implicit in the simplified equation shown here is implied also by more elaborate formulations of the equation that link return on investment to gross margins and capital turnover ratios, rather than simply linking profit to revenue and cost.

4. Edwin A. Abbott, *Flatland: A Romance of Many Dimensions* (New York: Penguin Books, Signet Classic, 1984 [reissue of the original 1884 edition]).

5. The contrast between quantity and difference in the nonliving and living realms is articulated by Gregory Bateson in many of his writings, especially *Mind and Nature: A Necessary Unity* (New York: E. P. Dutton, 1979), chs. 1 and 2.

6. Fritjof Capra, *The Web of Life* (New York: Anchor Books/Doubleday, 1996), ch. 7.

INDEX

···

H. THOMAS JOHNSON holds the Retzlaff Chair in Quality Management in the School of Business Administration at Portland State University, Oregon. He has practiced, taught, and written extensively in the fields of economic/business history, management accounting, and quality management, and has served on the editorial boards of *Accounting Review, Business History Review, International Journal of Strategic Cost Management, Journal of Cost Management,* and *Quality Management Journal.* His co-authored book *Relevance Lost: The Rise and Fall of Management Accounting* (Harvard Business School Press) was one of fourteen titles named in 1997 by *Harvard Business Review* as the most influential management books to appear in the first seventy-five years of *Harvard Business Review's* history. His controversial and internationally acclaimed sequel to that book, *Relevance Regained: From Top-Down Control to Bottom-Up Empowerment* (The Free Press), has been translated into four languages.

Professor Johnson gives presentations and workshops to corporate, professional, and academic audiences. He has also consulted with major organizations around the world, including Arthur Andersen & Co., Boeing, Chrysler, The Deming Institute, Ericsson Telefon, Ernst & Young, Ford Motor Company, Institute of Industrial Engineers, Institute of Management Accountants, Intel, Pacific Bell, Scania (Sweden), Schlumberger (France), TeleNord (Norway), Toyota Motor Manufacturing USA, Volvo, and Weyerhaeuser.

ANDERS BRÖMS is the co-founder and managing partner of SAM

Samarbetande Konsulter AB, an international management consultancy firm based in Stockholm, Sweden, since 1979. After receiving his baccalaureate and master's degrees in engineering and computer science from the Swedish Royal Institute of Technology (KTH) in Stockholm, he was employed for many years by L. M. Ericsson, the Swedish maker of communications equipment. From Ericsson he went on to found Samarbetande Konsulter. With his colleagues at Samarbetande, Mr. Bröms authored the path-breaking work on modern cost management: *Competitive Cost Management* (Business International) known in its Swedish translation as *Lönsamma Kunder, Lönsamma Företag* (Brombergs).